Tmg
7/98

EUROPEAN LITERATURE AND THEOLOGY IN THE TWENTIETH CENTURY

Studies in Literature and Religion

General Editor: David Jasper, Director, Centre for the Study of Literature and Theology, the University of Durham

This series of volumes will provide an interdisciplinary introduction to the study of literature and religion, concerned with the fundamentally important issues of the imagination, literary perceptions and an understanding of poetics for theology and religious studies and the underlying religious implications in so much literature and literary criticism.

RELIGIOUS AESTHETICS: A Theological Study of Making and Meaning   *Frank Burch Brown*

BREAKING THE FALL: Religious Readings of Contemporary Fiction   *Robert Detweiler*

THEATRE AND INCARNATION   *Max Harris*

THE STUDY OF LITERATURE AND RELIGION: An Introduction   *David Jasper*

EUROPEAN LITERATURE AND THEOLOGY IN THE TWENTIETH CENTURY: Ends of Time   *David Jasper and Colin Crowder (editors)*

LANGUAGE AND THE WORSHIP OF THE CHURCH   *David Jasper and R. C. D. Jasper (editors)*

PITY AND TERROR: Christianity and Tragedy   *Ulrich Simon*

Further titles in preparation

Series Standing Order

If you would like to receive future titles in this series as they are published, you can make use of our standing order facility. To place a standing order please contact your bookseller or, in case of difficulty, write to us at the address below with your name and address and the name of the series. Please state with which title you wish to begin your standing order. (If you live outside the United Kingdom we may not have the rights for your area, in which case we will forward your order to the publisher concerned.)

Customer Services Department, Macmillan Distribution Ltd
Houndmills, Basingstoke, Hampshire, RG21 2XS, England.

European Literature and Theology in the Twentieth Century

Ends of time

Edited by
David Jasper
Director, Centre for the Study of Literature and Theology
University of Durham

and
Colin Crowder
Lecturer in Systematic Theology
University of Durham

© The Macmillan Press Ltd 1990

Editorial matter and selection © David Jasper and Colin Crowder 1990

All rights reserved. No reproduction, copy or transmission
of this publication may be made without written permission.

No paragraph of this publication may be reproduced, copied
or transmitted save with written permission or in accordance
with the provisions of the Copyright, Designs and Patents Act 1988,
or under the terms of any licence permitting limited copying
issued by the Copyright Licensing Agency, 33–4 Alfred Place,
London WC1E 7DP.

Any person who does any unauthorised act in relation to
this publication may be liable to criminal prosecution and
civil claims for damages.

First published 1990

Published by
THE MACMILLAN PRESS LTD
Houndmills, Basingstoke, Hampshire RG21 2XS
and London
Companies and representatives
throughout the world

Printed and bound in Great Britain by
WBC Ltd, Bristol and Maesteg

Typeset by Vine & Gorfin Ltd
Exmouth, Devon

British Library Cataloguing in Publication Data
European literature and theology in the 20th century:
ends of time – (Studies in literature and religion).
1. European literatures, ca 1850–1974. Special
themes: Religion – Critical
I. Jasper, David, *1951*– II. Crowder, Colin III. Series
809'.93382

ISBN 0–333–51666–4 (hardcover)

Contents

General Editor's Preface	vii
Introduction	viii
List of the Contributors	x

1. Music, Madness and Mephistopheles: Art and Nihilism in Thomas Mann's *Doctor Faustus*   1
   George Pattison

2. The Appropriation of Dostoevsky in the Early Twentieth Century: Cult, Counter-cult and Incarnation   15
   Colin Crowder

3. After Apocalypse: Some Elements in Late Lawrence   34
   Donald Mackenzie

4. Wyndham Lewis on Time   56
   Martin Jarrett-Kerr, CR

5. Rewriting *The Waste Land*   70
   Michael Edwards

6. T. S. Eliot: Poetry, Silence and the Vision of God   86
   Peter Walker

7. The Very Dead of Winter: Notes Towards an Enquiry into English Poetry after Eliot   105
   Michael Alexander

8. Visions of Hell: Lowry and Beckett   117
   Francis Doherty

9. Samuel Beckett's Negative Way: Intimations of the *Via Negativa* in his Late Plays   129
   Marius Buning

10 Redemption and Narrative: Refiguration of Time in   143
    Postmodern Literature
    Irena Makarushka

11 Apocalyptic Fiction and the End(s) of Realism   153
    Robert Detweiler

Index   184

General Editor's Preface

This collection of essays is very much of and for its time. It traces the literature of the twentieth century in Europe through modernism and postmodernism to the point when the crucial question cannot be avoided: how does theology respond to the moment of the apparent collapse of coherence in language, meaning and reference, to the denial of logocentricity and the radical suspicion cast upon the whole Western metaphysical tradition?

The essays are concerned with literature rather than with theological debate as such. They represent a wide spectrum of views and religious opinion. And if hell, madness and apocalypse are never far away, there also remains the vision of God and redemption, recognisable within the sense of endings and wasted time.

David Jasper

Introduction

The papers in this volume were read at the Fourth National Conference on Literature and Religion, held in Durham University, England in September 1988. Entitled *Where The Wasteland Ends: European Literature and Theology in the Twentieth Century*, the conference addressed itself to a number of themes arising from the cross-disciplinary intellectual and spiritual ferment of modern times.

> Time present and time past
> Are both perhaps present in time future
> And time future contained in time past.
> If all time is eternally present
> All time is unredeemable.

The opening lines of T. S. Eliot's *Four Quartets* indicate the central themes of this collection of essays: the mystery of time, past, present and future, and the problem of redemption. Eliot's own wrestling with these questions, both in *The Waste Land* and *Four Quartets* (and in an important sense, as Michael Edwards shows in his paper, in the transition between them), is intrinsically significant; but it is also a sign of the artistic and theological complexity of the twentieth century.

The modern struggle for a redeemed present, a centre that will hold, has demanded a strenuous grappling with both past and future: to settle accounts with literary and religious forerunners (as Eliot attempted to do), to appropriate their meanings in conditions which threaten to be meaningless, is to heighten the questions of future, of eschatology and apocalypse. Meaning seems to be endlessly deferred, yet the transcendent may continue to break in, or simply (like Lawrence's Great God) ever slip away below our horizon. Within the postmodern condition appropriation and apocalypse remain the guiding, mutually defining themes of this book.

In our own times we seem to encounter the ends of time. First, there is the concern with apocalypse – the apocalypse now experienced as the end of time, but an end which is also a beginning in the realm of origins. Second, there is the sense –in postmodernism – of the end of 'time' as a governing idea, a traditional category lost but perhaps to be 'refigured': time redeemed in and through creative art. Third, there is the idea of time's end as its *telos*, its purpose, its transcendent goal.

The collection maintains a dialectic between the closing of time – even of the concept itself – and its opening up, between *closure* and *disclosure*. And this dialectic pivots on the possibility of redemption: in, through, but especially of, time itself.

Colin Crowder
David Jasper

List of the Contributors

Michael Alexander is the Berry Professor of English Literature in the University of St Andrews.

Marius Buning is a Senior Lecturer in the English Department of the Free University, Amsterdam.

Colin Crowder is a Lecturer in Systematic Theology in the University of Durham.

Robert Detweiler is Professor of Comparative Literature in the Institute of Liberal Arts at Emory University, Atlanta, Georgia.

Francis Doherty is a Senior Lecturer in the Department of English, Keele University.

Michael Edwards is Professor in the Department of English and Comparative Literary Studies, University of Warwick.

Martin Jarrett-Kerr is a member of the Community of the Resurrection, Mirfield, West Yorkshire.

David Jasper is the Director of the Centre for the Study of Literature and Theology, University of Durham.

Donald Mackenzie is a Lecturer in the Department of English, University of Glasgow.

Irena Makarushka is Assistant Professor in the Department of Religious Studies, College of the Holy Cross, Worcester, Mass.

George Pattison is Rector of a group of parishes in the Diocese of Bury St Edmunds.

Peter Walker is the Bishop of Ely.

1
Music, Madness and Mephistopheles: Art and Nihilism in Thomas Mann's *Doctor Faustus*
GEORGE PATTISON

Thomas Mann's *Doctor Faustus*[1] is the story of the German composer Adrian Leverkühn, a story which, as the title indicates, reflects that archetypally German story of the legendary alchemist who bargained away his eternal soul for the sake of knowledge and power. Leverkühn, at least at first glance, is more modest: he only requires twenty-four years of supreme musical creativity.

The twentieth century, of course, is not the Middle Ages and 'we moderns' no longer hold with poodles who turn into Princes of Darkness. The book's narrator, Leverkühn's humanistic friend Serenus Zeitblom, shares our aversion to medieval demonology and, as he introduces the dialogue between Leverkühn and Mephistopheles (recorded by Leverkühn himself on sheets of musical manuscript paper), he asks

> Is it really a dialogue? I should be mad to believe it. And therefore I cannot believe that in the depths of his soul Adrian himself considered to be actual that which he saw and heard. . . . But if he was not there, that visitor . . . then it is horrible to think that those cynicisms, those jeerings and jugglings, came out of the afflicted one's own soul. (p. 215)

Zeitblom is well aware that the whole thing may have been no more (but also no less) than a figment of Leverkühn's diseased brain, the first sickly fruits of a venereal disease contracted through a brief liaison with a prostitute. The possibility of such differing interpretations of this crucial scene raises one of the central questions addressed by the book as a whole: does Leverkühn's destiny, as a man and as an artist, stand under the sign of a maleficent superhuman power – or is his unhappy tale the result of an abdication of reason and humanity for which he alone must bear responsibility? Is his musical nihilism, a nihilism which reflects the dark destiny of his time and place, the work of Mephistopheles or of madness? This question in turn leads on to the further question as to what hope (if any) may be gleaned from this story of downfall and ruin.

Zeitblom's Christian (more specifically, Catholic) humanism, for which Mann has, obviously, a great deal of sympathy is, equally obviously, impotent in the face of his friend's and his nation's capitulation to inhumanity. Is art, then, our last solace, a last refusal of despair in the very jaws of hell? Zeitblom finds some such aesthetic consolation in Leverkühn's last, blackest work, 'The Lamentation of Doctor Faustus'. He acknowledges that 'this dark tone-poem permits up to the very end no consolation, appeasement, transfiguration', but, he asks, may it not also express a paradoxical

> hope beyond hopelessness, the transcendence of despair – not betrayal to her, but the miracle that passes belief. For listen to the end, listen with me: one group of instruments after another retires, and what remains, as the work fades on the air, is the high G of a Cello, the last word, the last fainting sound, slowly dying in a pianissimo-fermata. Then nothing more: silence and night. But that tone which vibrates in the silence, which is no longer there, to which only the spirit hearkens, and which was the voice of mourning, is so no more. It changes its meaning; it abides as a light in the night. (p. 471)

Yet it is hard to be satisfied with such an elusive and minimal aesthetic hope when confronted with the horror of individual and collective damnation revealed in Mann's book. It is especially hard since Mann himself suggests that there is something nihilistic about art itself, that art itself is at least partially responsible for luring the human spirit into the abyss of modern nihilism.

But if reason and art both fail us in the face of final catastrophe, what other resources do we have? Religion? Perhaps: there is certainly a constant religious theme in the book. Leverkühn's

Lutheran faith is emphasised throughout, and we learn that his first study at university had been theology, a study which he renounced in order to pursue his musical destiny. In the figures of Zeitblom and Leverkühn, and in the playing out of the relationship between them, Mann gives plastic form to the choices we may make in the face of ultimate hopelessness: reason, art or faith?

Let us begin with the temptation scene itself. We find Leverkühn residing in Palestrina, birthplace of the composer, in the year 1911 or 1912. He is sitting alone, recovering from a bout of the migraine to which he is prone, reading Kierkegaard's essay on Don Juan. Later in the conversation Mephistopheles himself recalls that Leverkühn had been reading 'in a book by the Christian in love with aesthetics', (p. 235) and lends his indubitable authority to the view that this Christian did indeed have a true insight into the demonic potentiality of music, recognising it to be

> the most Christian of all arts . . . – but Christian in reverse, as it were: introduced and developed by Christianity indeed, but then rejected and banned as the Devil's Kingdom – so there you are. A highly theological business, music – the way sin is, the way I am. (*ibid.*)

These remarks suggest that Kierkegaard's essay will help us to understand what is one of the central issues of *Doctor Faustus*, the relationship between music and the demonic. The essay, entitled 'The Immediate Stages of the Erotic or The Musical Erotic', is to be found in the first part of *Either/Or*, a book which bears comparison with *Doctor Faustus* both in terms of its brilliant and extraordinary construction, at once literary, philosophical and theological, and of the way in which it sets out the complex interrelationship between art, ethics and faith.[2] The first part comprises a series of aphorisms, essays, a review and a novella, 'The Seducer's Diary', in which Kierkegaard presents what he calls the aesthetic view of life, that is, the attempt to base life on aesthetic values alone. He distinguishes a sequence of stages in this aesthetic point of view, running from the naively innocent allure of erotic love through to the fully self-conscious state of damnation and despair which he portrays in the figure of Johannes the Seducer. Using the Hegelian vocabulary which on other occasions caused him so much amusement he described this as the movement from the immediate to the reflective forms of despair. Don Juan himself stands as the ultimate form of the first stage of the series, the very incarnation of immediate sensuous passion.

Further light on this can be found in Kierkegaard's early *Journals and Papers* where we find the stage of the aesthetic life discussed in terms of what Kierkegaard calls the three representative figures of Don Juan, Faust and the Wandering Jew. He defines these as the 'three great ideas representing life in its three tendencies, as it were, outside religion'[3], that is, sensuousness, doubt and despair. Kierkegaard sees these figures (or 'ideas') as stages in a process by which the consciousness of separation from the divine ground (concretely: from the Christian revelation and the Church) is intensified and internalised. He also regards them as historically determined, corresponding to the Middle Ages, the Reformation and the Modern period respectively. They also correspond, in his view, to particular forms of art: music, drama and epic. The increasing divergence of religion and culture which had been held together in the medieval synthesis thus works itself out simultaneously on the planes of history, consciousness and aesthetics. The Don himself, as the ideal representative of sensuous passion, and musical form are in this way both seen as instantiating the immediate stage of this process. In the essay in *Either/Or* Kierkegaard argues (on the basis of the principle that aesthetic perfection depends on the absolute congruence of form and content) that Mozart's *Don Giovanni* is the supreme and unsurpassable work of musical art. Music, he says, can find no more appropriate content than this, whereas all attempts to deal with Don Juan dramatically (as by Molière) or poetically (as by Byron) will fail, no matter how well executed. Don Juan *is* immediate sensuousness and music *is* the absolutely appropriate vehicle for the expression of immediate sensuousness. By way of contrast to Don Juan, Kierkegaard's Seducer represents the completely reflective pole of aesthetic self-destruction. Like Baudelaire, he is a man who never forgets himself, a man without immediacy.[4] His seductions are not like those of the amorous Don – not the outcome, that is, of a sheer, overwhelming superabundance of sensuous passion, but are carefully planned, highly intellectual conquests, in which the interesting rather than the voluptuous, animal delights of seduction are what is sought.

There are both striking similarities and equally striking differences between Kierkegaard and Mann in all this. Whereas Kierkegaard identifies music exclusively with the immediate sensuousness of erotic passion, Mann's musician, Adrian Leverkühn, is clearly no Don Juan. He is, in fact, much more like Kierkegaard's Seducer. He has qualities of intellectuality, irony and doubt which ought to exclude him from the field of musical expression, if Kierkegaard's definitions are correct (definitions which were, indeed, very much in accord with the general view of music prevailing in the nineteenth century). Like the reflective Seducer he holds 'interest' to be a higher motive than the warmth of merely animal sympathy (p. 70). Even his early works are plainly not effusions of youthful Romantic *joie de vivre*, nor even equally Romantic self-indulgent expressions of despair. They are instead characterised by a detached, critical and highly theoretical view of the nature and history of music. Although his first acknowledged masterpiece ('Ocean Lights') seemed to some to be a piece of orchestral impressionism in the mould of Debussy or Ravel, it was already regarded by its composer as out of date. Zeitblom describes it as a 'disillusioned masterpiece of orchestral brilliance' characterised by 'traits of parody and intellectual mockery' which are 'the proud expedients of a great gift threatened with sterility by a combination of scepticism, intellectual reserve, and a sense of the deadly extension of the kingdom of banal'.(p. 148) Even at this stage Leverkühn has no desire to carry forward the illusionism of late and post-Romanticism with its hypertrophied 'monster orchestra'(p. 147) but to return past Romanticism, past harmony, even past counterpoint to authentic polyphony. His intellectual conviction concerning the nullity of Romanticism is not, therefore, a sign of avant-gardism but of a tendency to regression, even to the point of barbarism. This tendency is also reflected in his fascination with ways in which music can be made to depend on linguistic and mathematical structures which are not in themselves musical. But what sort of sympathy or understanding can such a deliberate regression from the musical to the elemental expect to find? Granted, Leverkühn breaks through the sentimental lushness of late Romanticism; but breaks through to – what?

His father, we learn, had been an amateur chemist, delighting in experiments such as the dissolving of certain crystals in water-glass to produce eerie, colourful 'gardens' of chemical growths, resembling primitive plants such as algae but which are in fact totally inorganic. These 'osmotic growths', as Mann calls them, are used in the book as symbols of Leverkühn's own musical experiments, and are alluded to in the dialogue with Mephistopheles when Leverkühn remarks, 'I am to grow osmotic growths.' (p. 235) In other words, the music he is to produce will no longer be bound by 'the pretence of feeling as a compositional work of art, the self-satisfied pretence of music itself' (p. 234) but is to issue from that 'absolutely questionable' sphere where all differences between organic and inorganic, human and inhuman are blurred. Henceforth the conventions of music, and of reality, are to be regarded from the standpoint of irony, mockery and negation. 'Marvels of the Universe', one of the first works composed by Leverkühn after this demonic visitation, is pervaded by 'mockery ... preoccupation with the immeasurably extra-human ... a Luciferian sardonic mood, a sneering travesty of praise which seems to apply not only to the frightful clockwork of the world structure but also the medium used to describe it: yes, repeatedly with music itself, the cosmos of sound'. (p. 266) This is the art not of Don Juan but, in Kierkegaard's terms, of the Wandering Jew, a nihilistic art which, in the words of Kierkegaard's own philosophical mentor Poul Martin Møller, stands 'at the zero-point on life's thermometer', indifferent to the customary positive and negative gradations of good and evil which lie on either side.[5]

Leverkühn is no Don Juan in the personal sphere, either. The possibility that his descent into madness and despair is the result of syphilis does not indicate a life of sexual licence. It is, on the contrary, a unique event, brought about in Zeitblom's view, by Leverkühn's almost complete erotic innocence, his utter lack of experience and judgement in the things of the flesh. Normally protected by his armour of 'purity, chastity, intellectual pride (and) cool irony', (p. 144) Leverkühn is tricked into entering a brothel from which he flees as soon as he realises what it is. But before he can do so, one of the girls brushes his cheek with her arm. Zeitblom comments: 'His intellectual pride had suffered the trauma of contact with soulless instinct. Adrian was to return to the place whither the betrayer had led him'. (p. 145) Far from being indicative of habitual lust, the whole incident underlines and confirms Leverkühn's normal indifference to human relationships. Another example of this is his avoidance of the intimate form of address, *Du*, and his reticence in using the name of the person to whom he is talking. 'All about him was coldness.' (p. 12) The few relationships into which he is tempted end, like the scene with the prostitute, in disaster.

This aspect of Leverkühn's character can also be illuminated by reference to Kierkegaard, this time to his discussion of the demonic in *The Concept of Dread*. The idea of the demonic presented here is not to be confused with the reckless sensuousness of a Don Juan, a drunkard or brawler. Its essential characteristic is what he calls 'shut-upness' (Danish: *Indesluttethed*). He distinguishes this from the way in which a poet or lover might be 'shut up' with the germ of a great idea or romance: 'The demoniacal does not shut itself up *with* something, but shuts *itself* up .... Freedom is constantly communicating ... unfreedom becomes more and more shut-up and wants no communication'.[6] This shut-upness is a specific form of dread, or, to use what has become an accepted English term, of angst, which Kierkegaard calls angst in the face of the Good. This Good is defined here as 'revelation',[7] by which he means the self-knowledge and self-transparency in and through which a person is able to accept and affirm him– or herself 'before God', 'from whom', we may say, 'no secrets are hid'. Shut-upness, then does not mean merely a lack of sociability. It is rather something demonic because it is the refusal to recognise ourselves as we are in the sight of God, the refusal to reach out and make our own, in an act of fully self-conscious choice, the freedom and responsibility for which God has destined us. It is the atrophy of the personality, superbly described by Kierkegaard in his portrayal of the Emperor Nero. Nero, he suggests, is a man with the consciousness of a child, incapable of understanding, integrating or affirming his own personality. Trapped within the boundaries of a merely immediate existence, he is incapable of giving any kind of continuity to his life, and is consequently the victim of sudden moods of enthusiasm alternating with long interludes of vacuity and boredom, both, according to *The Concept of Dread*, characteristic of the demonic.[8]

> The immediacy of the Spirit is unable to break through and yet it demands a breakthrough, it demands a higher form of existence ... but it cannot attain (it), it is constantly disappointed, and he would offer it the satiety of pleasure. Then the Spirit within him gathers like a dark cloud, its wrath broods over his soul, and it becomes angst, which ceases not even in the moment of pleasure.[9]

Leverkühn, we have already seen, is no sensualist, no voluptuary like Nero, but Kierkegaard's account of the demonic shut-upness generated by angst in face of the Good applies as much to him as to

Nero. Like Nero he is constantly in search of a breakthrough to a different, higher level of being – instead he is constantly thrown back into himself and can only break through to the downward self-transcendence of regression to the inorganic and inhuman, the ice-crystal world of 'osmotic growths'.

Although I have been speaking of Leverkühn's character, it should be emphasised that he is, if anything, a composer first and a man second. It is precisely because of his destiny *as a musician* that he is unable to make the breakthrough from shut-upness, from the demonic, to freedom. In order to demonstrate this more clearly let us return to Kierkegaard's essay on Don Juan, indeed to the very passage quoted by Mephistopheles himself.[10] Here Kierkegaard argues that music does indeed involve the transcending of immediacy in the crude sense of a completely instinctual and unconscious life but is itself nonetheless essentially immediate and sensuous in relation to Spirit (that is, self-conscious subjective freedom). Only language, he claims, is able to function as a completely adequate vehicle for Spirit, that is, for the affirmation of ourselves as spiritual beings, endowed with freedom and responsibility 'before God'. Only language enables us to express this responsibility in the literal sense of enabling us to answer for ourselves and thereby achieving revelation. Kierkegaard links the preeminence of language in this respect to Christianity, specifically to its triumph over the ideals of antiquity. In antiquity, he asserts, the sensuous and the erotic were not excluded from humanity's spiritual quest, the goal of which was conceived of as the beautiful personality. Christianity, however, requires us to assume an absolute ethical responsibility for ourselves 'before God' which makes all sensuous and erotic considerations irrelevant. It is, then, from this standpoint (rather than from the standpoint of idealistic or Manichean asceticism) that the sensuous erotic principle is excluded from the central dimension of spiritual existence. It follows that since music is defined as the medium *par excellence* for the expression of this principle, music is also robbed of ultimate seriousness by Christianity. It is, in the Christian order, essentially profane, but, as profane, continuing to be determined by that power, Christianity, which excludes it and by this exclusion defines what significance it has for human adventure. It is therefore in this sense that Mephistopheles calls it 'Christian in reverse'. 'In other words,' Kierkegaard's pseudonymous essayist tells us, 'music is the demonic.'[11]

Leverkühn's intellectual genius is far removed from the naive sensuousness which Kierkegaard sees as the absolute subject matter of music, but, as we have seen, and consistent with Kierkegaard's understanding of music as that which is excluded by Christianity and thereby also rendered incommensurable with revelation, responsibility and self-affirmation, his journey into the depths of musical creativity is a journey into the ultimate profanity, into that which lies altogether outside language and which is beyond communication. In short, it is a journey into the demonic, a journey into hell. For hell, we learn, has, like music, the quality of being unspeakable. When Leverkühn asks about the torments that await him when his time is up, Mephistopheles tells him that

> one cannot really speak of it at all, because the actual is beyond what by word can be declared; many words may be used and fashioned, but all together they are but tokens, standing for names which do not and cannot make claims to describe what is never to be described and denounced in words. That is the secret delight of hell, that it is not to be informed on, that it is protected from speech, that it just is, but cannot be public in the newspaper, be brought by words to any critical knowledge.... No, it is bad to speak of it, lies aside from and outside of speech, language has naught to do with it .... (p. 238)

While a theological student Leverkühn had shared in the rural rambles and interminable theological discussions of the Christian Student Verein Winfried. In one of these discussions he takes issue with Kierkegaard's subjectivist view of faith. Rejecting the Kierkegaardian separation of Church and Christianity he asserts that even in its secularised bourgeois form the Church is

> a citadel of order, an institution for objective disciplining, canalizing, banking-up of the religious life, which without her would fall victim to subjectivist demoralization, to a chaos of divine and demonic powers, to a world of fantastic uncanniness, an ocean of daemony. To separate Church and religion means to give up separating the religious from madness. (p. 118)

But in this plea Leverkühn pronounces his own doom. He sees that without the maternal security of the Church the individual is left without protection to face the full impact of demonic temptation, an assault which the individual, as individual, will scarcely have sufficient power to withstand. Yet this is precisely the path he chooses for himself. His abandonment of theology and subsequent commitment to music is seen by the Catholic Zeitblom as the proper pursuit of a God-given endowment or vocation, since Zeitblom still clings to the ideal of a synthesis of religion and culture. Leverkühn, the Lutheran, sees it as an act of apostasy, realising that the passion with which he gives himself to music is an absolute passion in which all distinctions between religion, art, madness and the demonic are broken down.

The application of all this goes well beyond the individual fate of Leverkühn himself. Throughout the book we are reminded that he is very much a *German* composer and that his fate is also the fate of a whole musical tradition and of a whole people. Throughout the nineteenth century music had been the medium and focus for German self-understanding to an extraordinarily high degree. Nietzsche, who followed Schopenhauer in understanding music to be the immediate language of the will, proclaimed that it would be through music that the German spirit would be rejuvenated and purified. 'What else, in the desolate waste of present-day culture, holds any promise of a sound, healthy future?' he asked.[12] Through music we gain entry to the power of the Dionysian spirit which, sweeping away the petty rationality and morality of Alexandrian culture, brushing aside the asceticism and idolatry of religion, can renew in us the ecstatic, tragic power of the creative affirmation of life.

> All our hopes centre on the fact that underneath the hectic movements of our civilization there dwells a marvellous ancient power, which arouses itself mightily only at certain grand moments and then sinks back to dream again of the future. Out of this subsoil grew the German Reformation, in whose choral music the future strains of German music sounded for the first time. Luther's chorales, so inward, courageous, spiritual and tender, are like the first Dionysiac cry from the thicket at the approach of spring. They are answered antiphonally by the sacred and exuberant procession of Dionysiac enthusiasts to whom we are indebted for German music, to whom we shall one day be indebted for the rebirth of the German myth.[13]

Through this Dionysiac spirit the German genius will break 'the vassalage of evil dwarfs' (by which Nietzsche meant Christianity), by daring to live tragically and taking on itself the *Urschmerz* of life – precisely in order to know its otherwise unattainable ecstasies of joy. It is with such Dionysiac promises that Mephistopheles sweet-talks Leverkühn. Forget objective truth, he blusters, 'What uplifts you, what increases your feeling of power and might and domination, damn it, that is the truth – and whether ten times a lie when looked at from the moral angle'. (pp. 235–6)

But Leverkühn's career turns out to be the systematic dismantling of the hopes of German music. His unhappy passion impels him to unmask the 'irrelevant solemnity' (p. 60) of a musical tradition which has tried to take upon itself a spiritual vocation which it is inherently unable to fulfil. His final work, 'The Lamentation of Dr Faustus', is seen by Zeitblom as 'the revocation' of the most archetypal work of German music, Beethoven's Ninth Symphony. It reverses the Ninth Symphony's 'variations of exultation', (p. 467) its transformation of symphonic sound into vocal jubilation (p. 470). Instead it employs the human voice as no more than an echo of inorganic sound; it is, 'the giving back of the human voice as nature-sound, and the revelation of it *as* nature-sound'. (p. 466) It is therefore the artistic embodiment of the regression of the human to the inhuman, the organic to the inorganic, beyond good and evil. As such the work is a sustained lament, 'which sounds like the lament of God over the lost state of his world, like the Creator's rueful "I have not willed it" '. (p. 471)

The failure of music to fulfil the promise vested in it is in turn the reflection of another failure – the political failure of Germany to break through from the geographical and social confines of Central Europe to the freedom of cosmopolitan power. The hope that it would achieve such a breakthrough is seen as the hope sustaining the heady days of 1914. It is a hope which even the humanistic Zeitblom (and through him Mann himself) admits having shared. 'What the breakthrough to world power, to which fate summons us, means at bottom', we hear him declare,

> is the breakthrough to the world – out of an isolation of which we are painfully conscious, and which no vigorous reticulation into world economy has been able to break down since the founding of the Reich. The bitter thing is that the practical manifestation is an outbreak of war, though its true interpretation is longing, a thirst for unification. (p. 297)

The war is in this way perceived by Zeitblom as a decisive attempt to break out of the German psychology constantly 'threatened with envelopment, the poison of isolation, provincial boorishness, neurosis, implicit Satanism' (p. 299). It is, then, an attempt to break the mould of a national 'shut-upness' which corresponds exactly to the demonic character described by Kierkegaard. Leverkühn is sceptical of his friend's enthusiasm. 'How does one break through', he asks, 'How does one get out into the open? How does one burst the cocoon and become a butterfly?' (p. 298) His scepticism is justified. He knows in his own experience the impossibility of bringing about such upward self-transcendence by sheer will-power alone. Zeitblom too soon loses faith in the war effort and comes to recognise that the train of events which it sets in motion leads to a still greater imprisonment, the promised breakthrough ending in a regression to barbarism and to a Satanism no longer merely implicit. Germany itself must tread the path mapped out by Leverkühn's prophetic venture into the depths of music, the hell of art without humanity.

The counterpoint between Leverkühn and Germany itself is fundamental to the structure of the novel. Zeitblom informs us that he sat down to his biographical task on 27 May 1943, three years after Leverkühn's death (itself following on ten years of total mental breakdown). As he plots the downward curve of his friend's sorry life he periodically interrupts himself to expatiate on the increasing woes which afflict his country: the defeat of German arms abroad, the devastation of German cities at home, the ever more manifest insanity of its leaders. As his work draws to an end, the war too is reaching its catastrophic conclusion. The population of Weimar, once the epitome of the culture of which he is both inheritor and representative, is forced to file past the crematoria of a nearby concentration camp. 'Now the torture chamber has been broken open, open lies our shame before the eyes of the world' (p. 461). What redemption can there be from this vortex of destruction, the work of madness – or of some evil spirit which has, we know not how, gained mastery over our history?

The working out of the Faustian theme simultaneously on the planes of history and of art compels us to recognise that art has a significance which goes far beyond the aesthetic sphere itself. Whether as prophecy or reflection art cannot extricate itself from the destiny of its time, nor is our response to aesthetic form safely ensconced in some trouble-free dimension outside the reach of the storms of history. But what is to be done when history and art alike are adrift in 'a world of fantastic uncanniness, an ocean of daemony'? The reason and humanism of Zeitblom confess their own impotence in comprehending, let alone gaining control of such a catastrophic situation. In the blackness of 'The Lamentation of Dr Faustus' Zeitblom believes that the last high note, reverberating in the silence, bespeaks a courage of despair, a hope beyond hopelessness, akin to that act of faith which Tillich described as issuing from the unreserved acceptance of meaninglessness.[14] But, at the close of the book, as he contemplates the ruin of his country, 'clung round by demons ... staring into horrors', he seems to acknowledge that such an aesthetic solution cannot staunch the wound inflicted by this historical paroxysm that is more than madness. 'When, out of uttermost hopelessness', he asks, ' – a miracle beyond the power of belief – will the light of hope dawn? A lonely man folds his hands and speaks: "God be merciful to thy poor soul, my friend, my Fatherland" '. (p. 490) There is no answer. There is only the prayer. In such a catastrophe salvation can solely be by grace alone.

This Reformation formula brings us to the final twist in Mann's tale. For what if Leverkühn's pact with Mephistopheles, what if the profanation of art, what if the moral suicide of the nation were themselves manifestations of a colossally rash presumption on the all-encompassing availability of grace? Such a presumption might finds its supreme expression in the belief that grace is even available to the one who denies its very possibility in the face of the enormity of his crime. This is no speculation, since we find the thought in Leverkühn's own mouth, when he suggests to Mephistopheles that there might be an act of contrition of such despairing magnitude, despairing even of the possibility of redemption, which would prove irresistible to the Everlasting Goodness and Mercy. 'A capacity for sin so healless', he says, 'that it makes man despair from his heart of redemption – that is the true theological way to salvation.' (p. 240) As he sinks into complete mental breakdown he realises – too late? – the true character of this 'atrocious competition with the Goodness above'. (p. 482) But this theme suggests one last reflection: that the catastrophe into which we see art, artist and nation plunge headlong, although it occurs outside of and even in opposition to Christianity, has historically, aesthetically and theologically been made possible by the Christian gospel itself, above all by the reformulation of that gospel in the

German Reformation.[15] For the Reformers' message of salvation by grace alone (and the corresponding incapacity of human works to contribute to the process of redemption) invites the question, 'Shall we continue in sin, that grace may abound?' (Rom. 6:1). God forbid, said Paul, but that question remains the last temptation of Christianity, and insofar as art accepts the profanity into which Christianity has driven it, it remains also the last temptation of art. We should not therefore look for the unity of literature and religion in linguistic form or thematic interplay but rather in the light of their common exposure to this temptation and their common weakness in the face of it.

Notes

1. All references in the text are taken from the 1949 translation by H. T. Lowe-Porter, in the Penguin edition of 1968.
2. S. Kierkegaard (English translation), *Either/Or*, I (Princeton, NJ: Princeton University Press, 1959).
3. Idem, *Journals and Papers*, 6 vols (Bloomington: Indiana University Press, 1967–78), No. 795 (Danish edn. no. I A 150). Cf. G. Pattison *Kierkegaard's Theory and Critique of Art: Its Theological Significance*, PhD thesis, Durham 1983, pp. 152ff.
4. J. -P. Sartre, 'Preface' to Charles Baudelaire, *Les Fleurs du Mal* (Paris: Gallimard, 1964), pp. 5ff.
5. P. M. Møller, *Efterladte Skrifter*, 3rd. edn (Copenhagen: Reitzel, 1856), Vol. 3, p. 160.
6. S. Kierkegaard, *The Concept of Dread* (Princeton, NJ: Princeton University Press, 1957), p. 110.
7. Ibid., p. 113.
8. Ibid., pp. 115ff.
9. *Either/Or*, II, p. 190 (translation altered to be closer to the Danish text and to indicate the important cross-reference of the concept of breakthrough).
10. *Either/Or*, I, pp. 62ff.
11. Ibid., p. 63.
12. Friedrich Nietzsche, *The Birth of Tragedy and the Genealogy of Morals* (Garden City and New York: Doubleday Anchor, 1956), p. 123.
13. Ibid., pp. 137–8.
14. cf. Paul Tillich, *The Courage to Be* (London: Fontana, 1962), pp. 167ff.
15. In terms of Mann's novel the role of the Reformation in the development of German music is seen as in some way providing a parallel to its theological significance. Mann also deals with the themes of grace, repentance and forgiveness in *The Holy Sinner* (Harmondsworth: Penguin, 1961), which is set in the world of medieval Catholicism and therefore provides an interesting counterpoint to *Doctor Faustus*.

2

The Appropriation of Dostoevsky in the Early Twentieth Century: Cult, Counter-cult, and Incarnation
COLIN CROWDER

In mapping the cultural landscape of the early twentieth century, one would expect to find the waste land reflected not only in the original literature of the age, but also in its criticism of an earlier generation's thought. Here, if anywhere, should be found confirmation for the belief that nineteenth-century certainties collapsed into twentieth-century ambiguities; and yet in the case of Dostoevsky criticism, it will be argued, this is far from being the truth.

Helen Muchnic, surveying this same field fifty years ago, offered a succinct rationale for the isolation of Dostoevsky as a peculiarly appropriate object of attention within contemporary criticism:

> The intellectual development of an age is often visible in the reputation of a single author, of an author, that is, whose work is deep enough to rouse judgements of such metaphysical and aesthetic implications as the merely superficial estimates of fashion cannot touch. Dostoevsky is such an artist.[1]

It might be argued, in addition, that the reading of Dostoevsky – frequently treated as a paradigmatic Christian novelist – raises specifically theological issues, including that of Incarnation; and it is with this in mind that the following glimpses of critical history have been selected.

But why *appropriation*? Why not simply speak, with Muchnic, of Dostoevsky's English *reputation*? Here I must indicate what this category is meant to include and exclude: the appropriation of Dostoevsky refers to the process by which man and myth, people and plots, were claimed for religious discourse by the spiritually-inclined intelligentsia (a process continuing, if rather less spectacularly, to this day). Other categories of response – influence, effect, interpretation, reception – cannot do the same work:

– *influence* tends to suggest direct imitation or indirect echoing, the former uninteresting (isolating Walpole's *The Dark Forest* or Conrad's *Under Western Eyes*) and the latter so broad as to be meaningless (as in the common but unhelpful observation that every major writer of the century is a spiritual heir to Dostoevsky);

– *effect* is even broader, taking in the vagaries of literary fashion but providing no means of marking qualitative differences between responses;

– *interpretation* suggests a text-orientation hardly characteristic of the Dostoevskian phenomenon, the object of which was more often a mythic mix of creator and characters;

– and *reception* suggests the technicalities of reception theory, when neither its framework nor that of sociology of literature has been shown most apt for the example in question.

By appropriation, although it carries overtones of these other categories, I mean what the OED defines: 'the making of a thing private property' – that is, the active championing of Dostoevsky, and his assimilation, by writers, critics, theologians, and so the process by which all things Dostoevskian acquired enormous force in the cultural polysystem of the day. Why did a generation express its spiritual struggles through Russian mythology? What prompted this ideal identification, which can be seen in weaker forms even now? These are questions of appropriation; and they suggest further questions concerning current readings of Dostoevsky, and the extent to which our vision of the original is mediated by the critical prism of early twentieth-century writing.

THE RISE AND FALL OF THE DOSTOEVSKY CULT

The changing fortunes of Dostoevsky in England can be schematised, without artificial forcing, in terms of decades after the author's death in 1881. In the first decade there were a few, mostly careless translations;[2] articles in the literary journals tended to compare Russian with English novels, with the aim being to leaven the home product with the moral and religious concerns of Russian realism rather than the supposed immorality of French naturalism. Given this agenda, the typical assessment of Dostoevsky was not surprising: he was praised for his realistic depictions of Russian life (not least the threat of nihilism), insofar as they were suffused with humanitarian compassion; but he was condemned for a Zolaesque morbidity, and an appalling lack of artistry. So the general message was that Dostoevsky was a good thing but vastly inferior to Turgenev.[3]

Interestingly, the Dostoevsky fever of the war years was anticipated by three decades in a letter by Stevenson, writing in 1886 of *Crime and Punishment*:

> Many find it dull; Henry James could not finish it: all I can say is, it nearly finished me. It was like having an illness.[4]

But such a testimony was all but unique.

In the last decade of the century there were fewer translations, and surveys of Russian literature could even omit Dostoevsky entirely.[5] But there was growing admiration of his realism – despite new directions provided by the rise of abnormal psychology[6] – and even George Moore, in introducing *Poor Folk* in 1894, was obliged to regret his earlier characterisation of Dostoevsky as 'Gaboriau with psychological sauce' (in fact a quip at *Tolstoy's* expense in 1888, although Moore admitted he had never read a word by him).[7] Moore thought the realism of *Poor Folk* intensely moving, but, after all, not quite Turgenev. Four years later Gissing's[8] estimate was more intelligent, comparing Dostoevsky to his ostensible subject, Dickens, and finding the Russian far more powerful and profoundly tragic. Nonetheless the critics were still gripped by the notion of compassionate but badly-executed realism.

The first decade of this century had more to say about Dostoevsky, often via the Russian literary history, both indigenous and translated, as a result of which the traditional unfavourable comparisons with Turgenev and Tolstoy were systematised. Four such accounts can be taken as typical.

Waliszewski's[9] history appeared in 1900, and in it Dostoevsky is represented as a confused, antinomian mystic, and as a non-realistic, non-artistic inveterate borrower. Kropotkin,[10] in 1905, is not dissimilar, taking further the crucial distinction between intention and its realisation: Dostoevsky will be read not for his art but for his 'good thoughts' (p. 186); not least since 'the literary form is in many places almost below criticism' (p. 179) — and certainly below realism. What is significant in Kropotkin's reading is the usual failure to see any necessary connection between the art and what is said through it, and also a sense that realism is not flawed in Dostoevsky but barely attempted. In 1907, Saintsbury[11] was largely repelled by Dostoevsky, but like Kropotkin he makes allowances on account of moral earnestness; nonetheless, he suggests, one could have done without Dostoevsky.

But by the end of the decade the tone was changing. Baring,[12] in 1910, notes that Dostoevsky is no artist, but his message — previously allowed merely to offset adverse judgements — is all-important, and can be summed up as 'love and pity' (p. 252). But this is to read not humanism but religion in the novels, which are a 'hosanna to the idea of goodness and to the glory of God' (p. 254). And in a line which prefigures the Barthian reading of Dostoevsky, Baring says 'in leading us down in the lowest depths of tragedy, he shows us that where man ends, God takes up the tale' (p. 165). This deeply Christian approach to the work marks a turning point: like the writings of the cult years it is heavily dependent on the biography of the novelist, but unlike them, it still apologises for Dostoevsky's formal failings in the novels.

Eight years earlier, the gradual rise in Dostoevsky's appreciation had been encouraged by the partial translation of Merezhkovksy's[13] essays on Tolstoy and Dostoevsky, making available to English critics a new vocabulary — the language of the Russian idealist critics. Thus from 1902 the personalist and mystical interpretations of this tradition, embracing Vladimir Solovyov, Rozanov, Merezhkovsky, and subsequently Shestov, were partially mediated in England; and the Stevenson-type Dostoevsky-shock was able to find expression in a ready-made scheme of interpretation. Merezhkovsky, furthermore, in passing beyond the novels to the soul behind them, and replacing criticism with a synthetic, symbolic, apocalyptic vision, set the tone for the English Dostoevsky cult when it suddenly and spectacularly emerged.

This Dostoevsky cult, which flourished between 1912 and 1921, was the product of a number of factors. It was partly due to the systematic publication of all the fiction, translated by Constance Garnett and spanning all these years; but more due to a build-up of forces at the end of the century – individualism, mysticism, idealism, symbolism, psychological interest, aesthetic experimentation, and decadence – which were fused under the intense pressures of the First World War. The war prompted a political angle, but the real need went deeper, requiring the provision of a mythology of spiritual self-examination; and in the absence of a balancing rational restraint the Russian influence was, as Phelps has noted, 'degenerating into hysteria and mystical jargon'.[14]

There were still representatives of the earlier approach – Lloyd's *A Great Russian Realist* of 1912, for instance, finds the irreducible Dostoevsky in humanitarianism – but more typical of the age is the remarkable hymn to Dostoevsky created by John Cowper Powys in his *Visions and Revisions*[15] of 1915. Powys renounces critical objectivity at the outset, choosing instead to do justice to the spiritual impact of Dostoevsky, first intimated in England by Stevenson, but boosted by Merezhkovsky's authorisation: 'The first discovery of Dostoievsky is, for a spiritual adventurer, such a shock as is not likely to occur again'. (p. 241) Dostoevsky is treated by Powys as a unique spiritual phenomenon, a profound seer, a traveller beyond both Christianity and Nietzsche, in fact everything (it seems) but a novelist – 'Dostoievsky is more than an artist. He is, perhaps – who can tell? – the founder of a new religion'. (p.258) This is quite different from the enthusiasm of Baring, for whom the nature and quality of the art was still a difficulty; Powys, like the Russian idealist critics, is so seized by the metaphysical intensity of Dostoevsky's work that he has lost all interest in the means by which it is conveyed and conditioned.

Powys finds in Dostoevsky a Christianity free of the limitations of the historical variety – but it does not occur to him that such limitations may be necessary for meaningfulness; he is too taken with the existential essence of this new religion: 'The secret of it, beyond repentance and remorse, lies in the transforming power of "love"; lies, in fact, in "vision" purged by pity and terror; but its precise nature is rather to be felt than described.' (p.247) In all this the utter seriousness of Powys cannot be doubted. What is less clear is how this mystic atmosphere is related to the novels of Dostoevsky, or even his actual biography.

John Middleton Murry's[16] 1916 study has an even more explicit programme: it would be 'foolish' to write literary criticism of Dostoevsky's work, and so the book 'professes only to think of what may be for us prophetic in it'. (p. v) It is certainly not as an actual novelist in translation that Murry approaches Dostoevsky, but as 'a phenomenon which has lately burst upon our astonished minds, one towards which an attitude must be determined quickly, almost at the peril of our souls'. (p. v) Not only is this nothing to do with the *way* he said what he had to say – Murry says of him, 'he never achieved his own form' (p. vi) – but such a question is irrelevant, since we are told, 'Dostoevsky is not a novelist'. (p.28) What matters is his 'new logic' (p. 31) and his vision of eternity, the timeless appearing in time which constitutes the 'metaphysical obscenity'. (p. 36)

A clarification is necessary here. Murry is not placing the burden of his thesis on the offence of the otherworldly penetrating the worldly, although he appears to think he is; instead, the worldly is negated and becomes a vacuous category. Of Dostoevsky we read, 'deep down in his philosophy lay the conviction that that which is ordinary is in some sense unreal'. (p. 39) And despite claims that the issue is the clash of the eternal with the temporal, the real tenor of Murry's work is set by the denial of the latter. For instance, Dostoevsky's letter expounding the relation between the fantastic and the facts is quoted, but the whole point for Dostoevsky is that the facts *are* fantastic; Murry, however, places the fantastic outside facts, nature, the world, in the revolt of consciousness against life. The tensions and paradoxes which Murry apparently sought to generate are collapsed in the denial of nature, the body, and, ultimately, the text. Therefore it is axiomatic for Murry that Dostoevsky's major characters are not human: 'They are disembodied spirits'. (p.47) Their bodies are merely symbols of human spiritual possibilities.

This judgement also stands for Dostoevsky himself – 'For, fantastic as it may sound, Dostoevsky existed more truly as an idea than as a man'. (p. 52) This is the authentic note of the Dostoevsky cult, whereby Dostoevsky is only incidentally a novelist, and indeed is stripped of all contingencies and relations until he emerges as pure spirit, pure vision, and ultimately – as was perhaps inevitable – an ideal reflection of his self-appointed high priest. And this goes hand-in-hand with a growing resentment of Dostoevsky's actual religion: comparing Baring with Powys, and then Powys with Murry, it seems that for Dostoevsky to be made god, the God of Dostoevsky must be denied; furthermore, the root of the problem seems to be the offence of the Incarnation.

Murry's obsession with self-consciousness leads him into quite perverse readings of the novels: Svidrigailov is the real hero of *Crime and Punishment*; there was no murder in *The Brothers Karamazov* since the whole novel is a spiritual allegory. Murry is not just talking about possible constructions here but the very essence of Dostoevsky's intentions – so it comes as no shock to find that Alyosha is not a Christian: 'his knowledge of the great Oneness needs no belief in God for its support'. (p. 258) There is no ultimate for Murry but Dostoevsky and his vision, purged of the limitations of nature and history and body, and, apparently, the embarrassments of Dostoevsky's actual biography, books, and (significantly) religion.

So much for the major officiants of the Dostoevsky cult in the second decade of this century; there were many others too. But not all readers were convinced, and the cult generated an opposition which is just as important as a cultural barometer for the time. Part of this was the old guard among writers, who clung to the earlier critical preference for Turgenevan values, but usually replacing 1900s complacency with all the urgency of a counter-cult; they could all admire some things in Dostoevsky, but fought hard against the uncritical prostration before the whole. Conrad wrote of 'fierce mouthings from prehistoric ages';[17] Henry James of Dostoevskian (and Tolstoyan) 'fluid puddings'[18] and Galsworthy could only exclaim 'my God! – what incoherence and verbiage'.[19] Edmund Gosse summed up the case for the aesthetic opposition, some years later in a stiff letter to André Gide, when he railed against 'this epileptic monster', 'the cocaine and morfia of modern literature'.[20]

But such reactions pale besides D. H. Lawrence's legendary attacks on Dostoevsky, complicated by his relations with Dostoevsky's champion, John Middleton Murry. As Phelps notes, 'Lawrence's critical writings on the Russians take one into the very quick of his thinking'.[21] Discussing Lawrence adequately would require a book on the subject, but the basic features of his position must be stated, because it amounts to a counter-cult which sheds valuable light on the phenomenon of Dostoevsky's appropriation by Lawrence's contemporaries.

From his letters we know that Lawrence was once deeply affected by Dostoevsky, but the phase ended early in his career. In 1910, having been accused of Dostoevskyism, he could shrug off the charge simply: 'all the dear cranky Russian's stuff is as insane as it can be'.[22] But as the cult grew, he became obliged to come to terms with Dostoevsky, and repeatedly he attacked what he found most reprehensible: the ubiquitous moral scheme, the grovelling at the feet of Christ, but all the while a perversion and sensuality which would gladly overthrow the lot:

> I don't like Dostoevsky. He is again like the rat, slithering in hate, in the shadows, and, in order to belong to the light, professing love, all love. But his nose is sharp with hate, his running is shadowy and rat-like; he is a will fixed and gripped like a trap, He is not nice.[23]

Murry rather rashly asked Lawrence to write notes on Dostoevsky to help with his book; Lawrence responded with the opinion that Dostoevsky was fundamentally divided between two opposing volitions: the will to be selfless, consumed, and the will to be pure self, all-consuming. The result, he claimed, was a debasing of the noble in man, a cowardice in which mind did not follow being but being was forced to follow mind. Others, as he wrote elsewhere, try to keep the pure and the base apart: 'But Dostoevsky, mixing God and sadism, he is foul'.[24] It is interesting to note that later, when the cultic pressure was off, Lawrence could afford to be more generous – hence the good-humoured preface to a separate edition of *The Grand Inquisitor*;[25] nonetheless, he was genuinely relieved to find that Rozanov was not, as he had feared, 'a pup out of the Dostoevsky kennel'.[26]

Why then did the cult collapse after 1920? There are a number of factors, the extrinsic ones including a post-revolutionary distrust of Russia and a postwar desire for the restoration of normality and objectivity. More important were the intrinsic factors: the translations of novels had come to an end, but the letters (many of them unedifying begging letters) appeared, followed by the memoirs of relatives and other biographical material – and Dostoevsky's divinity did not emerge unscathed. Studies of Dostoevsky began to relate him, soberly, to the history of nineteenth-century Russia, rather than the history of the soul. But even more damaging to the cult was the application of psychology to the great psychologist himself: Lavrin's[27] 'psycho-critical' study of 1920 at least mixed psychology with symbolism and metaphysics, but by the late 1920s Dostoevsky had become a case-study – Adler detected a frustrated will-to-power, Freud detected an Oedipus complex.[28] No surprises there, of course, but even though criticism could not rest in such investigations, there could now be no return from psychology to hagiology. With the cult out of their system, critics of Dostoevsky in the third decade of the century were able to treat the novelist as a novelist for the first time in years.

One mark of the changed climate was the ability of writers to speak of Dostoevsky without feeling suffocated, pleasurably or otherwise. Virginia Woolf,[29] for example, in her essay 'The Russian Point of View', marvels that the soul should be the subject of his fiction: 'Out it tumbles upon us, hot, scalding, mixed, marvellous, terrible, oppressive – the human soul'. (p.228) And in 'Modern Fiction' she admits of the Russians: 'one runs the risk of feeling that to write of any fiction save theirs is waste of time'. (p.193) But she is aware of the gulf which separates the Russian and English traditions, and this is not a cue for relief (as it would be in Galsworthy) or hysteria (as in Murry), but for a balanced consideration of hermeneutics – relying on translations, 'we have judged a whole literature stripped of its style':

> What remains is, as the English have proved by the fanaticism of their admiration, something very powerful and very impressive, but it is difficult to feel sure, in view of these mutilations, how far we can trust ourselves not to impute, to distort, to read into them an emphasis which is false. (p.220)

In this way, Virginia Woolf shows that the alien may be admired, but the admired will remain alien.

In *Aspects of the novel*,[30] Forster considered Dostoevsky as a typical prophetic novelist. It is a difficult work, notorious for its vague terminology of 'flat' and 'round' characters, and Leavis bluntly spoke of its 'intellectual nullity'. But it contains interesting attempts to convey the implication of universality and infinity, of the soul's extension into God, which Forster finds in Dostoevsky, *without* the supra-critical excesses of a Murry or Powys. Of the world of the Karamazovs he says:

> it is not a veil, it is not an allegory. It is the ordinary world of fiction, but it reaches back. (p. 92)

And of Dmitri Karamazov:

> He does not conceal anything (mysticism), he does not mean anything (symbolism), he is merely Dmitri Karamazov, but to be

merely a person in Dostoyevsky is to join up with all the other people far back. (p. 92)

It is difficult to grasp Forster's precise meaning, if he had one, but this is obviously an attempt to do justice to the spiritual aura of Dostoevsky's work without prostrating oneself before it. The prophetic concentration, furthermore, like the psychic concentration for Woolf, is only one possibility for the novel, evidently not one which either felt impelled to emulate. In the late 1920s one could be moved by Dostoevsky, but without abandoning objectivity or a proper respect for hermeneutical and cultural limitations.

This decade also witnessed a number of excellent surveys of Russian literary history by D. S. Mirsky. One of these[31] gave a penetrating but sympathetic analysis of Dostoevsky's novels, firmly contextualising them in their origins and their subsequent interpretation. Mirsky insists on the *novel* in the novel of ideas:

> The idea of the novel is inseparable from the imaginative conception, and neither can it be abstracted from the story nor the story stripped of the idea. (p. 268)

Or again:

> it is impossible to separate the ideological from the artistic conception. (p. 271)

Such reminders are hardly news today, but they were a stern and necessary rebuke to the excesses of the Dostoevsky cult.

It should be added that Mirsky, pondering the optimistic and pessimistic readings of Dostoevsky, sides with Shestov and the Nietzsche-influenced tradition which, ironically, includes Murry. This rejection of Dostoevsky's apparent vision of hope seems related, however, to his insistence on the textuality of the ideas and the bodiliness of the characters in the novels. Now it is by no means obvious that the acceptance of the ambiguous should create a monopoly for the reading of Dostoevsky which opposes a Christian interpretation; but it does seem that critics like Mirsky were enabled to set the course of modern criticism – for instance reading the canon from *Notes From Underground* rather than to *The Brothers Karamazov* – while Christian readings were still satisfied with the artistic and religious terms offered by the Dostoevsky cult.

The Appropriation of Dostoevsky

By the 1930s, an objective, scholarly, and self-consciously sober mood dominated Dostoevsky studies. Biographies – not fantasias on Dostoevsky's soul – were written, such as those of Carr and Yarmolinsky;[32] studies located Dostoevsky by reference to his influences and those he influenced in turn.[33] In short, Dostoevsky became the subject of normal literary study and assimilation, a novelist among novelists, not a god among men.

But the English literary establishment would not be allowed to forget the cultic years, because the 1920s and 1930s saw the translation of important French and German works on Dostoevsky which were a reminder of the exaggerated championing and denouncing before 1920 in England. Hesse[34] and Spengler[35] were transfixed by the primeval Asiatic vision of Dostoevsky; Zweig[36] offered a 'sublimation' of the 'archetypal man'; even Meier-Graefe[37] waxed too metaphysical for current English tastes. From France came Gide's book,[38] which, despite its insistence that Dostoevsky was a novelist, and that ideas are always relative not only to characters but to moments in their existences, tended towards an eclectic subjectivism in interpretation; it glories in the psychological abysses, but more in tune with the mood of the age was Rivière's contention that in psychology, *'la véritable profondeur, c'est celle qu'on explore'*.[39] Yet no translated work on Dostoevsky compared, for sheer abandonment of the texts in favour of metaphysics and mysticism, with Berdyaev's study;[40] generalising and allegorising are rife in this compendium of Idealist Christianity, the heir to Merezhkovsky and Solovyov. The following quotation conveys all we need to know:

> Dostoevsky's novels are not, properly speaking, novels at all; they are parts of a tragedy, the inner tragedy of human destiny, the unique human spirit revealing itself in its various aspects and at different stages of its journey. (p. 21)

The book is perhaps the most magnificent example of the Christian appropriation of Dostoevsky, not in spite of, but *because* it is barely a reading of Dostoevsky at all.

It is in this context, amid translations of Berdyaev, Gide, the Germans, and also some Shestov in 1929, that the English were reminded of the Dostoevsky cult and obliged to take stock, as a leader in *The Times Literary Supplement* did during 1930.[41] In a far-reaching analysis the writer explores the tendency to spiritualise in Dostoevsky, as a problem of both content and form, but he has a specific objection to the body of ideas exalted by the Dostoevsky cult: 'Dostoevsky's profundities, we can realise now, are shallower than we had thought'. (p. 466) And this judgement appears to correspond to the revival of empiricism at the expense of idealism, as the shallowness detected seems to be a matter of experiential rootlessness:

> His variations on the spiritual nature of man are illuminating, bewildering, exciting, stimulating, somewhat terrifying. They do not necessarily correspond to any reality in human experience. (p. 466)

An unimaginative conclusion, perhaps, but an eloquent reflection of the return of the stiff upper-lip to English Dostoevsky studies. No need for a counter-cult here: Dostoevsky is no threat, more a slightly embarrassing memory.

CONCLUSIONS

What, then, should be said of this period as a whole? Others have suggested the factors which led to the rise of the Dostoevsky cult, and its demise less than a decade later; these are, variously, philosophical, aesthetic, psychological, even political. But there is an unexplored theological approach – not extracting causes, but diagnosing the symptoms of the time – to which I want to address myself here.

First, it is vital to note, in the earlier part of the period, the insistence on the (now discredited) dichotomy of content and form, the systematic divorcing of *what* Dostoevsky said from the *way* he said it. Perhaps it was inevitable that the arrival of Dostoevsky on the English scene would create this reaction: the meaning was unassimilable in existing categories, but the mediation of it could be put down to a fall from the Turgenevan ideal, a lapse into a mixture of French naturalism and fantasy. And turn-of-the-century criticism, moreover, was keen to isolate the ideals with which a novelist would leaven his realism. As a result, the fatal distinction permeated almost all writing on Dostoevsky for decades. In the first twenty years, critics praised Dostoevsky's humanism while condemning its grotesque vehicle, although his realism – then more a value than a technique – partially redeemed him. After that, with the realisation that Dostoevsky was not a realist in the accepted (and acceptable) sense, the traditional polarity was accentuated: one could either find the form problematic (as did Waliszewski, Kropotkin and Saintsbury) and stop there, or go on to embrace the problematic of the content (as did Baring) – unspeakable form, ineffable content, and little to suggest they might be related.

In effect, the Dostoevsky cult was the logical outcome of this process: the form was simply ignored, since the real interest was the content of Dostoevsky's unique mind; and so not only does the cult give the impression of a textless Dostoevsky, but of a bodiless one too. Zweig was right to speak of 'sublimation'. Powys and Murry, together with the earlier Russian idealists, Berdyaev, and the Germans to some extent, abstracted their ostensible subject into a vacuum wherein the cult expired. What is more significant is that the shrill opposition often perpetuated the same distinction: the literary old guard could not so easily forget Dostoevsky's form, and if they objected to his content too it was on different grounds. Lawrence presents a rather more complex case, but even with him we find something similar – it seems that Dostoevsky's repulsive Christianity would not be so bad if it were permitted a noble expression, rather than lodged in the sensual and grotesque context it occupies. The foulness lies in the mixing of God and sadism, and much else besides.

With this we come to the theological problem. The cult sought a pure, unconditioned message in Dostoevsky, first in the books and then beyond them, an unequivocal revelation of the truth; it would be compelling, free of all contingencies of body, text and world, apocalyptically unique. It was a cult of the divine in Dostoevsky, unimpeded by the veil of his humanity and limitations – an almost Gnostic affair. This was no chance similarity, since the Dostoevsky cult was a remarkably christological enterprise – partly because of the christological emphasis in Dostoevsky, and partly because of the messianic insistence of the cult writers, whether taking a Christian shape (Berdyaev) or that of its Nietzschean inversion (Murry). Indeed the line dividing their docetic Dostoevsky from a docetic Christ is a blurred one; in both cases the Word is sought, when there is only the Word incarnate to be found.

After 1920, not only was Dostoevsky's real biography recovered, and his historical environment restored, but there also occurred a turn to the novels as novels: body, history, world and text could no longer be negated. Moreover, it was not through them but in them, and nowhere else, that the spiritual significance of Dostoevsky was to be found, incarnate in contingency, limitation, and ambiguity. This realisation was enabled by a change in approach to the novels, in which content and form were reunited: Virginia Woolf was aware that Dostoevsky in translation had been stripped of style, and was therefore liable to gross misreading; Forster hailed the prophet in Dostoevsky, but it was because the prophetic was a tone of voice, not a corpus of revelations; even the leader writer of the *TLS* saw that the loose nature of Dostoevsky's composition was integrally linked to the nature of the elusive soul of which he wrote. There were, therefore, repeated attempts to close the gap between form and content, although it would be a long time before critics proclaimed the meaninglessness of speaking in such terms at all.

It is one of the ironies of this subject that the fatal disjunction had been anticipated and denounced in Dostoevsky studies before English criticism really began. De Vogüé's 1886 study, *Le Roman Russe*,[42] was influential in England long before it was published there; for Dostoevsky it coined the phrase 'the religion of suffering' – earning Gide's eternal contempt – but it also provided a penetrating analysis of the actual structure of the novels, in which we are told that fragments isolated from their contexts are meaningless, and that much is left unsaid but conveyed in the texture of the writing. This aspect of de Vogüé's analysis might have been developed, rather than the more conventional French recoil from Asiatic primitivism – but, in another quirk of this abnormal literary history, these insights were inherited by not the French nor English but the Russian tradition: it was Ivanov who explored Dostoevsky's symphonic composition, Bakhtin who canonised the idea of polyphony, and thereafter it would be futile to claim any internal voice as the isolable authorial voice.[43] But their translation has been a matter of very recent times. As a result of these crucial absences, English criticism trod a very long path from the psychological notion of artistic integrity to the literary one, that is, a recognition of the mutually conditioning nature of all elements in literary art.

If an attempt to glean theological illumination from the phenomenon of the Dostoevsky cult is viable, then it follows that the restoration of artistic integrity to Dostoevsky's works, the inseparability of the inner and the outer, is the condition for a restoration of the spiritual wholeness which is so absent from the early appropriation of Dostoevsky. And this, I would claim, is a christological concern, not just by analogy, but because this is the kind of concern which reading Dostoevsky impresses. The cult foundered on the inescapable necessity of body, history, and text for the mediation of the divine; the Church is founded on nothing else. But this is a matter of offence, the scandal of the incarnation, the divine in the degraded – and as such is highlighted by Dostoevsky's novels, the impulse for their appropriation, not an external gloss brought to them. The theological, indeed incarnational connection, is an internal one; the divisions of both cult and counter-cult alike are overcome by the text – neither Murry nor Lawrence liked their gods mixed up with the mundane, but Dostoevsky's God comes no other way.

Such a line of thinking should not, however, be taken as the triumph of the specifically Christian appropriation of Dostoevsky. Incarnation does not solve the problem of inner and outer in Dostoevsky's novels – it *is* the problem. But this is to stray into the struggles of a later era of Dostoevsky interpretation. What needs underlining here is the false start to that interpretation of which the Dostoevsky cult is the most obvious instance; and that theologians still manage to live on the capital ill-gained in the age of the synoptic Christian interpretation of Dostoevsky – ironically, a neglect of Dostoevskian ambiguities in the supposed age of the collapse of certainties. It is all too easy to invoke the Christian appropriation of Dostoevsky as crystallised in its great champions, Berdyaev in the East, and Thurneysen in the West – Thurneysen, omitted until now because he was not translated and so made available to English critics in the era considered, is a source of profound insights, but all his dialectic and paradox is immune to real ambiguity in the texts of Dostoevsky: 'The absolutely final word of his novels is "resurrection" '.[44] Yet resurrection, like incarnation, cannot be read in Dostoevsky except in its oblique, equivocal, and problematic contexts.

Failure to come to terms with such difficulties at this time led to a reaction from an unexpected source. Derek Traversi's[45] brilliant but one-sided essay of 1937 is an attack on Dostoevsky and on Berdyaev by a Christian, but it is likely that Berdyaev's Dostoevsky is the only target it can touch. Traversi's theme is the metaphysical egoism of Dostoevsky's attempt to transcend the senses and experience, a denial of humanity in the name of a baseless and literally vacuous mysticism. Among the corollaries of this transcendental deception are a necessary negation of both Church and Incarnation. The former follows from Dostoevsky's having no need of human experience and relation – an absurd premise, given his insistence on solidarity and the responsibility of each for all. As for the latter, 'there is no place for the Incarnation in Dostoevsky's theology, except, perhaps, as an impalpable abstraction on some distant metaphysical plane'. (p. 164) It must have seemed, Traversi claims, an intolerable compromise between pure mysticism and the weakness of humanity. Again an absurd premise. But where is Traversi finding them? – The answer must be that such distortions, the tones of transcendental individualism, are the fruit of the processes I have tried to describe, showing that the cultic Dostoevsky became the only Dostoevsky, even for his detractors. The curiosity of Traversi's essay is that his philosophical and theological perspectives could have been maintained as an exposition of Dostoevsky, rather than as an antidote to him. Nothing could better illustrate the result of the literary and religious disjunctions fostered by the Dostoevsky cult, and perpetuated in some readings of Dostoevsky to this day.

LAST WORDS ON APPROPRIATION

It is hard to avoid the hermeutical gaffe of saying 'We know better', when faced with the phenomenon of the Dostoevsky cult. But it would be harder, if there is anything in the correlation of christology in theology and literature here, to avoid saying 'We must speak differently'. Nonetheless, to talk of appropriation suggest the idea of 'appropriateness' – the propriety of the various ways in which Dostoevsky has been absorbed. So what appropriations of Dostoevsky have been appropriate? And what would the criterion be for deciding the issue?

One might refer to the discernible intention of the author (if one dared); or the possibilities of the text; or the possibilities of response to the text – such that author-, text- and reader-centred theories would be competing. Moving to the latest option or at least options would increase the potential for interpretation, the play of possible meanings; and if this were the case, there ought to be plenty of room for legitimate alternative readings. Hence the Barthian could adopt Thurneysen's reading without fear of misrepresenting the text. But this would not place her in direct succession to that seminal reading (thus losing continuity with the original appropriation of Dostoevsky), since part of the point in the era considered was very much *Dostoevsky's intention*: it was his insight, his prophecy that was to be absorbed and championed.

But is there no other way to see this phenomenon? I think there is, if we utilise Tomashevsky's distinction between actual and ideal biography: biographical criticism of the traditional kind must not be resurrected, but instead, 'we must consider how the poet's biography operates in the reader's consciousness'.[46] As a result of his investigation, Tomashevsky concludes that the vital issue in the reader's reference to a writer's life is not what happened but what he can *believe* happened. 'Only such a legend is a *literary* fact.'[47] Thus an ideal biography is some sort of criterion; it has the problem (if problem this be) of potential plurality, and shifting perceptions; but we cannot say it is any less adequate than the actual biographical criterion, which reduces to speculations upon the goings-on inside Dostoevsky's soul. It may be the case, after all, that we must test the appropriateness of our appropriations from within, as it were; and that for our appropriation to be fruitful we too must look to the Dostoevsky of faith, not the Dostoevsky of history, for the terms of its meaningfulness. And that there is here a christological parallel should go without saying.

Notes

1. Helen Muchnic, *Dostoevsky's English Reputation (1881–1936)* (Smith College Studies in Modern Languages, Vol. XX, nos 3–4, 1938–9; reprinted New York: Farrar, Strauss & Giroux, 1969), p. 1.
2. *Buried Alive: Ten Years Penal in Siberia* (English translation Marie von Thilo), 1881; *Prison Life in Siberia* (English translation H. Sutherland Edwards), 1887; and the series of translations by Frederick Whishaw: *Crime and Punishment*, 1886; *Injury and Insult*, 1886; *The Idiot*, 1887; *The Friend of the Family and The Gambler*, 1887; *The Uncle's Dream and the Permanent Husband*, 1888.
3. See Muchnic, op. cit., Chapter 2, for a convenient collection of the evidence.
4. R. L. Stevenson (to Symonds), quoted in ibid., p. 17.
5. Ivan Panin, *Lectures on Russian Literature* (New York: 1889).
6. Cesare Lombroso's *The Man of Genius* (London: 1891) and Max Nordau's *Degeneration* (New York: 1895) became available in translation.

7. *Poor Folk* (English translation Lena Milman, with preface by George Moore, London: 1894). The episode is discussed by Muchnic, op. cit., p. 181 n. 24.
8. George Gissing, *Charles Dickens: A Critical Study* (New York: 1898).
9. Kazimierz Waliszewski, *A History of Russian Literature* (London: Heinemann, 1900), pp. 322–60.
10. Peter Kropotkin, *Russian Literature: Ideals and Realities* (London: Duckworth, [1905] 1916).
11. George Saintsbury, *The Later Nineteenth Century* (Vol. XII of *Periods of European Literature*, London: Blackwood, 1907). Reprinted in D. Davie (ed.), *Russian Literature and Modern English Fiction* (Chicago: University of Chicago Press, 1965).
12. Maurice Baring, *Landmarks in Russian Literature* (London: Methuen, 1910).
13. Dmitri Merejkowski, *Tolstoi as Man and Artist: With an Essay on Dostoievski* (London: Constable, 1902).
14. Gilbert Phelps, *The Russian Novel in English Fiction* (London: Hutchinson, 1956), p. 172.
15. John Cowper Powys, *Visions and Revisions: A Book of Literary Devotions* (New York: G. Arnold Shaw, 1915).
16. John Middleton Murry, *Fyodor Dostoevsky: A Critical Study* (London: Martin Secker, [1916] 1923).
17. Conrad (to Garnett), quoted by Muchnic, op. cit., p. 73.
18. James (to Walpole), quoted in ibid., p. 74.
19. Galsworthy (to Garnett), quoted in ibid., p. 74.
20. Gosse (to Gide), quoted in ibid., pp. 138–9.
21. Phelps, op. cit., p. 183.
22. Lawrence (to Violet Hunt, 13 December 1910), *The Letters of D. H. Lawrence*, Vol. I, ed. James T. Boulton (Cambridge: Cambridge University Press, 1979), p. 199.
23. Lawrence (to Ottoline Morrell, 24 March 1915), ibid., Vol II, ed. G. J. Zytaruk and James T. Boulton (Cambridge: Cambridge University Press, 1981), p. 314.
24. Lawrence (to Ottoline Morrell, 1 February 1916), ibid., p. 521.
25. Lawrence, preface to *The Grand Inquisitor* (English translation S. S. Koteliansky; London: 1930). Reprinted in R. Wellek (ed.), *Dostoevsky: A Collection of Critical Essays* (Englewood Cliffs: Prentice-Hall, 1962).
26. Lawrence, review of V. V. Rozanov, *Solitaria* in *Phoenix* (London: Heinemann, 1936). Reprinted in Davie, op. cit., p. 100.
27. Janko Lavrin, *Dostoevsky and his Creation: A Psycho-Critical Study* (London: 1920).
28. See especially Richard Montgomery, 'Freud, Adler and Dostoevski', *New Age* XLV (1929), pp. 115–16.
29. Virginia Woolf, *The Common Reader*, First Series (London: Hogarth Press, [1925] 1945).
30. E. M. Forster, *Aspects of the Novel* [1927], ed. Oliver Stallybrass (London: Edward Arnold, 1974). Leavis is quoted in the introduction, p. xi.
31. D. S. Mirsky, *A History of Russian Literature* [1924], ed. F. J. Whitfield

(London: Routledge & Kegan Paul, 1949). See also *Modern Russian Literature* (London: Oxford University Press, 1925).
32. E. H. Carr, *Dostoevsky: A New Biography* (Boston: 1931); Avrahm Yarmolinsky, *Dostoevsky: A Life* (New York: 1934).
33. For instance, Boris Brasol (*The Mighty Three*, New York: 1934) stressed Dostoevsky's debt to Pushkin; Janko Lavrin contrasted him with Proust ('Dostoevsky and Proust', *The Slavonic Review* V (1927)) but traced his influence on psychological fiction of the day (*Russian Literature*, London: 1927); Tatania Vacquier ('Dostoevsky and Gide', *Sewanee Review* XXXVII (1929)) noted parallels with Gide's fiction; and there emerged a wealth of comparisons of Dostoevsky with James, Huxley, Woolf, Joyce, Conrad, Wasserman, and Waldo Frank.
34. Hermann Hesse, 'The Downfall of Europe – *The Brothers Karamazov*' (English translation Stephen Hudson), *The English Review* XXXV (1922), pp. 108–20.
35. Oswald Spengler, *The Decline of the West* (English translation C. F. Atkinson; New York: 1928).
36. Stefan Zweig, *Three Masters* (English translation E. & C. Paul; New York: 1930).
37. Julius Meier-Graefe, *Dostoevsky: The Man and His Work* (tr. H. M. Marks; New York: 1928).
38. André Gide, *Dostoevsky* [1925] (Harmondsworth: Penguin, 1967). See also the eclectic paper by Henri Peyre, 'The French Face of Dostoevski', in *Dostoevski and the Human Condition after a Century*, A. Ugrinsky, F. S. Lambasa, V. K. Ozolins (eds), Westport, Conn.: Greenwood Press, 1986).
39. Jacques Rivière, 'De Dostoiewsky et de l'insondable', *Nouvelle Revue Française*, Février 1922; reprinted in *Nouvelles Études* (Paris: Gallimard, 1947), p. 179.
40. Nikolay Berdyaev, *Dostoevsky* (English translation D. Attwater; New York: [1934] 1957).
41. *The Times Literary Supplement* 5 June 1930.
42. Eugène Melchior, Vicomte de Vogüé, *Le Roman Russe* (Paris: 1886).
43. See especially Vyacheslav Ivanov's *Freedom and the Tragic Life* and Mikhail Bakhtin's *Problems of Dostoevsky's Poetics*.
44. Eduard Thurneysen, *Dostoevsky* (English translation K. Crim; London: Epworth Press, 1964), p. 44.
45. Derek Traversi, 'Dostoevsky', *The Criterion* XVI (1937), pp. 585–602. Reprinted in Wellek, op. cit.
46. Boris Tomasevskij, 'Literature and Biography' (English translation H. Eagle), *Readings in Russian Poetics*, ed. L. Matejka and K. Pomorska (Ann Arbor: MIT Press, 1978), p. 47.
47. Ibid., p. 55.

3

After Apocalypse: Some Elements in Late Lawrence[1]
DONALD MACKENZIE

'Last *things*, as such', wrote Barth in his 1924 commentary on *The Resurrection of the Dead*, 'are not *last* things, however great and significant they may be. He only speaks of *last* things who would speak of the *end* of all things, of their end understood plainly and fundamentally, of a reality so radically superior to all things, that the existence of all things would be utterly and entirely *based* upon it alone, and thus, in speaking of their end, he would in truth be speaking of nothing else than their beginning.'[2] This articulates the crux of all eschatological speech: 'last *things*, as such, are not *last* things'; the Day of Judgement does not fall within any time-scheme and yet the reality it is believed to signal remains bonded with history and the temporal. It is a crux faced by all speech that essays the transcendent, that aspires, or is driven, to say what cannot be said in language. But eschatology may press it upon us with an especial sharpness. This is at least partly because the roots of Christian eschatology are twined with apocalypse.[3] And apocalypse notoriously, flamboyantly, proclaims the end of the present cosmos and its history in language and concepts that are unabashedly drawn from within both.

It is this which gives apocalypse its dynamic instability. If taken seriously it generates tensions that drive it beyond itself. If it is not so driven it degenerates into a low-grade science-fiction, a futurology aggressive or doom-laden or triumphalist – the kind of power-fantasy Lawrence denounces with a hectoring precision in his own commentary on Revelation (*Apocalypse*, pp. 62–3, 143–4). When carried beyond itself apocalypse has proved remarkably, and variously, seminal. It can enforce an iconoclastic theology of renewal as in the early Barth.[4] Or it can open the way to a theology of world-history, as attempted by Pannenberg.[5] At the opposite extreme it can funnel into existentialism: one sees this happening very clearly in Bultmann's Gifford lectures on *History and Eschatology*.[6]

These examples – they could be multiplied – testify to the continuing power of apocalypse in theology and as a mode of apprehending the world. It welds together – or maybe only yokes – history and cosmology; myth and the possibility of an iconoclastic disruption of myth. It is strongly dualist and yet possessed by a sense of the unity of history but not of that unity as teleological or benign. Rather it apprehends history as coiled about by the demonic, if not given over to it. Its sense of the demonic climaxes in the lurid myths of Armageddon but it would be unjust to apocalypse not to recognise the burden of theodicy that also impels it, its passion for the justification of the martyrs, the final undoing of all injustice, which is also the justification of God.[7] It is this concern for theodicy that can undergird the apocalyptic myths of renewal:

> And God shall wipe away all tears from their eyes; and there shall be no more death, neither sorrow nor crying, neither shall there be any more pain: for the former things are passed away. And he that sat upon the throne said, Behold, I make all things new. And he said unto me, Write: for these words are true and faithful. And he said unto me, It is done. I am Alpha and Omega, the beginning and the end. I will give unto him that is athirst of the fountain of the water of life freely (Rev. 21: 4–6).

The end of all things repristinates their beginning; in so doing it offers to integrate and transcend the history that lies between them. It is this which can save apocalypse from the blank world-rejection and the fantasies of destruction that are its inherent danger.[8]

As a mode of apprehending the world, apocalypse does not lose its fascination when secularised, cut loose from any anchoring in God as the transcendent Alpha and Omega of cosmos and history, made wholly intra-mundane. It remains for the post-Christian imagination a major heritage from the Christian centuries. Or perhaps not a heritage; perhaps only a radio-active deposit.

I

It is certainly the case that the imagination of apocalypse has haunted the imagination of the wasteland, if only as antagonist and problematic answer. In Section V of Eliot's eponymous poem apocalypse mutters on the margins of the Waste Land:

> Who are those hooded hordes swarming
> Over endless plains, stumbling in cracked earth
> Ringed by the flat horizon only
> What is the city over the mountains
> Cracks and reforms and bursts in the violet air
> Falling towers
> Jerusalem Athens Alexandria
> Vienna London
> Unreal

Or it is refocused in the spectral intensities of

> bats with baby faces in the violet light
> Whistled, and beat their wings
> And crawled head downward down a blackened wall
> And upside down in air were towers
> Tolling reminiscent bells that kept the hours
> And voices singing out of empty cisterns and
> exhausted wells

In 'Little Gidding', which marshalls the later poetry to a climax as *The Waste Land*, the earlier apocalypse is deflected into Pentecostal irruption: 'the dove descending breaks the air/With flame of incandescent terror' – an irruption held between the splendid opening epiphany

> the brief sun flames the ice, on ponds and ditches,
> In windless cold that is the heart's heat,
> Reflecting in a watery mirror
> A glare that is blindness in the early afternoon.
> And glow more intense than blaze of branch, or brazier,
> Stirs the dumb spirit: no wind, but pentecostal fire
> In the dark time of the year

and the more questionable integration of the close, 'When the tongues of flame are in-folded/Into the crowned knot of fire/And the fire and the rose are one.'

In Lawrence, *Women in Love* (at one stage to be titled *Dies Irae*), the first work to map a wasteland of the modern world, is also the first to be controlled by an imagination of apocalypse. The stories in *The Prussian Officer* volume, if we except the magazine-medievalism of *A Fragment of Stained Glass*, all centre on what one might call epiphanies of fracture, moments of breakdown which can also be moments of breakthrough: Louisa in *Daughters of the Vicar* washing the young miner's back; the widow in *Odour of Chrysanthemums* kneeling by the body of her dead husband ('she knew she had never seen him, he had never seen her, they had met in the dark and had fought in the dark, not knowing whom they met nor whom they fought. And now she saw, and turned silent in seeing') (p. 198); the whole pattern of *The Thorn in the Flesh*.

Such epiphanies may anticipate apocalypse but they remain individual, without the apocalyptic sense of an entire order being drawn irresistibly into a vortex of catastrophe and rebirth. One might argue the same for *The Rainbow*, even for Ursula's final vision, though the latter is obviously an extreme borderline case.

The distinctive wasteland of *Women in Love* – if one can call it that – is characterised by the triple working of a sensual culture that has broken loose from the spiritual, of mass industrialism, and of the vampire will: in Hermione a will-to-know, in Gerald a will-to-power and in his father a will-to-love. (I say *if* one can call it a wasteland because its world is so freighted with intimations of catastrophe. It could be urged that if we are to use the wasteland as an icon or a shorthand it should figure the sterile and the trapped, the place before or after catastrophe. It might also be urged that we should distinguish different images of the wasteland; and we should not believe that any of them, as images, are comprehensively true.) The wasteland in some of Lawrence's essays and stories of the 1920s is a wasteland of the deracinated, of the young people with their insistence on experience and having a good time and the undermining hostility beneath it (*St Mawr*, p. 79) – all that organic cohesion and decay of Europe against which Mrs Witt revolts (p. 100). This wasteland is the starting-point for his most ambitious essay in apocalyptic fiction, *The Plumed Serpent*, which is both a watershed for all the later Lawrence and also marks the end of the grappling with apocalypse that begins with *Women in Love*.

In *The Plumed Serpent*, as earlier in *St Mawr*, apocalypse is crossed with another motif, the return of the gods: crossed and decisively modified. St. Mawr himself breaks in on Lou's imagination out of an archaic world: 'a prehistoric twilight where all things loomed phantasmagoric, all on one plane, sudden presences suddenly jutting out of the matrix' (p. 35). But the Cambridge edition also annotates the first description of him 'glowing red with power' from a letter by Frederick Carter on the discussion with Lawrence of Carter's book on Revelation. 'From this', Carter says, 'came the landscape background of *St Mawr* and the red horse itself' (p. 232). And the burden of Lawrence's own *Apocalypse* is the recovery of a primary cosmic mythology beneath the overwriting of Jewish and Christian allegory. In *The Plumed Serpent* the Aztec religion gives him a cyclic mythology where each cycle ends in cosmic catastrophe and rebirth. And if apocalypse decisively shapes in this way the return of the gods in Lawrence their return shapes, no less decisively, his imagining of apocalypse. It becomes not – or not only – the end-catastrophe to which a disintegrating order drives; it becomes a return to, still more a return *of*, the primally numinous and renewing.

The crossing of apocalypse with the return of the gods is one feature that distinguishes Lawrence's handling of the latter, itself one of the major responses of the imagination to the modern world. Even to checklist some of its multiple forms from Keats or Hölderlin to Pound and beyond is not possible in an essay of this scale. One can only indicate in passing the key-features that define Lawrence's imagining of such a return. Crucial to it is the re-establishing of man's connection with his non-human universe. (This separates it decisively from such stories as those of Buchan or the early Forster or Pater's more potent *Denys l'Auxerrois* and *Apollo in Picardy*, where the pagan surfaces to disrupt a world that has forgotten it.) To carry through what Lawrence seeks would need a recreated religion, with ritual and liturgy; it would ramify into social and political transformation. This is what *The Plumed Serpent* tries to embody and no one, I imagine, will contest the judgement that, on this side, it fails – and fails so extravagantly as to seal the whole undertaking as preposterous in the first place. Until, perhaps, one remembers Pound and what can be claimed for some of *The Cantos*.[9]

This re-establishing means, secondly, that the pathos of distance, the sense of the gods as inaccessible or withdrawn, so strong in Hölderlin or Keats, has no place in Lawrence.

Thirdly, and perhaps most interesting, the gods evoked are non-Olympian: the Aztec gods of Mexico and, from the Mediterranean world, principally Pan. The implications of this I shall touch on at the end.

I have called *The Plumed Serpent* a watershed work for the later Lawrence. In it he pushes the key preoccupations of the years after the finishing of *Women in Love*, the years not only of the travel-novels but of the essays on *Democracy* and *Education of the People* and of *Studies in Classic American Literature*, through to their tangled conclusion. It carries to an extreme his grapple with a messianic politics of power and his cloudily apocalyptic reading of European history, the westward drift of the white race and its consciousness to the New World, its death-encounter with an alien blood. That Lawrence's handling of those issues is messy, sometimes sinister, needs no arguing – though one might recall Empson's riposte:

> in his way he was very well balanced, that is, he could swing over till he was sickeningly near coming off his balance and then swing up and pass it again. The whole subject of *Apocalypse* is that he feels the meanness and evil of the lust for power over men as strongly as he feels its necessity and beauty. To be sure the book comes to no conclusion, but it is an experience; it is a walk round an important subject. And in his evasive way he had a very political mind; the whole point of the mystical and anthropological and psychological background was to see how life can be lived well in the unique conditions of the modern world.[10]

I quote this not only because it seems to me generous and exact but because it provides an entry to the late work which can be seen as shaped – shaped, not determined – by a recoil from the situations the Mexican writings had explored *à l'outrance*. It is a recoil which takes several, overlapping, forms. The late stories return to earlier Lawrentian places and topics. Places: the English Midlands and the Mediterranean. Topics: *The Virgin and the Gipsy* harks back to the early fictions of break-out (*Daughters of the Vicar, Mr Noon*); its Major Eastwood is a cameo from the Nordic world of *Women in Love*; the latter novel's rendering of industrialism and pitting against it of the isolated, individual couple recur, drastically narrowed, in *Lady Chatterley's Lover* which also resurrects the figure of the gamekeeper from *The White Peacock*.

As this indicates, the recoil works itself out in a narrowing of focus and field.[11] And *Lady Chatterley's Lover* – Lawrence's most traditional novel – is exceptional in the late fiction, whose clearest successes are in fable (*The Virgin and the Gipsy, The Man who Loved Islands, The Escaped Cock*). As fables these have the anonymous individualising signalled by the titles with their echoes of ballad, as in *The Virgin and the Gipsy*, or fairy-tale, as in *The Princess*. It is a quality of anonymity that stops off on this side of archetype and myth. ('I will ask her nothing', says the man who had died in *The Escaped Cock* 'not even her name, for a name would set her apart. And she said to herself: He is Osiris. I wish to know no more.') (p. 59). As fables they also exhibit a crystallised form and a liberation, perhaps only a lightening, of mood and tone from the heavy intensities of the apocalyptic fictions that had preceded them.

II

The transition comes in *The Flying Fish* fragment Lawrence wrote when recovering from near-fatal illness at the end of his time in Mexico. Its opening beautifully encapsulates the evocation of the Mexican landscape which is the strength of *The Plumed Serpent* and the apocalyptic vision of which that landscape becomes the vehicle. For Gethin Day

> in the last years, something in the hard, fierce finite sun of Mexico, in the dry terrible land, and in the black staring eyes of the suspicious natives had made the ordinary day lose its reality to him. It had cracked like some great bubble, and to his uneasiness and terror, he had seemed to see through the fissures the deeper blue of that other Greater Day where moved the other sun shaking its dark blue wings. Perhaps it was the malaria; perhaps it was his own inevitable development; perhaps it was the presence of those handsome, dangerous, wide-eyed men left over from the ages before the flood in Mexico, which caused his old connections and his accustomed world to break for him. He was ill, and felt as if at the very middle of him, beneath his navel, some membrane were torn, some membrane which connected him with the world and its day. The natives who attended him, quiet, soft, heavy and rather helpless, seemed he realized, to be gazing from their wide black eyes always into that greater day whence they had come and where they wished to return. Men of a

dying race, to whom the busy sphere of common day is a cracked and leaking shell (p. 209).

This recalls the 'dark sun' passage from *The Plumed Serpent* (pp. 122–6). It may also recall, further back, that potent image at the climax of 'The Industrial Magnate' chapter of *Women in Love* when Gerald, looking at his own face in the mirror

> dared not touch it, for fear it should prove to be only a composition mask. His eyes were as blue and keen as ever, and as firm in their sockets. Yet he was not sure that they were not blue false bubbles that would burst in a moment and leave clear annihilation. He could see the darkness in them, as if they were only bubbles of darkness. He was afraid that one day he would break down and be a purely meaningless babble lapping round a darkness (p. 232).

To one side of this visionary breakdown lies the modern desolation pinpointed in the sketch of Vera Cruz

> where the wild primeval Day of this continent met the busy white-man's day, and the two annulled one another. The result was a port of nullity, nihilism concrete and actual, calling itself the city of the True Cross (p. 217).

To the other side lies Gethin Day's return to his family home described in the pseudo-Elizabethan prose of his ancestor's *Book of Days*:

> 'Daybrook standeth at the junction of the ways and at the centre of the trefoil. Even it rides within the Vale as an ark between three seas; being indeed the ark of those vales, if not of all England.' – So had written Sir Gilbert Day, he who built the present Daybrook in the sixteenth century (p. 208).

The image of the ark there is interesting. It figures in the 1924 essay *Books* as an image of the adventuring consciousness that alone avails in the catastrophe of a doomed civilization:

> Catastrophes alone never helped man. The only thing that ever avails is the living adventurous spark in the souls of men. If there

is no living adventurous spark, then death and disaster are as meaningless as tomorrow's newspaper.

Take the fall of Rome. During the Dark Ages of the Fifth, Sixth, Seventh centuries A. D., the catastrophes that befell the Roman Empire didn't alter the Romans a bit. They went on just the same, rather as we go on today, having a good time when they could get it, and not caring. Meanwhile Huns, Goths, Vandals, Visigoths and all the rest wiped them out.

With what result? The flood of barbarism rose and covered Europe from end to end.

But, bless your life, there was Noah in his ark with the animals. There was young Christianity. There were the lonely fortified monasteries, the little arks floating and keeping the adventure afloat. There was no break in the great adventure of consciousness. Throughout the howlingest deluge, some few brave souls are steering the ark under the rainbow. (*Reflections on the Death of a Porcupine*, p. 199).

That has the no-nonsense energy and the bouyancy that are attractive in much of Lawrence in the early 1920s – the postwar sense of breakdown and the gipsy freedom of the travel-writing alike steadied by a sense of quest. In *The Flying-Fish*, by contrast, the ark provides an image of withdrawal but also of mastery and protection. It has to be set against the other images of the flying-fish and the dolphins:

And always, always like a dream, the flocks of flying-fish swept into the air, from nowhere, and went brilliantly twinkling in their flight of silvery watery wings rapidly fluttering, away low as swallows over the smooth curved surface of the sea, then gone again, vanished, without splash or evidence, gone. One alone like a little silver twinkle. Gone! The sea was still and silky-surfaced, blue and softly heaving, empty, purity itself, sea, sea, sea.

Then suddenly the faint whispering crackle, and a cloud of silver on webs of pure, fluttering water was soaring low over the surface of the sea, at an angle from the ship, as if jetted away from the cut-water, soaring in a low arc, fluttering with the wild emphasis of grasshoppers or locusts suddenly burst out of the grass, in a wild rush to make away, make away, and making it, away, away, then suddenly gone, like a lot of lights blown out in one breath. And still the ship did not pause, any more than the moon pauses, neither to look nor catch breath. But the soul pauses and holds its breath, for wonder, wonder, which is the very breath of the soul (pp. 219–20).

This is risky but I think it works, a mesmerising and self-recovering prose that has ahead of it the evocation of the dolphins and behind it – this is important – the transcended emptiness of

on the softly-lifting bow-sprit of the long, swift ship the body was cradled in the sway of timeless life, the soul lay in the jewel-coloured moment, the jewel-pure eternity of this gulf of nowhere (p. 219).

The Flying-Fish is only a fragment and in danger when its fable tilts heavily towards allegory. The most ambitious of the late fables is, of course, *The Escaped Cock*. It too returns to long-standing Lawrentian themes. There is the old insistence, one-sided if not obsessive, that the murdered and betrayed invite their murder and betrayal. The rejection of the Christian resurrection story as only a sealing of death is voiced as early as *The Rainbow* (pp. 261–2 where the narrative suddenly breaks into direct address) as well as in the late article on *The Risen Lord*; and there is a 1925 essay on *Resurrection* (*Reflections*, pp. 233–5) which reads almost as a précis for the story but with an aggressive exaltation that links it rather with *The Plumed Serpent* and is happily absent from *The Escaped Cock* itself.

It is, for all that, the most extreme of the late fictions. It systematically recasts biblical texts and motifs: sometimes making its didactic point heavily as with the Emmaus story (pp. 32–3); sometimes allowing it to emerge from an echo, as when the priestess's question 'Can I not give of my own? who is going to oppose me and the gods?' sets the response of the vineyard-owner (Matt. 20:15) resonating in a new context (p. 51; cf. *Apocalypse*, p. 146); sometimes melting down a scripture paradox into a paradox of its own: 'I am risen in my own aloneness, and inherit the earth, since I lay no claim on it' (p. 31).

The recasting can be seen at its most effective in the passage where the man who had died looks at the peasant who is sheltering him and reflects:

Why then should he be lifted up? Clods of earth are turned over for refreshment; they are not to be lifted up. Let the earth remain earthy, and hold its own against the sky. I was wrong to seek to lift it up. It was wrong to try to interfere. The ploughshare of devastation will be set in the soil of Judea, and the life of this peasant will be overturned like the sods of the field. No man can save the earth from tillage. It is tillage, not salvation ... (pp. 22–3).

That meshes a key text from John (12:32) with suggestions of 1 Corinthians 15: 47–9 and maybe Revelation 22: 11 and modulates them into another, aphoristic idiom. It shapes a genuine challenge to the Christian belief in the redemption and transformation of the world ('Let the earth remain earthy, and hold its own against the sky') where the rejection of Christian sacrament at the climax (p. 55) can hardly escape being stigmatised as founded on a vulgar error.[12]

The return of the gods is given a vehement twist in *The Escaped Cock* with its risen Christ who in Part One renounces his mission to become in Part Two Osiris to the waiting priestess of Isis. The rejection of the messianic is fed by the desire for singleness, isolation, distance that is recurrent in all the later Lawrence (*Kangaroo, St. Mawr*) and gives *The Plumed Serpent* its rare moments of the convincingly religious as when Kate at the age of forty knows that she no longer wants 'love, excitement and something to fill her life' but 'to be alone with the unfolding flower of her own soul, in the delicate chiming silence that is at the midst of things' (p. 60). But here the desire can be expressed with the extremism fable makes possible:

> always he must move on, for if he stayed, his neighbours wound the strangling of their fear and bullying round him. There was nothing he could touch, for all, in a mad assertion of the ego, wanted to put a compulsion on him, and violate his intrinsic solitude. It was the mania of individuals, it was the mania of cities and societies and hosts, to lay a compulsion upon a man, upon all men. For men and women alike were mad with the egoistic fear of their own nothingness.
>   And he thought of his own mission, how he had tried to lay the compulsion of love on all men. And the old nausea came back on him. For there was no contact without a subtle attempt to inflict a compulsion (p. 34).

After Apocalypse: Some Elements in Late Lawrence 45

The spare intensity of this vision is not far from hysteria. Or would not be, were it not met and transcended in the second part by the renewal of contact carried in the fable's insistent patterning of touch – a patterning that climaxes in its reshaping of atonement:

> his death and his passion of sacrifice were all as nothing to him now, he knew only the crouching fullness of the women there, the soft white rock of life.
> 'On this rock I build my life' . . .
> So he knew her, and was at one with her.
> Afterwards, with a dim wonder, she touched the greater scars in his sides with her finger-tips, and said:
> 'But they no longer hurt?'
> 'They are suns!' he said. 'They shine from your touch. They are my atonement with you' (pp. 57–8).

This culminates the recasting of the biblical throughout: the sovereign future tense of the promise to Peter (Matt. 16:18) becomes the a-historical present of a life that has renounced the messianic; 'his face shone unconsciously' recalls the Moses of Exodus 34:29 (and possibly the Pauline exegesis of it in 2 Corinthians 3:7–18) but telescopes it into the quite unbiblical imagery of the inner sun.

In itself this passage sways dangerously on the edge of the laughable ('He crouched to her, and he felt the blaze of his manhood and his power rise up in his loins, magnificent. "I am risen!"'). But perhaps one should take it with the rhapsodic climax

> the man looked at the vivid stars before dawn, as they rained down to the sea, and the dog-star green towards the sea's rim. And he thought: How plastic it is, how full of curves and folds like an invisible rose of dark-petalled openness that shows where the dew touches its darkness! How full it is and great beyond all gods . . . . I am like a grain of its perfume, and the woman is a grain of its beauty. Now the world is one flower of many petalled darknesses, and I am in its perfume as in a touch (p. 58).

and the carefully-counterpointed close where buoyant drift – 'So let the boat carry me. Tomorrow is another day' – faces an image re-routed from apocalypse: 'the gold and flowing serpent is coiling up again, to sleep at the root of my tree' (p. 61).[13]

III

The resurrection, for Christian belief, is the sovereign but also elusive – at moments tormentingly elusive – mystery in which the immanent and historical are assumed into the transcendent, the point at which, in the phrase of Cornelius Ernst, 'the world which belongs to man becomes the world which belongs to God'.[14] 'What is wrong', Mackinnon asks, 'with the simple down-to-earth realism of those who say that either Christ rose or he did not?' And he answers:

> Simply, I think, that they would enclose within the category of event what is itself more than event . . . [Christ's] resurrection, although in one sense in time, possesses also a relation to the eternal as unique and ultimate as that of the universe itself to its creation. Indeed, what I would be prepared to argue is that here for Christians is focused the very relation of the temporal to the eternal itself. So that maybe we would not be wrong if we saw creation itself through this event, which is more than event.[15]

That 'event which is more than event' is also the point from which apocalypse must be reconstructed. Or, rather, it is the point at which we may glimpse a meeting of apocalypse and history in which both are transfigured. As Ernst puts it in the essay from which I have just quoted:

> We want to see Jesus as someone who walked in Galilee and Jerusalem, who, from the originating source of meaning in himself, prior to a literal-metaphorical distinction, was and is the supreme and unique revelation of God, beyond distinctions of meaning . . . . If by 'meaning' we may provisionally understand the process or praxis by which the world to which man belongs becomes the world which belongs to man, then we may see a man's life as tranformation in and of meaning, a 'metaphor' beyond metaphors . . . the Resurrection is the ultimate 'metaphor' of the world, its translation and trans-figuration.[16]

What Lawrence does in *The Escaped Cock* is to dovetail resurrection wholly back into the natural, to assert against all forms of transcendence the claims and splendour of life in the flesh. There is the vision of storming energies that breaks on the man who had died as he

> looked nakedly onto life, and saw a vast resoluteness everywhere flinging itself up in stormy or subtle wave-crests, foam-tips emerging out of the blue invisible, a black-and-orange cock, or the green flame tongues out of the extremes of the fig-tree. They came forth, these things and creatures of spring, glowing with desire and with assertion. They came like crests of foam, out of the blue flood of the invisible desire, out of the vast invisible sea of strength, and they came coloured and tangible, evanescent, yet deathless in their coming. The man who had died looked on the great swing into existence of things that had not died, but he saw no longer their tremulous desire to exist and to be. He heard instead their ringing, ringing defiant challenge to all other things existing (p. 21).

This throws up the last question which the man who had died asks himself as he 'went on deeper into the phenomenal world, which is a vast complexity of entanglements and allurements', 'From what, and to what, could this infinite whirl be saved?' (p.33). The story pivots on that question as we move from the harshness (Madeleine takes the risen Jesus for a spy instead of the biblical gardener) and clangour of Part One to the beautifully composed evocations of landscape and weather and daily ritual around the temple of Isis in Part Two (pp. 35–6 or 48–50). The 'determined surge of life' (p. 22) modulates down into the pervasive presence of the sea, into the image of the priestess as we move towards the climax ('her swaying softly subsided, like a boat on a sea that grows still') (p. 53), into the final escape. And Lawrence has not lost the genius of his travel-writing for the swift, definitive phrase: 'here at the temple he felt peace, the hard, bright pagan peace with hostility of slaves beneath' (p.44).

The celebration of the sensuous here-and-now, as this should demonstrate, is not simplistic. And the greater day – that rocking paradox of the apocalyptic vision – has not been forgotten though it too has been wholly naturalised:

> The sun fell on the corner of the temple, he sat down on the step, in the sunshine, in the infinite patience of waiting. He had come back to life, but not to the same life that he had left, the life of the

little people and the little day. Re-born, he was in the other life, the greater day of the human consciousness. And he was alone and apart from the little day, and out of contact with the daily people. Not yet had he accepted the irrevocable *Noli me tangere* which separates the re-born from the vulgar. (p. 44)

The divisions there hark back as far as *The Rainbow* and the *Study of Thomas Hardy* which offers a 'metaphysical' commentary upon it. Their formulation in the *Study* comes in the context of tragedy.[17] Here they come in a context that might claim to lie on the far side of tragedy and they feed into a desire for integration. At the end of a careful evocation of 'the little day, the life of little people' the narrative has the man who had died say to himself: 'Unless we encompass it in the greater day, and set the little life in the circle of the greater life, all is disaster' (p. 50). Very well, one might respond, but how? but how? It may seem absurd to ask such questions of a fable, but of a fable as insistently didactic as this one might ask them. The integration of the individual with his own life and with the greater life of the cosmos is rendered in the stepping-stone precision of the passage that follows the rhapsodic climax quoted earlier:

> he stayed in his cave in the peace and the delight of being in touch, delighting to hear the sea, and the rain on the earth, and to see one white-and-gold narcissus bowing wet, and still wet. And he said: This is the great atonement, the being in touch. The grey sea and the rain, the wet narcissus and the woman I wait for, the invisible Isis and the unseen sun are all in touch, and at one. (pp. 58–9)

This is pure epiphany and wholly persuasive (where the proclaiming of man's unity with the cosmos in *Apocalypse* can weary). But when it comes to the integration of the greater life with that of the little day the story slides into escapist drift. Fable as a form may license such escape but a fable as strenuous as *The Escaped Cock* is bound to wobble if it avails itself of it.

This last point can bring into focus the rejections that drastically limit *The Escaped Cock* even if they are essential to the crystalline integration it achieves. It rejects the world of politics and of history; and with them tragedy. The text that comes to mind here for contrast and definition is Dostoevsky's *Legend of the Grand*

Inquisitor.[18] More accurately, one might say that Lawrence has rejected human life as shaped in and by history. Though maybe clearest in this fable, that rejection goes deep in his work. At least from *Women in Love* onwards he apprehends history, and so any developed society, through apocalypse. Rejection of the latter leaves him falling back on the immediate sensuous life of the here-and-now.

Apocalypse offers a counterweight, especially on politics (e.g. pp. 68–72 or 145–8). *Its* limitations are caught by Empson in the phrase I quoted earlier: 'a walk round an important subject'. Its handling of politics and history is too impatient; the sweeping absolutism smothers the possible perceptions of irony and tragedy in political action which could lie beneath the surface absurdity of some of its judgements (e.g. p. 165).[19] A common element that may link those rejections and the rejection of Olympian myth is a hostility to the fixed, the individuated, the final:

> Gods should be iridiscent like the rainbow in the storm. Man creates God in his own image, and the gods grow old along with men who made them. But storms sway in the heavens, and the god-stuff sways high and angry over our heads. Gods die with the men who have conceived them. But the god-stuff roars eternally, like the sea, with too vast a sound to be heard . . . .

That is effective enough, if a bit hectic (like much of *Apocalypse*). It combines anthropological relativism with a drive towards the primally numinous. Such a drive is Lawrence's deepest impulse as a religious writer. Hence the importance of Pan for him and the rejection of the Olympians that goes with it: 'Don't you imagine', asks Cartwright in *St Mawr*, 'Pan once *was* a great god, before the anthropomorphic Greeks turned him into a half a man?' (p. 65) And again in *Apocalypse*: 'The Olympic-heroic period was only an interlude. The Olympic-heroic vision was felt to be too shallow, the old Greek soul would continually drop to deeper, older, darker levels of religious consciousness all through the centuries' (p. 116). (Cf. *Reflections*, pp. 315–16.)

This anti-anthropomorphism is not Hebraic at all: pre-Socratic rather.[20] It gives Lawrence an intense freedom of response. Yet one wonders how far the evocation of the primally numinous can be sustained without lapsing into a windy primitivism; and to that question *St Mawr* does not prompt any very positive answer.

Certainly when I consider Lawrence's rejection of the Olympian world I find myself thinking of Otto's luminous mediation of it in his *Homeric Gods* and – not least in the present context – of the stimulus Bonhoeffer acknowledges from the latter in his prison sketches for a Christianity that will recover a true worldliness. (One could cite, for instance, the comment he quotes in one of his letters: 'this world of faith which springs from the wealth and depth of human existence, not from its cares and longings'.)[21]

Engaging with the Resurrection and with *Revelation*, these two late works bring into final focus the deepest of Lawrence's rejections, the rejection of transcendence – all that for Christian belief comes under the credal rubric of: he ascended into heaven and sitteth on the right hand of the Father. In the New Testament the resurrection of Christ is inseparable from his exaltation whether this occurs in formula (as in Romans 1:4) or in the spaced-out Lucan narratives of the Ascension or in the tighter account of John 20 which suggests 'that for the fourth Evangelist, the separate events of Easter, Ascension and Pentecost are presented as in fact falling within twenty-four hours, aspects of the single Paschal mystery'.[22] For Lawrence, of course, such transcendence is out of the question: there is only one world; any asymmetric transcendence, whether of a creator God over his creation or of Platonic Form over particulars, is not an option to be seriously considered. *The Escaped Cock* only carries through with the polemical beauty of fable what his work has presupposed from the beginning. And if we wish to maintain the New Testament presentation – as I certainly do – we have to ask what sense we, in our present world, can give to, for instance, Colossians 1:15–20. But even if we are only in the business of comparing myths we have to ask whether Lawrence's rejection of transcendence does not leave his fable enormously thinner, narrower than the myth it so insistently reworks.

The rejections in those late works are drastic; and they leave the world of the here-and-now that they celebrate radically limited. Against this we have to set not only the intermittent splendour but the flexibility of that celebration. If we say it is a world that excludes tragedy – and Lawrence is never at any time a tragic writer – we must ask whether some modern valuations of tragedy as a supreme or central form are at all justified. (We have also to consider the kind of tragedy this Lawrentian world might encompass, the kind of tragedy he suggests in the fine introduction, also late, to his own translation of Verga's *Maestro-Don Gesualdo*). Finally, we should acknowledge that Lawrence pursues both apocalypse and the return of the gods with a single-mindedness that, if it can precipitate him into absurdity or worse, also makes him exemplary – not least because his single-mindedness raises forcibly the question of their fruitfulness as responses to the modern world.

To be more specific: he raises the question whether apocalypse is not decisively truncated when severed from the transcendent and from history; and whether myth is no less truncated when what we might call its Olympian phase is rejected. His handling of myth and the numinous I have touched on. As for apocalypse, once severed from transcendence, become wholly intramundane, can it retain much or anything of the complex power I tried to catch in my opening sketch? Does it not become purely an imagination of catastrophe, an imagination that excludes tragedy no less than it excludes theodicy and renewal? Or else a sailing and optimistic imagination of renewal that deludes itself it can escape from history?

There are obvious reasons why apocalypse should solicit the modern imagination ('These are apocalyptic times, my dear sir' Strelnikov tells the hero in *Dr Zhivago*, 'this is the Last Judgment. This is a time for angels with flaming swords and winged beasts from the abyss, not for sympathisers and loyal doctors');[23] and reasons, not less compelling, why it should be resisted. This is not at all to deny that apocalypse and the return of the gods are two of the strongest answers to an experience of the wasteland. It is only to claim that the imagination of both should entertain a purifying agnosticism. I end with two passages which – in very different idioms – enforce such an agnosticism. The first – in relation to the return of the gods – is from Heidegger's essay 'Building, Dwelling, Thinking':

> Mortals dwell in that they await the divinities as divinities. In hope they hold up to the divinities what is unhoped for. They wait for intimations of their coming and do not mistake the signs of their absence. They do not make gods for themselves and they do not worship idols. In the very depth of misfortune they wait for the weal that has been withdrawn.[24]

Against the brooding gravity of that we might set – on apocalypse and apocalyptic readings of human experience – a passage from Barth; not the volcanic and prophetic Barth of the 1920s but the

Mozartian church theologian of the *Dogmatics*. Sketching "Phenomena of the Human" in *CD 111/2* he considers, after materialist and idealist anthropologies, the existentialist claim that in frontier situations we encounter the transcendent other which calls our existence into question; and he asks,

> Millions of our contemporaries have been constantly plunged from one frontier situation (in the most intense sense) to another. But what has it all meant to them in practice? Has any one encountered the wholly other, and been changed by this encounter, as a result of taking part in the fighting in Russia or Africa or Normandy, of suffering the Hitler terror, of enduring aerial bombardment, hunger and imprisonment, of losing loved ones, of being in extreme danger of death dozens of times, and of having some sense of personal implication in the common guilt? Humanity is tough. It seems to have been largely capable of dealing with the confrontation of transcendence supposedly implied in these negations of its existence ... according to the present trend, we may supppose that even on the morning after the Day of Judgment – if such a thing were possible – every cabaret, every night club, every newspaper firm eager for advertisements and subscribers, every nest of political fanatics, every pagan discussion group, indeed, every Christian tea-party and Church synod would resume business to the best of its ability, and with a new sense of opportunity, completely unmoved, quite uninstructed, and in no serious sense different from what it was before. Fire, drought, earthquake, war, pestilence, the darkening of the sun and similar phenomena are not the things to plunge us into real anguish, and therefore to give us real peace.

And he ends by citing that most piercing of Old Testament theophanies when God reveals himself to Elijah on Horeb in a still, small voice or – in one of the alternative renderings one has heard proposed – in the voice of a very sharp stillness. 'The Lord', says Barth, 'was not in the storm, the earthquake or the fire (1 Kg 19:11f). He really was not.'[25]

Notes

1. Lawrence texts are quoted from the Cambridge edition where that is available: *Apocalypse and the Writings on Revelation*, ed. M. Kalnins (1980); *The Plumed Serpent*, ed. L. D. Clark (1987); *The Prussian Officer and Other Stories*, ed. J. Worthen (1983); *The Rainbow*, ed. M. Kinkead-Weekes (1989); *Reflections on the Death of a Porcupine and other Essays*, ed. M. Herbert (1988); *St Mawr and Other Stories*, ed. B. Finney (1983); *Study of Thomas Hardy and Other Essays*, ed. B. Steele (1985); *Women in Love*, ed. D. Farmer (1987). *The Escaped Cock* is quoted from the edition by G. M. Lacey (Los Angeles, 1973). For the Introduction to Koteliansky's translation of *The Grand Inquisitor* I have used *Phoenix*, ed. E. D. Macdonald (London, 1936); and for the Introduction to *Maestro-Don Gesualdo* and the article on *The Risen Lord*, *Phoenix II*, ed. W. Roberts and H. T. Moore (London, 1968). Page references for quotations are given in brackets in the text.
2. English translation H. J. Stenning (London, 1933), p. 110.
3. Christopher Rowland in *The Open Heaven* (London, 1982) has argued a documented case for eschatology as only one element, and not a constitutive one, in apocalypse (see e.g. pp. 48, 75–77, 188–9). One could accept this and still argue that it is the eschatological element that has counted in the later history of apocalypse. The emphasis on the revelation of a secret knowledge in apocalypse is, of course, highly relevant to Lawrence's dealings with the subject.
4. One might compare here *Church Dogmatics II/1*, English translation T. H. L. Parker et al. (Edinburgh, 1957), pp. 631ff. with its engaging passage of theological autobiography.
5. See e.g. his *Jesus – God and Man*, English translation L. L. Wilkins and D. A. Priebe (London, 1968), pp. 74ff, 165–9, 191ff and esp. 365ff.
6. One might compare Pannenberg's criticism, in his essay on 'Hermeneutic and Universal History', of Bultmann's existentialist interpretation of the New Testament texts: *Basic Questions in Theology*, Vol. 1, English translation G. H. Kehm et al. (London, 1970), pp. 109–11 – not least in view of the stress on man's relation to the cosmos in Lawrence's writings on apocalypse.
7. See e.g. Jurgen Moltmann *The Crucified God*, English translation R. A. Wilson and J. Bowden (London, 1974), pp. 160ff., with the criticisms of Pannenberg on pp. 176–7.
8. Cf. the key-role of prolepsis in Pannenberg's use of apocalypse (e.g. *Jesus – God and Man*, pp. 60ff or 106–8). In a different context cf. Frank Kermode's discussion of apocalyptic fictions and the concords they achieve in *The Sense of an Ending* (London, 1967), pp. 5ff.
9. See e.g. the essay on Pound in D. S. Carne-Ross *Instaurations* (Berkeley, 1979), pp. 193ff. and esp. 211–6; the discussion of Pound in Chapter 3 of Charles Tomlinson's *Poetry and Metamorphosis* (Cambridge, 1983), which quotes (p. 54) the characterisation of him as 'a pagan fundamentalist'; or Michael Alexander's suggestive phrase for Canto 47: 'a reconstituted pagan Deuteronomy' (*The Achievement of Ezra Pound*, London, 1979), p. 180.

10. *Argufying* (London, 1987), p. 460.
11. Cf. Kermode: 'Lawrence and the Apocalyptic Types' (reprinted in e.g. the *Casebook* on *The Rainbow* and *Women in Love*, ed. C. Clarke (London, 1969), pp. 203–18); more specifically, on the predominance of preordained types in the later fiction (pp. 217–18).
12. Cf. the judgements of Donald Davie in *A Gathered Church* (London, 1978), pp. 91–7 and the issues in religious and cultural history they open up.
13. See e.g. *Apocalypse*, pp. 5–6 for documentation of Lawrence's use of Pryse's *Apocalypse Unsealed* from which this kind of imagery derives. Cf. *Apocalypse*, pp. 123ff.
14. *Multiple Echo* (London, 1979), p. 75.
15. G. W. H. Lampe and D. M. Mackinnon, *The Resurrection* (London, 1966), pp. 63–4.
16. Ibid. This pregnant formulation, emerging from a discussion of metaphor and ontology in Aquinas and Pseudo-Dionysius, gets us beyond the common and not very helpful insistence on the resurrection as metaphorical. It might be correlated with Michael Edwards' discussion of 'the tense and surely astonishing' Pauline oxymoron of the spiritual body in *Towards a Christian Poetics* (London, 1984), pp. 5ff. Might oxymoron be considered the characteristic figure of the resurrection, as paradox (*Verbum Infans, figlia del tuo figlio*) of the incarnation and chiasmus of the atonement (cf. 2 Corinthians 5: 21 or Greville's great axial lines in *Caelica XCIX*: 'With glory scourging all the sprites infernal/And uncreated hell with unprivation')?
17. See e.g. *Study*, pp. 20–21 or 95–101.
18. See, however, Lawrence's lucid engagement with the Dostoevsky fable in the Introduction he wrote for Koteliansky's translation about the time he had finished *Apocalypse*: *Phoenix*, pp. 283–91.
19. *Apocalypse*, of course, requires more than this cursory judgement; I hope to consider its treatment of myth and politics more fully in a future study of *Myths of England* in Kipling, Lawrence and others.
20. Cf. e.g. Heraclitus, fragment 36 (in the numbering of Burnet's *Early Greek Philosophy*): 'God is day and night, winter and summer, war and peace, surfeit and hunger; but he takes various shapes just as fire, when it is mingled with spices, is named according to the savour of each' (Burnet, p. 149). Mara Kalnins argues for the importance of Heraclitus in particular for *Apocalypse* and the last writings in 'Symbolic Seeing: Lawrence and Heraclitus' in Kalnins (ed.) *D. H. Lawrence: Centenary Essays* (Bristol, 1986), pp. 173–90.
21. *Letters and Papers from Prison*, English translation R. Fuller et al. (London, 1971), pp. 331–3.
22. D. M. Mackinnon: *Themes in Theology* (Edinburgh, 1987), p. 162.
23. *Dr Zhivago*, English translation M. Hayward and M. Harari (London, 1958), p. 227. The issues raised here echo through the book up to Gordon's final comment in the Epilogue, after he and Dudorov have listened to the terrible childhood story of Zhivago's daughter.

    Take that line of Blok's 'We, the children of Russia's terrible years': you can see the difference of period at once. In his time, when he

said it, he meant it figuratively, metaphorically. The children were not children, but the sons, the heirs of the intelligentsia, and the terrors were not terrible but apocalyptic; that's quite different. Now the figurative has become literal, children are children and terrors are terrible. There you have the difference. (p. 463).
24. *Poetry, Language, Truth*, English translation by A. Hofstadter (New York, 1971), p. 150.
25. *Church Dogmatics 111/2*, English translation H. Knight et al. (Edinburgh, 1960), pp. 114–15.

4
Wyndham Lewis on Time
MARTIN JARRETT-KERR, CR

Ethelbert the Builders' Foreman is defending the relevance of the past and of old ruins to his sceptical, anti-historical mates. He says (in his improbable stage cockney):

> There's some new notion about time, what says that the past – What's be'ind you – is what's goin' to 'appen in the future, bein' as the future 'as already 'appened. I aven't 'ad time to get the 'ang of it yet; but when I read about all those old blokes they seems much like us.[1]

Ethelbert (in *The Rock*) is, like Eliot himself, in favour of Church restoration. The reference to the 'new notion' is to J. W. Dunne's *An Experiment with Time*, published by Black in 1927, but reissued by – guess who? – *Faber & Faber* in 1938. Dunne's ingenious exposition of 'serialism' came just at the right moment to give mathematico/scientific respectability to an attempt to translate Einsteinian relativity theory into popular drama. Dunne's first success was with J. B. Priestley, whose first 'time-play', *Dangerous Corner*, appeared in 1932. Here the 'Dunne-influence' was slight. But *Time and the Conways* (1937) was a deliberate attempt to put Dunne on the boards. It presents 'Observer II' (Kay at twenty) watching what will happen to her as 'Observer I', over twenty years later. Dunne's third book, *The New Immortality* (1938) includes an exposition of his 'serial' theory, including diagrams. This exposition, he tells us, was 'given to an audience of about 1,200 at a "Foyles Literary Lunch" on April 2nd 1936'; and this 'was repeated to the cast of Mr Priestley's play, *Time and the Conways*'.[2] Unfortunately we have Priestley's own account of this: 'Mr Dunne not only came to see the play in London but also gave a talk to the actors after the performance, in what seemed to be a gallant but rather desperate attempt to explain his theory to them'.[3]

None of this needs taking seriously, least of all Priestley's middlebrow entertainment. But the topic of 'time' continues to be important, if only as an example of how high-level speculation can seep down into popular leisure–culture in a decade or two. Probably the books of Henri Bergson were the most significant element in the public interest in the nature of Time. His appeal was a combination of brilliant imaginative illustration, a good foundation in biology, and a welcome challenge to the empiricist–determinist–mechanist assumptions which dominated French intellectual life at the turn of the century – and French then meant European. His discussion of time is only a part, but an important part, of a wider review of the contrasts between the intuitive and the analytic, the creative and the repetitive, the 'inner' and the 'outer'.

> When you raise your arm, you accomplish a movement of which you have, from within, a simple perception; but for me, watching it from the outside, your arm passes through one point, then through another, and between these two there will be still other points; so that if you begin to count, the operation would go on for ever. Viewed from the inside, then, an absolute is a simple thing; but looked at from the outside it is [subject to] an inexhaustible enumeration.[4]

It is fascinating to recall that the conversion to Christianity of two such different philosophers as Jacques Maritain (who ended up 'Thomist') and Gabriel Marcel (so-called 'Christian existentialist') was due to the – at that time – agnostic Bergson. And Von Hügel, though critical of much in Bergson, saluted the Frenchman's 'wonderful delicacy and penetration in his distinction between "clock-time" and *"la durée"* '; for 'all the characteristically human values and ideals . . ., the very notion of worth, are developed . . . not in Time but in Duration'; so that 'History is busy with realities which, at bottom, even here and now, are not in "Time" at all'.[5]

T. S. Eliot attended Bergson's lectures in Paris in October 1910 at the Collége de France, and was impressed by them. Nine years later this influence seems not to have disappeared; the notion in 'Tradition and the Individual Talent' of a new work of art simultaneously affecting all preceding works of art, is faintly

Bergsonian: 'Whoever has approved of [the] idea of order, of the form of European . . . literature will not find it preposterous that the past should be altered by the present as much as the present is directed by the past'.[6] It is true that Bergson was largely supplanted by Bradley in Eliot's thinking (see below); but traces of Dunne and Bergson remain.

When Eliot went to Paris in 1910 he was accompanied by his friend Wyndham Lewis. But it is unlikely that Lewis went with him to Bergson's lectures, for he had heard them before. At some date between 1902 and 1908 Wyndham had been to the Collège de France, and noted that Bergson 'was an excellent lecturer in philosophy, dry and impersonal with a high collar and frock coat'.[7] (Note the praise of 'impersonal'.) And though he later took Bergson as his main target in his fusillade against 'time the enemy' he admitted to a debt, especially to Bergson's notion of 'laughter'. But now comes a paradox. I have quoted from Bergson's early essay, which became a booklet (of eighty pages), *Introduction to Metaphysics*. But the English translation, vetted by Bergson himself, was by T. E. Hulme, who followed up the translation by a series of essays on Bergson, posthumously printed in *Speculations*.[8] Hulme had been sent down from St John's College, Cambridge for a youthful misdemeanour (1904); but it was a letter from Bergson, predicting that Hulme would produce important work in the philosophy of art, that persuaded St John's to take him back.[9] How could this enthusiasm of Bergson's co-exist with the severe 'classicism' that had attracted Lewis to him? Lewis in fact thought they were incompatible: 'Bergson dominated [Hulme] and . . . anything tainted with Bergsonism could not help being suspect to me.' Nevertheless Lewis had had to say that Hulme was 'one of the most promising intelligences produced in England since the Shaw–Wells–Bennett vintage'.[10] So Lewis tolerated the mixture.

But why was Lewis so hostile to 'Bergsonism'? Ezra Pound was much more simply dismissive of Hulme. He said that he thought Hulme's philosophical studies merely 'crap'; and he added: 'DAMN Bergson and frog diarrhoea'.[11] But Lewis's fusillade was part of a wider and more considered campaign, and an important one. So to that we turn.

Lewis's *Time and Western Man* came out in 1927, and startled the public if only for its range, covering contemporary, as well as classical theory of art, modern poetry and prose, with a remarkably wide reading in philosophy. At first glance it seems a mere *tour-de-force*, lumping together disparate essays on (for instance) 'Romantic vs. Classic', Sculpture, ancient and modern, Russian ballet; Gertrude Stein, Proust, Joyce, Pound; Henri Brémond on *La poésie pure*; Leibniz, Locke, Berkeley, and Hume; Schopenhauer, Nietzsche and Spengler; Einstein, Bergson, Russell, Whitehead, Samuel Alexander; Michaelangelo, Rodin, Epstein and Picasso. Yet if we see the book as a 'Theme and Variations', a closer look reveals that the argument holds together remarkably well – whether one agrees with it or not. He starts from a careful examination of the changing meanings and implications of the terms 'classical' and 'romantic', and concludes – while giving due weight to the importance for 'continuity' of the 'classical' – that there cannot be a hard-and-fast division between the two: 'the best in European art has never been able to be "classic", in the sense of achieving a great formal perfection'.[12] For lying behind these oppositions is a deeper one: that between the permanent and the changing, between motion and stillness, between (ultimately) space and time.

Bergson had stated unequivocally that the primal error of philosophy from Plato to Plotinus was the assumption that

> There is more in the immutable than in the moving, and that [we pass] from the stable to the unstable by a mere diminution. [But we moderns have rightly] learned to place the moving continuity of creation (*la durée*) as the locus of real life.[13]

Bergson uses the example of the creative writer to illustrate the nature of 'intuition' as distinct from scientific analysis. When the artist has collected all his materials, made all the notes on his subject, he has not yet got the work. He must 'place himself directly at the heart of the subject, and . . . seek as deeply as possible for an impulse' – for he is looking 'not for a thing, but [for] the direction of a movement'.[14]

It is precisely this 'priority of flux' that Lewis wishes to challenge; and he finds this priority everywhere in modern literature and philosophy – even in sculpture, when he describes the 'fluid photographs in commercially produced marble' of Rodin, which he calls 'the plastic counterpart of Bergson (his sculpture contemporary with the doctrine of the *élan vital*, and looking as though it had been done expressly to illustrate it'.[15] And Lewis extends his net to sweep in variegated specimens of the same 'Time-bend' or 'cult of the Flux', such as the artistic primitivism of Gauguin, the ethnic primitivism of Rousseau (the cult of *le sauvage*), the linguistic ditto (or baby-talk) of Gertrude Stein, and the ethical relativism of William James – leading to the extreme behaviourism of J. B. Watson, the relativism of Nietzsche, and the evolutionary flux of 'Philosophy of Organism'.

If we want a brief statement of what Lewis wanted to assert, against the 'time-obsession' which he is attacking, it is to be found in a short statement by the Thomist, Père Rousselot, whom he quotes:

> 'Abstraire, c'est mépriser le fluent et postuler la permanence; c'est donc cristalliser ce qui se répand, concentrer le diffus, glacer ce qui coule, c'est Solidifier.'
>
> 'That is what I claim to do, in my painting, my novels, my criticism,' says Lewis: 'To despise the fluid and to postulate permanence, to crystallize that which (otherwise) flows away, to concentrate the diffuse, to turn to ice that which is liquid, mercurial – to solidify'.[16]

This sounds impressive. But what sort of reception did it get? Eliot, of course, welcomed it, in spite of Lewis's criticism, in *Time and Western Man*, of his (Eliot's) friends, Pound and Joyce. Yeats, surprisingly, 'read it with ever growing admiration and envy'. Equally surprising was the reaction of some theologians. Fr Martin D'Arcy, the top-rank Jesuit, collector of highbrow scalps, gave it five pages in *The Month* ('*Permissu superiorum*').[17] We have, he said, many artists, critics and philosophers, but seldom all in one: 'the unique quality of this book is that it is by an artist, a critic and a philosopher'. Lewis, knowing the contemporary arts, has 'detected a fatal flaw' in almost all of them. Fr D'Arcy lauds a passage by Prof. Bosanquet, cited by Lewis:

> The modern Italian neo-Idealists ... and the English and American neo-realists who are represented by Prof. Alexander and the 'Six', [all agree on one principle:] ... In both alike we have the actual and ultimate reality of Time, progress to infinity, as the ultimate character of the Real.[18]

Fr D'Arcy was not uncritical; but they became lifelong friends, and Lewis, of course, painted a famous portrait of him.

Another unexpected welcome to *Time and Western Man* came in a now forgotten work of philosophical theology, *The Incarnate Lord* by Fr Lionel Thornton, CR.[19] Fr Thornton totally lacked poetry, music, or humour; but he was a good philosopher, and he devoted four pages of his book to Lewis.

> Mr Lewis is an author whose distinction and versatility are well-known. . . . He proclaims himself a disciple of Plato. He is an artist turned philosopher, who has a special predilection for space as against time.

Fr Thornton agrees with Lewis and his 'more obvious criticisms of recent evolutionary philosophy', and says that

> when Lewis identifies the 'reality' of the space–time realists with the great river Flux . . . this identification seems to be substantially correct.

He also agrees with Lewis's criticism of 'Dr. Broad's very unsatisfactory theory of sense-data'.[20] He does not agree about Whitehead: but of that, more later. Whether Fr Thornton is right to call Lewis himself a 'Platonist' is less clear. The only pure 'platonic' statement I can find in his works is expressed by Vincent Penhale, the anti-hero of Lewis's slight but amusing and unusual novel, *The Vulgar Streak*. Vincent is a self-defeating failure, and ends by hanging himself. Pinned to the corpse is a chilling note:

> Whoever finds this body, may do what they like with it. *I* don't want it. Signed: its former inhabitant.[21]

The Ghost has clearly abandoned the machine: 'The Body – The Tomb'.

Wyndham Lewis's dealings, in *Time and Western Man*, with his fellow-artists were less favourably received. To express his 'spatialism' he paraded the 'temporalists'. One of these was Proust.

> 'Proust', said Lewis, 'embalmed himself alive. He died as a sensational creature in order that he should live as historian of his dead sensational self. . . . When the complicated and peculiar

needs of admiration exacted by his slight, ailing feminine body ... were in the nature of things no longer forthcoming ... he bleakly awoke [and so became] an historical person by embalming himself in a mechanical medium of time.'[22]

This is clever; but is it true? The young Marcel, thinking of the many faces of Albertine, tries to remember one but finds it difficult since the relation to her is 'impregnated with an element of love which, ever unsatisfied, lives always in the moment that is to come'.[23] But that is not Proust submerged in Time; it is the emotional state of one fictional character. An earlier passage looks more 'Bergsonian', when Marcel ponders his relationship with his father:

> In theory one is aware that the earth revolves but in practice one does not perceive it, the ground upon which one treads seems not to move, and one can rest assured. So it is with Time in one's life ... In saying of me 'He's no longer a child', [or] 'His tastes won't change now' – my father had suddenly made me conscious of myself in Time.[24]

And this made young Marcel depressed. But again, there seems no sense of existence swamped by time here. And Proust once took issue with Bergson on philosophical grounds.

> Bergson claims that consciousness overflows the body and extends beyond it. Where memory and philosophic thought is concerned, that is obviously true. But such is not M. Bergson's meaning. According to him, the spiritual element, because it is not confined in the physical brain, can, must, survive it. But the fact is that consciousness deteriorates as a result of any cerebral shock. Merely to faint is to annihilate it. How, then, is it possible to believe that the spirit survives the death of the body?[25]

Proust, then, is more of a positivist than Bergson.

Earlier, Lewis had spoken of 'the school of Bergson–Einstein–Stein–Joyce–Proust'.[26] This may be just, applied to Gertrude Stein; but it can't be applied to Einstein, who was a mathematician; still less to Joyce. This is one of Lewis's strangest aberrations, and for a time caused much bitterness between the two. Joyce was patient and detached about it, and deferential to his cleverer friend. When Lewis said, loftily, 'there is not much reflection going on at any time inside the head of Mr James Joyce'[27] I don't think Joyce minded – he wasn't interested in what Lewis meant by reflection. And Joyce-critics have convincingly shown that Lewis missed the point, especially of *Ulysses*. His description of Stephen Dedalus ('the frigid prig') and of Bloom ('the author, thinly disguised as a middle-aged Jew tout')[28] is a total misjudgement. The fine study of *Ulysses*, S. L. Goldberg's *The Classical Temper*[29] shows the subtlety and delicacy of the relationship between Stephen and Bloom, and its development. Of course it is a 'time novel', but without surrender to or romanticising of the fluidity of passage. 'The Classical Temper' (a phrase of Joyce's), says Goldberg,

> displays itself as a responsive openness to life, a firm grasp on the centrally human ... and allegiance to the objective, and a mistrust of metaphysical or naturalistic 'realities' abstracted from human experience.[30]

And other critics demonstrate how, concealed in *Finnegans Wake*, Joyce replied to Lewis by satirising his finicky superiority.[31]

Returning to Lewis's philosophical interests, we have seen how Fr D'Arcy and Fr Thornton praised his perceptiveness. But in Lewis's desire to sweep as many thinkers as he could into his dustbin marked 'Time-servers', he recklessly included the author of *Science and the Modern World*. On Schopenhauer, Edouard von Hartmann, Bergson (perhaps), William James, J. B. Watson, and Samuel Alexander, Lewis is acute, in his swashbuckling manner. But Whitehead stands apart. Fr Thornton's expert understanding of Whitehead is a proper corrective.

> Mr Lewis has made a serious blunder, which goes far to spoil the argument of his book. In his haste to destroy the 'enemy' he has unfortunately mixed up Whitehead the Platonist with the wretched crowd of behaviourists and gland-worshippers upon whom his wrath is so justly poured forth.... To identify the God of Whitehead with the emergent time-god of Alexander is a first-class blunder.[32]

There is another formidable philosopher whom Lewis also tackles: F. H. Bradley. (I have seen no discussion of this part of *Time and Western Man*.) Eliot, of course, had studied Bradley intensively for three years.[33] Lewis's account is different, and less sympathetic. He takes Bradley – rightly – as the finest expression of Absolute Idealism. But

> Bradley, who was a great metaphysician, appears nevertheless to us discouraged and crushed himself, by the contradictory, invisible weight of his Absolute.... His Absolute *appears*: but it shows a perplexed and dismal face.... While introducing his Absolute, Bradley exhibits what seems a lack of belief, and so fails to inspire it.[34]

There may be truth in this; but Bradley is not always so negative:

> I trust we may have reached a conviction... not merely that time is unreal, but that its appearance also is compatible with a timeless universe. It is only when misunderstood that change precludes a belief in eternity. Rightly apprehended it affords no presumption against our doctrine. Our Absolute must be; and now, in another respect, again, it has turned out possible. Surely it is real.[35]

And Lewis could have found further support from Bradley's ethics. The Appendices to *Essays on Truth and Reality* are devoted to a demolition of William James's pragmatism and pluralism. Lewis might have relished Bradley's conclusion:

> If... I am told that I have no right to ask for metaphysical doctrine where none was ever offered, I shall content myself with a smile. If there is anything in philosophy of which I am fully assured, it is ... that to seek to discuss the nature of truth apart from a theory of ultimate reality ends – must end – in futile self-deception.[36]

There is one point at which Lewis and Bradley appear to coincide, and it is precisely on the topic of time: though Lewis seems not to have noticed it. In his long, racy, satirical poem, 'One Way Song' Lewis has the lines:

> Always, Eyes-Front! Creatures of Progress! suited
> Only for one-way travel, in Time bodily rooted
> Try and walk backwards: you will quickly see
> How you were meant only *one-way* to be! ...

Perhaps Lewis had spotted a modest footnote in Bradley's *Appearance and Reality*, which runs:

> We think forwards, one may say, on the same principle on which fish feed with their heads pointing up the stream.[38]

The connection between 'classicism', 'tradition', 'spatialism' (versus 'temporalism') and the political Right seems obvious. Why, then, have I said nothing about Lewis the 'fascist', the 'racist', the anti-semite – in short, the friend of Roy Campbell? The standard picture can be found in Valentine Cunningham's *British Writers of the Thirties*.[39] On that I have two remarks. First, though I could provide a few more examples to confirm the picture, I could also match quotation for quotation to show a completely different one. And second, the conspicuous absentee from the list of periodicals and 'weeklies', on which Mr Cunningham relies, is the only intelligent one of the period: the *New English Weekly*.

What is relevant to the theme of Time in Lewis is his own development, both in his life and in his writing. He abandoned some of his more absurd opinions; and his fiction shows a maturing spirit. Tolstoy, when a precocious fifteen-year-old, worked out two simple propositions:

> Time is man's ability to conceive of many objects in one space, while Space is man's ability to conceive of many objects at one and the same time.[40]

But the two are not symmetrical: time, unlike space, is (or seems to us, *pace* J. W. Dunne and, perhaps Mr Rupert Sheldrake) irreversible. We have seen that what Lewis missed in Joyce was precisely the growth of Stephen from clever dialectics to self-knowledge, and the unconscious, but warm contribution of Bloom to that process. In his own novels Lewis too developed: notably in his pictures of women in *The Revenge for Love* and *Self-Condemned*. His strange and terrifying apocalyptic speculations in 'The Human Age', especially the second and third volumes, *Monstre Gai* and *Malign Fiesta* are hardly 'reactionary'; and his predictions about future 'world government', in that remarkable history of American Presidents, *America and Cosmic man*,[41] are politically unclassifiable.

There is, of course, a *double-entendre* in my title, 'Wyndham Lewis on Time'. His own growth (including a mellowness that came from suffering, especially from his gradual blindness) was not a surrender to Time but an employment of it. The late Frederick Tomlin has written movingly (from personal knowledge) of his development in a certain theological awareness.[42] In the present post-new-critical, post-structuralist literary climate – one which is hard to distinguish from a total relativism – Lewis is still 'timely'. True, he supports the priority of intellect, against any surrender to 'mysticism', for it

> has been given us as the appointed and natural path on which to make our approach to God. The emotional is too indiscriminate, and it is unlikely that then God would be encountered. Rather our hungry Self would waylay us.[43]

And it is precisely the sense of the priority in being, the 'beyondness' of Deity that renders the notion of God Emergent and Evolving so outrageous to Lewis. In 1943 he praised a book by Christopher Hollis:[44]

> It is his [Hollis's] position . . . and must be the position of anybody I should say, if they give it a moment's thought – that in the matter of the famous 'Rights of Man', all 'rights' must and only can, derive from God, there being no other discoverable sense in the expression.[45]

In 1949, commenting on the death of a mutual friend, Lewis wrote:

> PS. Very sorry to hear about poor old Born. Mans life is but a vibration in an eyelash of God. We are Born, we Die. In life we are in death.[46]

But only two years before his own death in 1957 he had a long discussion with Hugh Kenner about the projected fourth part of 'The Human Age', which would have been called 'The Trial of Man'. In his discussion, reported by Kenner, he revealed that he had changed his perspective (at seventy-three years of age), and had hinted at this, in what would appear in this fourth volume, Pullman's sudden realisation that 'God values man: that is the important thing to remember.'[47] But, due to declining health, he was never able to write the volume.

Notes

1. T. S. Eliot, *The Rock* (London: Faber, 1934), pp. 15–16.
2. J. W. Dunne, *The New Immortality* (London: Faber, 1938), p. 79: referring to J. B. Priestley, *Time and the Conways* (1937).
3. J. B. Priestley, 'Author's Note', in *Three Time Plays* (London: Pan Books, 1947), p. viii. Mr Priestley complains that some critics felt that he had not really absorbed Dunne's philosophy into *Time and the Conways*, but merely put a later scene earlier than the one supposed to precede it. I'm afraid I agree with the critics.
4. Henri Bergson, *An Introduction to Metaphysics* (English translation T. E. Hulme; London: Macmillan, 1913), pp. 5–6. (Translated from *Revue de Métaphysique, et de Morale* (Paris, Janvier 1903)).
5. F. von Hügel, *Essays and Addresses*, Vol. II (1926), p. 53. (First given as 'The Place and Function of the Historical Element in Religion', London Society for the Study of Religion, 2 May 1905).
6. T. S. Eliot, 'Tradition and the Individual Talent', in *Selected Essays* (1932 edn), p. 15. (Reprinted from *The Egoist*, October 1919.)
7. Jeffrey Meyers, *The Enemy – A Biography of Wyndham Lewis* (London: Routledge & Kegan Paul, 1980), p. 16.
8. T. E. Hulme, *Speculations* (Collected and edited by Herbert Read) (London: Routledge & Kegan Paul, 1936) Chapters 4 and 5.
9. The flyleaf of Bergson's *Introduction to Metaphysics* announces: 'Ready Shortly: an Introduction to Bergson's Philosophy, by T. E. Hulme'. Did it ever appear – except in the essays and lectures given in 1909 and 1911? (See Michael Roberts, *T. E. Hulme* (London: Faber, 1938; reprinted by Carcanet Press, 1982, pp. 16–17).
10. Wyndham Lewis, *Blasting and Bombardiering* (London: Calder & Boyars, 1967), p. 107. (Originally published 1957.)
11. Quoted in Humphrey Carpenter, *A Serious Character – The Life of Ezra Pound* (London: Faber, 1988), p. 114.
12. Wyndham Lewis, *Time and Western Man* (hereafter *T. & W. M.*), (London: Chatto & Windus, 1927), pp. 24–5.
13. Bergson, *Introduction to Metaphysics* pp. 64–5.
14. Ibid., 76–7.
15. *T. & W. M.*, p. 156.
16. Pére Rousselot, quoted (no ref. given) in Wyndham Lewis, *Paleface. – The Philosophy of the Melting-Pot* (London: Chatto & Windus, 1929) pp. 253–5.
17. *The Month*, No. 150, December 1927. 'A Critic Among Philosophers' by Martin D'Arcy, SJ, pp. 511ff. (Unfortunately the rule by which the correspondence of Jesuits is embargoed for forty years means that research students will be unable to consult the Lewis–D'Arcy letters before 2016. Fr Teilhard de Chardin was wily enough to deal with this ban before his death. Fr D'Arcy was not so pragmatic.)
18. Bosanquet, cit. in *T. & W. M.*, p. 156.
19. Lionel Spencer Thornton, *The Incarnate Lord* (London: Longmans, 1928).
20. Ibid., pp. vi–xi.

21. Wyndham Lewis, *The Vulgar Streak* (1941; republished 1973, Jubilee Books) p. 240.
22. *T. & W. M.*, p. 265.
23. Marcel Proust, *Remembrance of Things Past* (New Translation by T. Kilmartin; Harmondsworth: Penguin, 1983) 'Place Names: The Place', I. 101.
24. Ibid., 'Mme Swan at Home', I. 520.
25. Proust, from unpublished letters and notes, in André Maurois, *Proust – Portrait of a Genius* (English translation, 1983) I. 101. (Cited in Hans Meyerhoff, *Time in Literature* (Berkeley: University of California Press, 1960)) pp. 76ff.
26. *T. & W. M.*, p. 106.
27. Ibid.,
28. Ibid., p. 117.
29. S. L. Goldberg, *The Classical Temper* (London: Chatto & Windus, 1961).
30. Goldberg, op. cit., p. 32. (The phrase occurs in Joyce's *Stephen Hero*: Stephen says to the President, 'My entire esteem is for the 'Classical Temper' in art . . . a temper of security, satisfaction and patience . . . . The romantic temper. . . . is an insecure, unsatisfied and impotent temper.' Could Lewis have described it better? And surely Pound is right about Joyce: '(He) writes a clear hard prose. He deals with subjective things, but he presents them with such clarity of outline that he might be dealing with locomotives or with builders' specifications . . . . One can read Mr Joyce without feeling that one is conferring a favour'. (E. Pound, *Literary Essays* (London: Faber, 1954), p. 399).
31. Cf. Geoffrey Wagner, *Wyndham Lewis – A Portrait of the Artist as Enemy* (London: Routledge & Kegan Paul, 1957), esp. Chapter 11: 'Master Joys and Windy Nous'. Also Peter de Voogd, 'James Joyce, Wyndham Lewis and the Mediatization of Word and Image', in *Dutch Quarterly Review of Anglo-American Letters* (Vol. i, 1988, Leiden). And George Otte, 'Time and Space': Joyce's response to Lewis', in *James Joyce Quarterly*, Vol. 22, no. 3, Spring 1983. [I am indebted to Mr Alistair Stead, of Leeds University School of English, for these references.]
32. L. S. Thornton, op. cit., p. xi.
33. Eliot studied Bradley seriously from June 1913 to January–February 1916. [I owe the details to Mr Geoffrey C. Hines, who has long been working on Eliot's philosophical–religious development – a work which I hope will one day be published.]
34. *T. & W. M.*, pp. 398–9.
35. F. H. Bradley, *Appearance and Reality* (1893; cited from 1930 edn.) Chapter xviii, p. 149.
36. F. H. Bradley, *Essays on Truth and Reality* (Oxford: The Clarendon Press, 1914), p. 149.
37. *Collected Poems and Plays of Wyndham Lewis* (Ed. Allen Munton; Manchester: Carcanet Press, 1979), p. 67. (For a more sophisticated – and abstruse – discussion of Lewis's grasp of contemporary 'Time Philosophy' than we have room – or competence – for, see the long note by Paul Edwards and Steve Walker on the 'Relativity Cantos' (xxv

38. Bradley, *Appearance and Reality*, op. cit, p. 189, fn.
39. Valentine Cunningham, *British Writers of the Thirties* (Oxford: Oxford University Press, 1988). Here are a few counter-quotations: On Anti-Semitism: Lewis writes to an acquaintance: 'How you can manage to cling to your romantic feelings in the matter of Jews I cannot understand ... I gather ... that if some murderous tyrant decided to kill all the Jews he could lay his hands on, you would be prepared to regard him as rather a sound fellow. I do not see how that historical racial emotion can survive the *next* war.' (1950, *Letters of Wyndham Lewis*, ed. W. K. Rose, Methuen, 1968, pp. 519ff.). On Politics: 'I was devoutly thankful to learn that the Tories had not got in ... Capitalism is as rampant as before ...'. (1945, *Letters*, pp. 391ff.) Or: 'Luckily we have a Socialist Government, which is here to stay'. (1948, *America and Cosmic Man*, loc. cit.). On changing his mind: 'Long ago ... it became apparent to me that I had been wrong ... in opposing the war. Before the Munich Conference – I saw clearly ... that Hitler was that most detestable of things a chronic and unteachable little militarist, who just would have his good old second war ...'. (1942, *Letters*, p. 324.) (And, of course, four years before that he had repudiated his book of 1931 in praise of Hitler, by writing *The Jews, Are They Human?* and *The Hitler Cult*, (1938)).
40. I owe this brilliant *aperçu* by Tolstoy to A. N. Wilson's anthology, *The Lion and the Honeycomb – Religious Writings of Tolstoy* (London: Collins, 1987) p. 155.
41. Wyndham Lewis, *America and Cosmic Man* (Nicholson & Wilson, 1948), p. 173.
42. E. W. F. Tomlin, in the Introduction to *Wyndham Lewis: An Anthology of his Prose* (London: Methuen, 1969). Other studies by Tomlin are *Wyndham Lewis* (British Council series on 'British Writers and their Work', no. 64, 1955 (revised, 1969); and, most important of all, the chapter 'The Philosophical Influences', in Jeffrey Meyers (ed.) *Wyndham Lewis: a Revaluation* (London: Athlone Press, 1980). On the theological aspects I would add one passage that is of interest, and not much known: 'In the course of my work on Hegel, I came across a magnificent fragment of Søren Kiekegaard – Barth's philosophical inspiration you remember. He said all that is necessary to say about Hegel and other "existential" systems ...' (1943: *Letters of Wyndham Lewis.*, p. 357.)
43. *T. & W. M.*, p. 390.
44. Christopher Hollis, *The American Heresy* (1930).
45. *Letters of Wyndham Lewis*, p. 349.
46. Ibid., p. 49 (Wolfgang Born, Assistant Professor of Art in City College, New York, was teaching at St Louis and went there to stay).
47. Hugh Kenner, Appendix to *Malign Fiesta*, Vol. III of 'The Human Age' (London: Calder & Boyars, 1955).

5
Rewriting *The Waste Land*
MICHAEL EDWARDS

The Waste Land witnesses to the pain of writing, of undergoing an accumulated past, of books and of history, which is both plethoric and unending. So did Eliot's distress abate when he became a Christian? His views changed, but did they remove his earlier views? It is of interest to ask what we should expect. One might suppose that the standpoint of faith would make writing a straightforward, though challenging, activity, and would offer comfortable thoughts about the movement of history. Yet seeing things in a biblical light can render the 'vanity' of history and of writing even more momentous, and intolerable. To convert is to be shown a whole new world but also to realise more fully just how fallen is the old one. A Christian lives, surely, between two worlds, and although the second is *powerful* to be born, it is still not here. We have, but what we have is a 'pledge', a 'taste'; everything has changed, but the Change is for the future. Redemption makes a *différance*.

It is certain that after 1927, the year when Eliot became an Anglo-Catholic and also, strangely, the year of Yeats's rough beast, Eliot set about dealing with his atheist years (I use the word with its Pauline meaning) by rewriting the works they had produced. Appropriately, *Four Quartets*, the culmination of his Christian poetry, took on his most important pre-Christian poem and the one to which all his previous poetry had led. He seems to have seen the opportuneness of escaping from the waste land of time, and writing, and self, partly by, quite literally, rewriting *The Waste Land*. Yet *Four Quartets* recognises that to rewrite *The Waste Land* is not to dismiss the waste land: that one cannot, by an act of writing, merely enter a new world, and bracket the Fall. So Eliot, with a new faith, writes a poem which, while it explores that faith and the possibility it creates, also mocks its own pretentions to understanding, and is even more rigorous than *The Waste Land* in its searching of our ills.

Rather, indeed, as the New Testament, while promising and celebrating salvation, is more far-reaching than the Old in its condemnation of the world from which we need to be saved; and rather as Jesus Himself is fiercer than the Old Testament's wrathful – and loving – Jehovah. It is the gentle Jesus who says such things as, 'Ye are of your father the devil', and 'Depart from me, ye cursed, into everlasting fire.' The horror of *Four Quartets* is less intense than that of *The Waste Land*, but more real: 'O dark dark dark. They all go into the dark.'

Conversely, *The Waste Land* is not without hope, so that in his rewriting Eliot was able to take hints from it. As an example, the final, albeit disguised, 'yes' in the Russian reading of 'DA' (line 400), which is chiefly to engender the Sanskrit 'Datta', 'Dayadhvam' and 'Damyata', is a sign of Pentecost beyond the poem's Babel. The very scope of the poem is itself a positive. Its ground is no less than the geographical area of our civilisation, so many of whose roots it reaches for and whose remote source it traces to India. In a way it really is an epic, which feels its way out to the limits and down to origin, like the *Odyssey*, the *Aeneid, The Faerie Queene, Paradise Lost*. It attempts to hold civilisation by charting it.

That *Four Quartets* rewrites *The Waste Land* is known to the extent that the structure of 'Burnt Norton' and subsequently of the other quartets follows its five-part division, with sometimes close parallels such as the brief fourth-section lyrics on death; and also that the later poem retraces the steps of the earlier from a garden, or gardens, to a chapel: from a natural place, with mythic overtones, to a spiritual; from a place for innocence before the Fall to a place for guilt after. Both poems have a completed mythic shape, and the first is a kind of palimpsest for the second. Their beginnings and endings hum, furthermore, with correspondences. *Four Quartets* opens no less than *The Waste Land* with images of origin: tree, children, light, water, dust, and with their occultation, and even the 'time present' from which it views them, so as to enter the strain of time past and time future, is a reworking of the fractured *now* of *The Waste Land*, heavy with 'Memory and desire'.

It continually returns to the opening of the earlier poem, as part of its determination towards renewal. When the final lines of 'East Coker', for example, look through the 'empty desolation' of 'vast waters', or waste waters, they echo the cry, *'Oed' und leer das Meer'*, as a preparation for the searching beyond it in 'The Dry Salvages'. They add a specific meaning to the quartet's closing words: 'In my end is my beginning', since one of 'my' beginnings introduced into this end is the beginning of *The Waste Land*. The latter reappears in the 'midwinter spring' passage of 'Little Gidding', where it is finally and perfectly reversed. Instead of a real spring spurned in favour of a forgetful, undemanding winter ('winter kept us warm'), a real winter is appropriated by an imagined but demanding spring (the 'soul's sap quivers'); rather than a spring unnaturally seen as 'cruel', a winter is spiritually perceived as bringing a new kind of life, 'neither budding nor fading'. Here, the rewriting is plainly in the interest of change, of religious conversion. As the last of the quartets, 'Little Gidding' even summarises *The Waste Land* once more, in its move from spring to a chapel.

Indeed, as a poem which occupies the same geographical limits as *The Waste Land*, and which is similarly open to the suggestions of Indian religion, *Four Quartets* constantly takes up the matter of the earlier work so as to transform it. A dust which is only fearful becomes the sign of a necessary and ultimately joyful assent to mortality. Lust is rewritten as love. The passive and frustrated 'memory and desire' become a vigilant 'aftersight and foresight' ('Little Gidding' II); the 'use of memory' is seen as allowing love to expand 'beyond desire' ('Little Gidding' III). The waste land itself is transformed, into a 'life of significant soil' ('Dry Salvages' V), and into a series of real and imagined places, which strive towards the 'place of grace' of *Ash-Wednesday* V and the 'grace dissolved in place' of 'Marina'.

The location of the poet likewise changes. The writer in *The Waste Land* is placed, with an indirection which is itself indicative of the poem's discomposure, in a sanatorium, first at Margate (line 300) then near Lac Léman (line 182) in a 'decayed hole among the mountains' (line 385), where there is a chapel empty and in ruins. The writer in *Four Quartets*, or someone like him, finds his way to the chapel at Little Gidding, which is also a 'shell' ('Little Gidding' I) but whose 'husk of meaning' is nevertheless available to the penitent who is serious. The poems move from a secular place of healing to a spiritual. And the reader changes, through the poems' address to him. He is no less slyly involved, through the delayed apostrophe of 'Burnt Norton': 'My words echo / Thus, in your mind', but he is no longer an 'hypocrite lecteur' (line 76), to be fleered and reduced along with the writer.

Four Quartets also reworks the rhetoric of *The Waste Land*. *The Waste Land* is continually contradicting, undoing, itself. It enacts the self-laceration of a fallen language, thrown into confusion not only by the event at Babel, or by whatever you think that story refers to, but by the serpent of Genesis questioning and then denying statements by God, and so disturbing words all the way back to the Word. *Four Quartets* also abounds in contradictions, but they work for reconciliation. It too knows the antinomies of the Fall: the 'soundless wailing', for example ('Dry Salvages' II), of the sadness belonging to the sea. They cannot be written away; they are still written down, with the same urgency. But it also rehearses the compatible oppositions of faith: 'the darkness shall be the light', 'where you are is where you are not' ('East Coker' III), and so on, as a deliberately traditional vision. Its single untranslated quotation, 'Figlia del tuo figlio' ('Dry Salvages' IV), focuses paradox at the point where the Anglo-Catholic Eliot believes it to be redeemed, in the *'impossible* union / Of spheres of existence' achieved by the Incarnation (V). The poem reaches, one might say, for oxymoron: for a language, and the imagination it anticipates, proper to a world fallen and yet capable of re-creation. The warring parties of the seventeenth century are seen as finally 'United in the strife which divided them' ('Little Gidding' III); a spray of lavender is thought of as 'Pressed between yellow leaves of a book that has never been opened' ('Dry Salvages' III).

Even the word 'figure' figures. It insists at the outset, in the lyric of 'Burnt Norton' II, on the ultimate 'reconciliation' of the 'wars' in man and the non-human universe according to an older, figurative, vision, expressed in an earlier figurative poetry: 'The dance along the artery / The circulation of the lymph / Are figured in the drift of stars'; 'We move above the moving tree / In light upon the figured leaf'. By the end of that first quartet, however, it is part of the realisation, via St John of the Cross – 'The detail of the pattern is movement, / As in the figure of the ten stairs' – of the momentariness of transcendence ('Sudden in a shaft of sunlight') to one caught between 'un-being and being'. Its evolution in the last quartet begins with the reader having to understand that his approach to the chapel is inadequate: 'Either you had no purpose / Or the purpose is beyond the end you figured / And is altered in fulfilment' ('Little Gidding' I). It is a nice pun: our end and purpose, as penitents or as poets, are ahead of what we 'figure'. So the London street in the next section is left 'disfigured' (another pun) by the ghost and the Luftwaffe, in order that, in the next section and on the following page, the whole of experience can change:

See, now they vanish,
The faces and places, with the self which, as it could, loved them,
To become renewed, transfigured, in another pattern.

'Figured', 'disfigured', 'transfigured': it is a perfect ternary sequence.

Finally, the endings of the poems, where the transmutation of the earlier in the later is, as one would expect, the most evident. Rain does fall at the end of *The Waste Land*, yet the plain remains 'arid'; the last section of *Four Quartets* looks forward to discovering a river and a waterfall. The refining fire into which Arnaut Daniel immerses himself in the closing lines of *The Waste Land*, in a context which turns this vision or purgation into merely one of many jarring possibilities, returns secure in the 'refining fire' of 'Little Gidding' II and in the poem's last line. The troubled 'Shantih shantih shantih', which is either, indistinguishably, a deeply religious *envoi* or the utterance of a madman ('Hieronymo's mad againe'), becomes the quite untroubled 'All shall be well, and / All manner of thing shall be well' of Juliana of Norwich, repeated over and again as if part of a rite. Even here, however, the vision is set beyond apocalypse, and the certainties of the final lines are not overwhelming. They cannot prevent a phrase in 'East Coker' II: 'That was a way of putting it', from returning to the mind to rout complacency.

To see further into this rewriting, we need to realise, first, its wider significance as part of a return to beginnings. We know that Eliot was continually rewriting works of the past; after a time that past included his own works, so that he also rewrote himself, altering, quoting, using material left over. His poetic activity after his conversion is more specifically a determined attempt to 'redeem' his earlier verse, by discovering redeemed experience to the side of the fallen experience which that verse knew so well.

Four Quartets returns, time and again, to the beginning of his earlier poems, not only of *The Waste Land*, but of 'Gerontion', and even of 'The Love Song of J. Alfred Prufrock': it returns to the first page of the *Collected Poems*. It recalls, I believe one can show, detail after detail of their openings, so as to amend them. The incessant return is motivated partly by the desire to purify moments, and especially initial moments, of the past. It is also motivated, in its further ambition, by a need for beginning, for origin: for an unsullied Eden of experience and of writing. The allusive manoeuvre of *The Waste Land* involves, or so I have proposed elsewhere, a quite systematic refluence to the beginning of a poem (Brooke's 'The Old Vicarage, Grantchester'), of a long poem (*The Canterbury Tales*), of a book of poetry (*Les Fleurs du Mal*), of a narrative (*Heart of Darkness*), of a play (*The Spanish Tragedy*), of an opera (*Tristan and Isolde*), of a prophecy (Ezechiel); to the beginning of English poetry (Chaucer), of poetry itself (the Sibyl), of literature (a Veda), of Indo-European language (Sanskrit). It presses back to the 'sylvan scene' of origin (line 98) as quoted from *Paradise Lost* (IV 140), only to lose it in the fact that the person gazing on Eden there is Satan, who is about to destroy it. *Four Quartets* acts no less through quotations; it is equally intent on searching the beginnings of works; it probes even more explicitly for the Beginning.

Consider the works it uses. Like *The Waste Land*, it calls up the opening paragraphs of Conrad's *Heart of Darkness*, in the first lines of 'East Coker' III ('They all go into the dark'). In the same passage it quotes from the first speech of Milton's *Samson Agonistes* ('O dark dark dark'), while another adversary, Shelley, is present via the opening section of 'Ode to the West Wind', in the 'dead leaves' blown by the wind in 'Little Gidding' II and in the description of time as both 'destroyer' and 'preserver' in 'Dry Salvages' II. Milton also enters through his own beginning as a poet, the ode 'On the Morning of Christ's Nativity'. The ode has left several traces, one of which is the 'bedded axle-tree' on only the second page of 'Burnt Norton'. In stanza VII of the ode's 'Hymn', the sun withdraws at the appearance of a greater sun which its 'burning axle-tree' cannot bear; in Eliot, Jesus Himself is the axle-tree, the still point of the turning world, and I am not sure that anyone has noticed the pun on the 'bedded' Christ-child. The works of which Eliot approves mightily are likewise quoted in their beginnings. It is the initial figure of *The Ascent of Mount Carmel*, of St John of the Cross, which is translated at the end of 'East Coker' III ('You must go by a way wherein there is no ecstasy', etc.); it is the first two lines of Dante's *Commedia* which provide a way of describing the menacing experience of 'East Coker' II: 'In the middle, not only in the middle of the way / But all the way, in a dark wood', and its loaded return in V: 'So here I am, in the middle way'.

There is another work, however, whose beginning is of greater significance, and whose presence creates yet another link with *The Waste Land*. I suppose it must be a coincidence that the beginning of *The Romaunt of the Rose* is also much concerned with time, from line 369, and even with 'Thre tymes' (line 380); these are not times present, past and future, and the thinking about time is quite different. Yet when Eliot evokes a 'passage' which we did not take towards a 'door' we never opened into a 'rose-garden', is he not following Chaucer through the 'passage' (line 502), the 'dore' (531), by which the 'I' in Fragment A does pass so as to enter the most famous rose-garden of them all? In both gardens there is birdsong, from, among others, 'thrustles' (line 665) or a 'thrush'; both gardens resemble the 'paradys erthly' (line 648) or 'our first world'.

Like Prufrock, Chaucer's narrator seems to hear 'Song of mermaydens of the see' (line 680): the first poem in Eliot's *Collected Poems* also returns to origin in the *Romaunt*. But it is the relation to *The Waste Land* that is most revealing. *The Waste Land* opens with a distorted quotation from the first line of *The Canterbury Tales*, which enables Eliot to return to the beginning of English poetry as part of a troubled pursuit of origin, and with a view to embracing the history of poetry in a flurry of quotations which mainly incapacitate it. *Four Quartets* goes even further back, to an earlier work of 'the father of English poetry', for an embrace no longer sarcastic but reconciliatory; in which light, even the fact that the *Romaunt* is a translation takes on significance. Yet *Four Quartets* too disturbs origin, for like the 'sylvan scene' of *The Waste Land* its garden is flawed, or rather, it is not true Eden. What Eliot follows, into the rose-garden of the *Romaunt*, is the 'deception of the thrush'; he follows, one might say, the perilous but also, in this case, cautionary polysemy of words in a fallen language, since the 'deception' by which we are tempted is also a 'disappointing', from the French, and a 'taking', from the Latin.

By means of the *Romaunt*, Eliot returns, or aims to return, to a garden at the beginning of the world and a poem at the beginning of our poetry. And it is the sense of a beginning, even more than the sense of an ending, that bedevils writing, or that haunts it like a possibly holy ghost. It is evidently at work in *Paradise Lost*, which continually strives against its own title; in Pope's reworking of Milton in *The Dunciad*; in the Miltonic opening of Wordsworth's *Prelude*. In *The Waste Land*, an anguish about beginning is thoroughly Modernist. The plethoric past which excludes Eliot from origin makes it impossible for him to begin: he can only get under way by laying out phrases from Malory, Petronius, Dante, the Book of Common Prayer, Chaucer.

In the opening of *Four Quartets*, footfalls likewise 'echo in the memory', and it seems that Romantic anxieties return. Eliot's deceiving thrush is surely a reminiscence of Keats's nightingale, who calls to him like fancy, a 'deceiving elf'. Listen to the movement of their verse:

> Adieu! adieu! Thy plaintive anthem fades
>   Past the near meadows, over the still stream,
>   Up the hill-side . . .

> Quick, said the bird, find them, find them,
> Round the corner. Through the first gate,
> Into our first world . . .

This is the last rewriting that I know of Keats's hugely seminal ode. Eliot mimes Keats's acceptance of loss and departure for a movement of illusory approach and discovery; 'our' first world is an origin we have not known, though we seem to remember it from childhood, and a cloud in a garden of dead leaves suffices to remove the light of origin, the primal waters, and what they reflect. For the poem works against nostalgia ('Go, go, go'), and continually traps the reader into 'now' as the only acceptable time. It does quest for Eden. When 'Little Gidding', which is the poem's end, comes to 'the world's end' (I), what it finds there are 'the source of the longest river': the river, presumably, of Genesis 2:10, which 'went out of Eden to water the garden' before dividing into four; and the 'voice of the hidden waterfall', where the Fall is equally hidden in 'waterfall'. It also finds the rose, which is Dante's tree of life. Yet, first, the quest in this world is *for* this world. It is the biblical quest, for 'new heavens and a new earth', or, in the terms of 'Burnt Norton' II, for 'both a new world / And the old made explicit' – for a world utterly changed and yet still itself. *Four Quartets* is a poem of the earth; even its grace, in that same section of 'Burnt Norton', is 'a grace of sense'. So its ending looks to a future when we shall 'arrive where we started / And know the place for the first time', by passing through 'the unknown, remembered gate', when 'the last of earth left to discover / Is that which was the beginning'. Is there in all literature a more exact apprehending of a moment of revelation which, rather than disclosing another world, illuminates this one beyond what one can conceive – an act of Imagination which enables one, at last, to enter the real?

And the search is not for beginning but for a new beginning. For there are yet more works to whose beginning *Four Quartets* returns, and if it goes, continually, to the beginning of beginnings in Genesis, often to be repulsed (by 'Adam's curse' in 'East Coker' IV, or the 'bitter apple' of 'Dry Salvages' II), it also goes to the beginning of Luke's gospel for the Annunciation ('Dry Salvages' II), which is the beginning of Jesus and of new life, and to the beginning of the Acts of the Apostles for Pentecost, which is the beginning of the Spirit and of new speech.

Even Pentecost, however, remains at a distance. It enters in the opening of 'Little Gidding', where midwinter spring is said to contain 'pentecostal fire', like the tongues of fire with which the Spirit descended on the apostles in Acts, Chapter 2; but there is 'no wind' to correspond to the 'rushing mighty wind' which accompanied that descent, and, according to what was an afterthought, the human spirit which observes the scene remains 'dumb'. The second reference is fully assertive: 'the communication / Of the dead is tongued with fire beyond the language of the living', but before one of the dead can appear and speak in the second section, the Spirit passes in the guise of an enemy aircraft, a 'dark dove' with a 'flickering tongue', and the wind merely blows 'metal leaves' and the ghost himself. The dove descends again in the fourth section, but only to break 'the air / With flame of incandescent terror'. As everywhere, there is pain, the need for repentance, and imperfection for the time being. There *is* a reversal, of course, of the Babel of *The Waste Land*, which is also a kind of parody-Pentecost: a speaking in tongues which leads, not to universal understanding but to baffled incomprehension, and which sounds, indeed, rather like the drunkenness of which the disciples themselves were accused. *The Waste Land* goes out with bangs and whimpers in a final scattering of Babelic noise, or in the mouthings of international inebriates. When this is replaced, however, in the final lines of the *Quartets*, by an infolding of the tongues of flame, one knows that this consummation is not for now; it does not occur in *Four Quartets* – there is no such thing as a Pentecostal poem; it is deferred to a 'when' beyond the end of the world.

Instead of following *The Waste Land* towards the now impenetrable origin of language and of writing, *Four Quartets* goes to the origin of new language at Pentecost. Its other way of dealing with the earlier work's dismay about writing, in what constitutes a further reworking of it, is to engage once again with Ecclesiastes.

Ecclesiastes, with its insistent refrain: 'vanity of vanities; all is vanity', and its string of quotable, unflattering remarks on the human condition, has always proved attractive. It has entered English literature through a number of titles, some of them recent (*Many Inventions, The Golden Bowl, The Sun Also Rises*), and, more importantly, it has provided an atmosphere, a vocabulary, for works as disparate as Johnson's 'The Vanity of Human Wishes' and, I suppose, the whole *oeuvre* of Beckett. (*Murphy*, for example, opens with a Beckettian recasting of one of the famous phrases: 'The sun shone, having no alternative, on the nothing new'.) The power of Ecclesiastes is surely that, while everywhere acknowledging a just, bountiful and transcendent God, it describes a fallen world and leaves one in it. It says, unswervingly, what the facts are, and so it can be taken by the Christian for a hard and truthful look at the *miseria* of the world, which remains and is not to be simply spirited away by faith; and by the atheist, the agnostic, after the ablation of some of its parts, as saying what he too thinks in the starkest way possible. Its place in the structure of Christian thought is shown by the fact that St Paul, when describing the condition of the world that we experience since the Fall (Romans 8:20), goes to the Greek translation of Ecclesiastes for the word that he wants: *mataiótês*, 'vanity'.

The work held Eliot's imagination before he was converted, to the extent that the statement: 'he that increaseth knowledge increaseth sorrow' (1:18) might stand as an epigraph to his early poems; and to the extent that a Dantean reference to '*nostra vanitate*' does stand in the epigraph to his first book. It continued to speak to him, after his conversion, of a reality not to be ignored. Is it an exaggeration to think that the first of his *Collected Poems* was actually written under the sign of Ecclesiastes? We know that the two paragraphs in 'The Love Song of J. Alfred Prufrock' beginning: 'And indeed there will be time', rely on the third chapter's similar iteration of *time*'s, and one sees that Prufrock's most startling instance: 'There will be time to murder and create', is a sensational version of verse 3: 'A time to kill, and a time to heal'. The next series of paragraphs: 'For I have known them all already, known them all', returns to the thought of

Ecclesiastes 1:9: 'The thing that hath been, it is that which shall be; and that which is done is that which shall be done' (the thought will reappear in the foretelling and foresuffering of Tiresias); while the series: 'And would it have been worth it, after all', recalls the Preacher's repeated question: 'What profit hath a man of all his labour?' (1:3). The *spleen* and *ennui* of the nineteenth century are present, certainly, but through them Eliot homes, throughout the long middle of his poem, to the Old Testament work that maybe subtends them.

Later poems remember in particular the twelfth and last chapter. It leads one into and out of *The Waste Land*, with far more allusions than the single one which Eliot indicates in the Notes, and is audible in *Ash-Wednesday*, *Murder in the Cathedral*, and *The Family Reunion*. That it should have exercised Eliot in work after work is especially interesting when one realises the significance of one of its unquoted phrases: 'of making many books there is no end', for the anguish of *The Waste Land*. The phrase is equally relevant to *Four Quartets*, which also returns to that last chapter.

Indeed, *Four Quartets* takes on itself, like 'Prufrock', the burden of Ecclesiastes. As Denis Donoghue has indicated, it is often a mediation on *vanitas vanitatum*.[1] The particular horror of endlessness in the Preacher's lament: 'yet is there no end of all his labour' (4:8), is actually expanded in the Preacher-like dirge of 'Dry Salvages' II, which asks, repetitively, 'Where is there an end of it . . .?' and replies, 'There is no end, but addition'. The phrase drives one back for a while into the desolation of *The Waste Land* (as also forward to Beckett). There are many further instances, and the most telling are those which show Eliot to have been thinking of Ecclesiastes at the beginning of *Four Quartets*, and at the end of all four of its constituent poems. His beginning, on time, goes to the beginning of Ecclesiastes, to verse 9: 'The thing that hath been, it is that which shall be', and, as Raymond Preston pointed out, to its reprise in 3:15.[2] One could write out the Preacher's words there in Eliotic verse:

> That which has been is now
> And that which is to be has already been,
> And God requires that which is past.

Or:

> Time past is time present

And time future contained in time past.
Time past must be redeemed.

Ecclesiastes is the very first work alluded to in *Four Quartets*, after the epigraphs. It also provides the concluding thought of 'Burnt Norton': 'Ridiculous the sad waste time / Stretching before and after', where 'waste' seems to refer to Eliot's most famous poem, and to place it in the world from which 'Burnt Norton' seeks to recover. The ending of 'East Coker' returns once more to the passage on time: 'There is a time for the evening under starlight, / A time for the evening under lamplight'; while our 'temporal reversion' to the 'soil' in the last line of 'The Dry Salvages' recalls, among other biblical passages, a verse from the last chapter: 'Then shall the dust return to the earth as it was'. And if the beginning of *Four Quartets* goes to the beginning of Ecclesiastes, its end goes to the end. For it is said later in the last chapter that the Preacher 'sought out, and set in order many proverbs' – a statement recalled and twisted at the end of *The Waste Land* – and that he 'sought to find out acceptable words: and that which was written was upright'. The final section of 'Little Gidding' recalls and modifies this in its vision of a writing where 'every phrase / And sentence . . . is right (where every word is at home . . .)'.

It is this contrast between *The Waste Land* and *Four Quartets* that shows what Eliot is about. As *Four Quartets* looks to overcome *The Waste Land*'s unease about time, the past, history, by its opening to Incarnation, so it looks to overcome the earlier work's unease about writing by its own writing practice. It is just as full of other men's works, and the past of literature is quite as much its theme. 'My words echo', says its first page, and 'Other echoes / Inhabit the garden'. They do indeed, often as no-longer-modern verse forms – isn't this part of the point, in fact, of those imitations of earlier 'poetical fashions'? One needs to consider Eliot's first notes for the opening of 'East Coker' V:

> 20 yrs
> l'entre 2 guerres
> 20yrs. or 600 upwards.

He is clearly comparing his own twenty years 'largely wasted' with the whole history of Engish poetry from Chaucer. We cannot tell how he would have developed the idea, but it is tempting to read all those centuries of poetry into the lines that he did write, about

'Trying to learn to use words, and every attempt / Is a wholly new start, and a different kind of failure'. He does not simply lose his concern about writings of the past, but his perspective changes. He recognises, in the lines which follow, that what one is looking for 'has already been discovered' by men 'whom one cannot hope / To emulate – but there is no competition'. Competition was not the problem, it is true, in *The Waste Land*, but the sheer existence of so many predecessors was, whereas they are greeted here with acknowledgement and humility: the one thing, one remembers from the second section, whose 'endlessness' is acceptable.

'Little Gidding' is where the work is actually done. As the fourth of the poems, it reminds the reader once more that *Four Quartets* itself continually begins again, with 'a wholly new start', because one is only ever beginning. This is a sorrow, but also an opportunity. For its opening relates yet again to the opening of *The Waste Land*: there, April 'stirs' dull roots, here (as an afterthought), another kind of spring 'stirs' the dumb spirit; while its second section is an essential rewriting of *The Waste Land*, of an astonishing precision and inventiveness. When the narrator, walking in the streets of the unreal city, encounters, not Stetson but a 'familiar, compound ghost', he meets, one knows, with recession on recession of other writers: Yeats, Pound, Eliot himself, Poe, Baudelaire, Mallarmé, Laforgue, Donne, Milton, Shelley, Virgil, Dante, Ford, Swift, Johnson ('The Vanity of Human Wishes', in fact), Sir Thomas Browne, Tourneur, Kipling, Tennyson, Arnold, James, Shakespeare, and who knows how many more. It is a miniature *Waste Land* of allusions, and the opening does begin with an inspiration, by 'dove' and 'wind', which is troubled and fearful. Yet this is not the cruel inspiration of *The Waste Land*, and, the ghost once met, the two figures become 'compliant to the common wind': to the inspiration, that is, which blows on all poets. Instead of *The Waste Land*'s anxiety about the teeming multiplicity of writers, there is an acceptance of them all, friend and foe alike. No longer the stuff of nightmare, they are reconciled for a new act of writing where (as I suggested in the chapter on *Renga* in *Towards a Christian Poetics*) his precursors help Eliot to compose his lines while Eliot enables them, reciprocally, to 'find words' they 'never thought to speak'. Whereas the final, polyglot strafe of quotations in *The Waste Land* is a showing of the 'many books' – there they are in their most obvious disarray – the verse here gathers the scattered works and voices; as a small sign, perhaps, of the gathering of the 'scattered quires', as described at the end of the *Paradiso*, into 'one volume'.

Isn't it strange that critics relate the quotation procedure of *The Waste Land* to the idea of tradition in 'Tradition and the Individual Talent'? The essay talks of poetry as 'a living whole of all the poetry that has ever been written'; the poem suffers invasion by an exorbitance of books. The essay sees tradition as something by which a poet might place himself; the poem sees a litter of writers wherever it looks. Only by the time of *Four Quartets* had Eliot found a way, as poet, of coming to terms with his own idea, in a move which is actually a renewal of neo-classicism.

It could have been bland – and it will be bland to anyone who is suspicious of this kind of reconciliation. The passage closes, for all that, where it begins, in dread. Before leaving him in the 'disfigured street', a street both bombed and bereft of the figurative, the ghost discloses to the speaker the 'gifts reserved for age'. While he draws on Milton, Swift, Yeats, moreover, he also draws on Ecclesiastes. Compare 'the cold friction of expiring sense' with 'desire shall fail' (12:5); 'laughter at what ceases to amuse' with 'thou shalt say, I have no pleasure' (12:1); and the insistence on 'human folly' and 'fools' approval' with the Preacher's motif of the fool. The 'master' of 'Little Gidding' II concludes by counselling his disciple regarding age; the Preacher counsels his son to take heed in his youth, before 'the years draw nigh' (12:1). The master reveals the 'exasperation' for the spirit of a man unless he is 'restored by that refining fire'; the Preacher passes across an unstated 'unless' to *his* final advice, to fear God and keep his commandments (12:13).

In the very passage where Eliot seeks to repel his earlier distress at the 'making of many books', he actually returns to Ecclesiastes, to hear the Preacher's deeper distress, as voiced in the just preceding verses, about age and end. As if to reinforce the point, 'Little Gidding' is precisely the quartet where, earlier in this same second section, the word 'vanity' at last occurs. One might then reflect that even this passage of confident, consummate writing, falls under the judgement of the insidious phrase I quoted above: 'every attempt' is 'a different kind of failure'.

And the underlying theme here is, after all, death. It is not merely that the one thing uniting all the poets of the past is the fact that they are dead, though that thought in itself, in all its banality, can pull one up. Poetry is in contact with death, through its encounter with the mortality of the world to which it aspires and of the self which it actuates, as of the very language deployed for the encounter; and through its awareness that the death of the world and of the self is, in one way or another, its own origin. So Eliot descends, for the purpose of his poem, into Hell or Purgatory, and discovers that the self in creation is 'someone other' while nevertheless being 'still the same', and that when he cries he hears 'another's voice cry'. He realises, at last, the *othering* of the self, which is quite different from the decentred self of *The Waste Land*, where, to quote from 'Portrait of a Lady', he must 'borrow every changing shape / To find expression', and where one can understand his later disparaging of the poem, however unjust, as a 'piece of rhythmical grumbling'. He achieves a kind of multipersonal utterance, which also differs from the decentring of voice in *The Waste Land*, its dispersal into a heterogeneity of voices, some of them barely comprehensible, a few of them the cries of birds. (*The Waste Land* is the work of a virtuoso continually lamenting his impotence.)

For it is a ghost who speaks. It is arguable that the elegy, in its explicit concern for death, its clarifying of the failure of poetry's vocative desire, its ability to raise a new image (of 'Lycidas', of 'Adonais') out of loss, moves close to the source, to the sense, of poetry. *The Waste Land* throngs with the dead – it begins with their burial – and they, naturally, fail to speak. As soon as they begin, they are cut off, deflected: 'Whan that Aprill . . . is the cruellest month', 'The . . . Chair she sat in'. Death is the silencing of voice, so the ultimate victory would be to locate voice within the dead themselves, and that is what 'Little Gidding' achieves, in the only way in which a poet can achieve it. It delivers, insofar as one ever could, 'the communication / Of the dead', which is 'beyond' the language of the living. It raises the dead for the composing of a communal poem, and is a new kind of elegy.

As the ghost speaks, he refers to speech; this poetry emerging from death is thoroughly self-aware. But has enough attention been paid to the logic of his syntax? The 'since' of his opening: 'Since our concern was speech . . .' leads not to a main clause also concerned with language, but to this: 'Let me disclose the gifts reserved for age'. Speech impels one outside itself, to the moral and spiritual world of 'aftersight and foresight'. This sounds like a valediction, and it is. In the one passage in the poem where someone speaks, the bitter, self-knowing, admonitory voice is not the voice of Eliot (or of Milton, or Yeats), but the voice of bitterness, self-knowledge, admonition. And remarkably, having projected voice out there, having written in such a way as to utter the self by outering it – and having come to terms with beginning, made peace with the 'many books', and concluded his response to *The Waste Land* – Eliot stopped writing poems.

Notes

1. 'T. S. Eliot's *Quartets*: a new reading', *Studies*, 1965, p. 62.
2. *'Four Quartets' Rehearsed* (London: Sheed & Ward, 1946), p. 9.

6

T. S. Eliot: Poetry, Silence and the Vision of God
PETER WALKER

His last great poem proclaims the death of language, and stands as a commitment to his search for unity of self in 'the constitution of silence'.

So David Spurr, writing of the Eliot who, he says, 'like Mallarmé, knows that even the language of poetry . . . cannot ultimately attain to the immaculate purity of his absent mystical reality'.[1] A figure from our own century's poetry comes to mind, David Gascoyne's *Orpheus*:

And he came carrying the shattered lyre,
And wearing the blue robes of a king,
And looking through eyes like holes torn in a screen . . . .

Out of his sleep, from time to time,
From between half-open lips,
Escaped the bewildered words which try to tell
The tale of his bright night
And his wing-shadowed day
The soaring flights of thought beneath the sun . . . .[2]

It was the thesis of the Polish poet, novelist and critic, Jerzy Peterkiewicz, in his little-noticed *The Other Side of Silence. The Poet at the Limits of Language* (1970), that the constitution of silence may indeed be the true destiny of the poet. Rowan Williams, Lady Margaret Professor of Divinity at Oxford, to whose 'Poetic and Religious Imagination', an essay valuable in its own right, I owe my introduction to Peterkiewicz's searching study of a theme in lesser-known but magisterial European writing, sums up its thesis as follows:

> If Peterkiewicz is right, every poem is a step along the road to a liberation from words . . . Even 'the prophet's leap', the founding of poetry upon the moment of ecstatic inspiration, is commonly a self-deluding luxury. And the final step brings the poet to a complete imaginative void, the dark night of utter alienation from the 'available' world, 'the desert of the heart'.[3]

Such language is bound to raise a question from within the Christian tradition, in which the concept of the spoken word retains so integral a place, as, for instance, in Colin Macleod's contemporary lines on the Creation:

> Suddenly you spoke, planted a flaring kiss
> on your familiar silence;
> and folded in your arms for an instant
> fulminations of novas bursting from the abyss.
>
> Your word
> fell on the silence, forcing
> a fiery seed deep into its womb.[4]

We have to ask how real is this contemporary talk of the acceptance of a *reductio ad silentium*. Geoffrey Hill has described, as vividly as any of our poets, a moment of *aphasia*, his 'God's Little Mountain'[5] expressing it in terms of one once

> shut
> With wads of sound into a sudden quiet,

but then, fallen until he had 'found the world again', incapable of speech about it. But the poem closes with the continuing agony of the need to find words, and in keeping with its last line Hill the critic has written of Eliot:

> In the essay 'Poetry and Drama' Eliot speaks of 'a fringe of indefinite extent, of feeling which one can only detect, so to speak, out of the corner of the eye and can never completely focus . . . . At such moments we touch the border of those feelings

which only music can express'. As Eliot well knew, however, a poet must also turn back, with whatever weariness, disgust, love barely distinguishable from hate, to confront 'the indefinite extent' of language itself and seek his 'focus' there. In certain contexts the expansive outward gesture towards the condition of music is a helpless gesture of surrender, oddly analogous to that stylish aesthetic of despair, that desire for the ultimate integrity of silence, to which so much eloquence has been so frequently and indefatigably devoted.[6]

There are two sorts of silence, we may say, the composed silence and the stunned. Silence in the presence of the ultimate, as before the vision of God (to pick up the title of the present chapter), runs quickly into the second of them, for which we have already found ourselves using the term *aphasia*. An exercise in Eliot criticism, the present essay is written on the twofold intuition: first, that *Four Quartets*, Eliot's 'last great poem', deserves appraisal in the light of a new but well-documented experience on the part of men and women of today, including would-be creative writers, of *aporia*, helplessness in the face of a new unavailability of speech; and secondly, that the Christian theologian might have a serious observation to offer on this phenomenon – provided only, one must quickly add, that he or she resists the temptation to annex the struggling poet and shake him down until he fits into a tight theological scheme of things. With such a caveat, there is, I want to suggest, a certain, not often noticed, congruence between the movement of Eliot's mind from his taking up his pen to write what proved to be the first of *Four Quartets*, and a seam of contemporary Christian theology often thought of as radical.

To return to the observation on Eliot from which we began, it must at once be said that this movement in theological appreciation is in another direction than that of seeking 'unity of self' in a 'constitution of silence' or under any other condition, if such words would indicate an introverted exercise. Rather, it is one of outreach towards the world, and as such, the present writer would maintain, a rediscovery of a primary Christian perception. Yet, to anticipate, the question may yet remain whether such a movement may fetch up in fact in a new *aphasia*. If so, the religious significance of that experience may have its own new urgency.

I propose to approach the *Four Quartets* by way briefly of two writers, the first a Christian theologian, and the second a Sanskrit scholar and student of Indic philosophic traditions, who have, between them, opened Eliot up for me and opened me to Eliot. The first of them gives me the phrase which the reader will find cardinal to my appraisal of the poems: it is the highly idiomatic phrase, *the genetic moment*. The second points me to what I see as the heart of this whole matter. I find it in her application of the word *compassionate*. The writers are Cornelius Ernst, of the Dominican Order of Preachers, and Cleo McNelly Kearns, Professor in the Humanities at Yale.

1. Cornelius Ernst died, aged 53, in 1977. A persistent theme in the (posthumous, 1979) collection of his papers[7] is 'the reformulation of theology in our time'. He would see this as happening in a movement towards 'a preference for the language of meaning over the language of being'. In a sequence of phrases from him, it is a shift from 'a theological world in which meaning was articulated in argument and not as insight', and from 'a style which prized clarity and decisiveness above exploration in depth'. The newer approach allows the possibility of a world 'flowering into the light' (the phrase is from Thomas Aquinas, before the schoolmen tightened everything); and of language being seen as having a constituent place in life and community through its part in the apprehension of meaning, it being 'in the process and practice of living' that meaning is to be found. The quest, so seen, is to discover, in the face of contemporary diversifications and complexities, any possibility of a unified vision of 'reality as a whole'. What is at issue (and it was once seen as the main concern of the Christian thinkers, the doctors of theology) is not less than *the mystery of the intelligibility of being*, the question whether unitary sense can be made of our world. Thus, seeing the significant life of a Dominican House of Studies as the contemplative life, Ernst describes its primary concern in a phrase which could in fact express the whole of a Christian commitment – 'a contemplative engagement with the world', and speaks of this as involving

> *not a withdrawal into the cell of self-knowledge but an entrance into the Christian meaning of time by way of the Christian meaning of our times.*[8]

To such a moment of insight, Ernst gives the name 'the genetic moment', and writes:

Every genetic moment is a mystery. It is dawn, discovery, spring, new birth, coming to the light, awakening, transcendence, liberation, ecstasy, bridal consent, gift, forgiveness, reconciliation, revolution, faith, hope, love.[9]

Yet although this is the language of insight, of letting the deeper vision emerge creatively, recreatively, it is on the loaded word *mystery* that this quick summary of Ernst's language of the genetic moment must end. In his own words at the point where he is addressing the distinctive illumination which the Christian revelation has to offer:

There is, if you like, a hole at the centre of the genetic moment, a void, which turns out to be a plenary, superabundant: a radiant darkness. What I am trying allusively to suggest is that the Christian experience of the genetic moment is at once an experience of the creatively new become manifest in human articulation, and an experience of an ultimate source, the hidden God, *Deus absconditus* who has made his transcendence known in the darkness of a death. If the experience were not *both at once* it would split apart into an insipid humanism of progress (or a revolutionary arrogance), or an esoteric mystique of world abnegation.[10]

2. Cleo McNelly Kearns' *T. S. Eliot and Indic Traditions, A Study in Poetry and Belief* (1987)[11] has a seminal quality which is not simply a function of her knowledge of the Eastern traditions which Eliot had sat under. At home herself in a field he had made his own at a greater depth than has always been recognised, she is able to relax into a sympathetic listening. In perhaps the most moving and illuminating pages of her book, her treatment of the close of *The Waste Land*, she hears in the *Datta, Dayadhvam and Damyata* of *What the Thunder Said* the poet's appeal to his reader for a particular response.[12]

Long ago, Helen Gardner advised the reader of *Four Quartets* that it was better in reading poetry of this kind 'to trouble too little about the "meaning" than to trouble too much'.[13] To look, then, at the invitation with which Kearns sees *The Waste Land* closing, and to do so with an eye on what may come out of it for our reading of *Four Quartets*, it is partly that, as that most appreciative of interpreters of Eliot said, one can 'try too hard' about the meaning. More deeply, it is that what the poet invites is a positive receptivity – the awful daring of a moment's surrender to what is on the page, with an attention which is not self-assertive. Give, sympathise, control: such an openness might lead to such a 'grasp' of the movement of the poetry as that for which Eliot, always the sailor, found an exquisite model in the hand sensitive on the tiller of the lively boat. And it is a matter of the heart and not only the head:

> your heart would have responded
> Gaily, when invited, beating obedient
> To controlling hands.

Space is left to the reader at the close of *The Waste Land*, Kearns insists, space indeed on the page, surrounding the Indic word for the peace that passes understanding. At the end of a poem which has charted pain, and not simply the poet's private pain but the pain of a world's futility and sterility, the reader is left with a question waiting to be asked, and he or she is left space to ask it. It is the same healing question that Parsifal must ask the king before the healing stream can flow: What ails you? The poet, by the nature of his craft, cannot ask it directly 'short of the bathos of the direct appeal' . . . . Here, it must be left to emerge out of the poetic maze of hints and echoes from literature, philosophy, legend, religion. The question that is invited is, What does it all mean? But if so, it is meant to be asked not cerebrally but compassionately: not in separation from 'the serious question of the world'. So, at the crucial point to which all her exposition has been leading, Kearns turns to make a brilliant appropriation of a phrase of Thomas Merton on contemplation. Shall it be defined as *compassionate* time? that silence of meditation through which the breakdown into multiplicity is contained and transcended?[14]

The account of *Four Quartets* which I wish to explore from the 'hints and guesses' just outlined is, to a degree, less exalted than that of the critic from whom this essay began, and certainly sees Eliot as more concerned with what Peterkiewicz called the 'available' world than is commonly allowed. The concept of the *ordinary* comes to mind from Stephen Spender:

> The poet appeals to the reader, on the ground of shared experience of living within time . . . *on the level of the ordinary man*.

Spender is, I think, right, and not least in seeing this as totally of a piece with Eliot's own avowal of humility as

> the only wisdom we can hope to acquire.[15]

There is something here, too, that is not entirely remote from a theme which Kearns has emphasised in terms of the contribution of Indic thought to 'the open, communal wisdom, the resonance of which Eliot was trying to convey'.[16] But it was only lately that I stumbled upon the piece of 'ordinary' writing which seems, when laid alongside one of those passages in *Four Quartets* which has seemed so inaccessible, to illustrate the point most nicely. Happily, consideration of it will take us at once into what I believe to be the crux of *Four Quartets*, namely the nature of that 'genetic moment' of personal illumination when, in the language we have been borrowing from Ernst, there seems at any rate a possibility that the world might flower into unitary meaning.

In Juliette Huxley's autobiographical *Leaves of the Tulip Tree* there occurs the following passage:

> So it happened to me unexpectedly one summer day, as I was walking in the silent garden: the awareness of participating in the boundless pulse of life, conscious of a fusion of my spiritual roots with the very soil I walked upon, its daedal vegetation and imprisoned minerals, while at the same time perceiving the infinite treasures of the mind of man, in another dimension and reality. The illumination flooded me with intense gratitude, with grave eager joy and anticipation. As Traherne wrote:
>
> > I within did flow
> > With seas of Life, like wine.
>
> The plough opens the soil for seed and germination, and the eternal miracle of growth, of life itself revealing unimaginable new complexities, burst upon me, like a fiery awakening.[17]

Now I do not see why anything more complicatedly mystical than this experience (which the writer herself ventures to say she conceives of as common to many) need be looked for as the moment of illumination, the moment 'in and out of time', to which Eliot keeps returning in *Four Quartets*. Here, surely, is what 'Garlic and sapphires in the mud', 'Burnt Norton' 2, the sequence that has caused such agony to critics, is essentially about. Perhaps, if so, we are only surprised by Spender's emphasis upon the *ordinariness* of the experience 'in and out of time' because we are half-expecting the poet, if he was a visionary at all, to be treating of something more akin to Gascoyne's distracting foreign land, or Spurr's immaculate purity of an absent mystical reality, things which he must struggle to express in words that can somehow capture soaring flights of thought beneath the sun.

I do not think that that is the Eliot of *Four Quartets*. What is touched in that long sequence is the infinitely more profound but less complicated thing, the intuition of a world held in something of a wholeness, and of oneself as a part of that wholeness. The early Eliot, the young philosopher, is quoted by Kearns (from an unpublished essay of 1913) as speaking with a note of condescension, of 'the pathetic primitive *credo* in ultimate explanation and ultimate reality which haunts us like the prayers of childhood'.[18] Condescending, or wistful, whichever, or both, in those younger days, the later poet returns, haunted, to the thought: and it is the theme which, if the Christian theologian we have been working from was right, is the one that has been claiming anew some of the theologians.

It is time to try to indicate as concisely as may be what I have called the crux of *Four Quartets*. It is the question of where, in Ernst's useful term, Eliot looks finally to find the moment of insight that might offer sense and life and meaning – the genetic moment.

What I wish to propose is that the whole movement of *Four Quartets* is one that is away from seeing *either* the moment of ecstatic inspiration (the isolated moment in the rose garden of 'Burnt Norton' 1) *or* the contrasting, or complementary, deliberately-sought moment of ascetic darkness which operates by

> Emptying the sensual with deprivation
> Cleansing affection from the temporal
> ('Burnt Norton' 3)

as, at any rate *in itself or in isolation*, a moment of the durable insight that is looked for. Rather, the moment of insight into meaning is offered, if it is to be real, within the substance of actual living in the 'available' world of the temporal. And actual living will mean the shared human condition under the condition of our human responsibility for ourselves and for each other. If illumination is sought, it must come through a progressive

> purification of the motive
> in the ground of our beseeching
> ('Little Gidding' 3)

the touchstone of which will be the being searched in terms of compassion.

Upon whether *Four Quartets* may be so read, the validity of this paper will depend. The danger is that, to some degree unwittingly, we shall in the event have done no more than shake the poem down to fit a scheme. The hope would be another one: that one might catch the movement of this great sequence as a living thing – a movement coming indeed out of life, and not out of an individual life in isolation from other lives. That would be truly consonant with the interpretation already offered of the last sequence of that other great poem, *The Waste Land*. Nor will the present writer be hurt, or think it out of keeping with the tone he is seeking to present as Eliot's, if what follows in the present essay is read as no more than

> hints followed by guesses.[19]

Moments of 'Burnt Norton' have already been touched upon above. The moment in the rose garden, or, again, the moment of disclosing darkness, are given, when they come, unsought or sought, as moments to be remembered ('Burnt Norton' 2); they are significant glimpses of liberation from the deadening sense of life as no more, whether in retrospect or in prospect, than meaningless sequence. That seems to be somewhere at the heart of 'Burnt Norton'. But its momentary shaft of sunlight can leave us all the more aware, in the actual business of life afterwards, of the futility of

> the waste sad time
> Stretching before and after.

So Burnt Norton ends.

That we are not meant to throw away those glimpses, however wistful they may seem, is asserted with some precision in 'East

Coker' 3 and 5: but with the crucial difference, now, of a warning given about the moment of intensity – a warning of its incompleteness in itself: it is to be seen, the poet insists, as a moment not lost but yet *'requiring'*. The point is not simply in 'East Coker' 5, as it was in 'Burnt Norton' 2, that we cannot continue to live in that particular intensity; but rather that it is in the continuities of life (or, better, of lives in continuity with other lives), rather than in singular moments in separation, that meaning will disclose itself. It is, indeed, into another intensity, not that of a possible esoteric mystique of world abnegation (to pick up Ernst's words) but an intensity of effort, that, 'still and still moving', we must be moving, and into 'another and deeper communion', for

> Love is most nearly itself
> When here and now

[meaning the isolated here and now of the intense moment]

> cease to matter.

And Love, we note, has come down to earth (fallen, to find the world again) – from the abstractions of 'Burnt Norton' 5 to the affectionate moment with the photograph album.

A year later, in 'Dry Salvages' 2, come the appraisals that have come with advancing years, of what it is all about: all that is compacted in the pregnant line about the moment of sudden illumination,

> We had the experience but missed the meaning;

all that is given in the explicit acknowledgement, in 'Dry Salvages' 5, that

> The hint half guessed, the gift half understood, is Incarnation.

The poet's theme, as articulate here as anywhere in *Four Quartets*, is liberation into the possibility of finding meaning. That the critical moment for this is the moment of intentional, un-selfregarding, action has been the movement of thought in 'Dry Salvages' 3 (for so, in its context, I read the vital parenthetic line which says that the time of death is every moment). And now, if we could but take the measure of the meaning of the Incarnation, it would give us our liberation into that apprehension of eternal verity hinted at indeed in the moments 'in and out of time' but, as the saints know, truly given elsewhere: that is to say

>   given
> And taken in a lifetime's death in love,
> Ardour and selflessness and self-surrender.

A transition has been made, it is plain, since 'Burnt Norton', and, through 'East Coker' to the end of 'The Dry Salvages', we see the poet's growing appreciation of what the true account of it is: and, if I am to be held to my chosen language, the question faces me where do I place 'the genetic moment' of that new understanding *for the poet himself*? (The personal question is not improper or an intrusion: the autobiographical component is formative in the poetry.)

That the poet himself was subject to the visionary moment, the moment 'in and out of time', is plain from the poetry itself most surely: and we can be grateful for the plotting of such experiences in Lyndall Gordon's *Eliot's Early Years*, for instance, in her treatment of the younger Eliot and the night-time city streets.[20] Yet it is perhaps only those old enough to have experienced 1938 and the relief, later perhaps repented, when Mr Chamberlain landed at Heston on his return from Berchtesgarten with his piece of paper, saying 'I think it is peace in our time' and Czechoslovakia was betrayed, who will take the full force of an emphasis in current Eliot exposition[21] on the darkness of those days in the life of a nation as having had a critical effect upon the poet. The crucial texts are two: the first from the Boutwood Lectures delivered by Eliot in Cambridge in March 1939 at the invitation of the Master and Fellows of Corpus Christi College, and sent to the publisher as *The Idea of a Christian Society* within weeks of the outbreak of war.

> I can believe [said Eliot] that there must be many persons, who, like myself, were deeply shaken by the events of September 1938, in a way from which one does not recover – the feeling which was new and unexpected was a feeling of humiliation, which seemed to demand an act of personal contrition, of humility, repentance and amendment; what had happened was something in which one was deeply implicated and responsible. It was not, I repeat, a

criticism of the government, but a doubt of the validity of a civilisation. We could not match conviction with conviction.... Was our society, which had always been so assured of its superiority and rectitude, so confident of its unexamined premises, assembled round anything more permanent than a congeries of banks, insurance companies and industries?[22]

'East Coker' was published next year (1940), and in it the loaded lines of 'East Coker' 3:

> O dark dark dark. They all go into the dark,
> The vacant interstellar spaces, the vacant into the vacant,
> The captains, merchant bankers, eminent men of letters,
> The generous patrons of art, the statesmen and the rulers,
> Distinguished civil servants, chairmen of many committees,
> Industrial lords and petty contractors, all go into the dark,
> And dark the Sun and Moon, and the Almanach de Gotha
> And the Stock Exchange Gazette, the Directory of Directors,
> And cold the sense and lost the motive of action.
> And we all go with them, into the silent funeral,
> Nobody's funeral, for there is no one to bury.
> I said to my soul, be still, and let the dark come upon you
> Which shall be the darkness of God.

There, surely, is virtual *peripeteia* from the preoccupation of 'Burnt Norton'. It is not the individual darkness of the ascetic that is now being presented: rather (as the poet admonishes himself) the darkness into which he is to enter, or rather, which he is to allow to come upon him as the darkness of God, is the darkness of this world. The Christian meaning of time is to be found in the meaning of his own times, and the meaning of those times is conveyed in the lyric of 'East Coker' 2

> What is the late November doing
> With the disturbance of the spring

with those lines demanding to be read against the ordered sequences of nature and history of 'East Coker' 1 or the glimpse of a rhythmic unity at the corresponding point of 'Burnt Norton' – 'Garlic and sapphires in the mud'. The times are those of a catastrophic and apocalyptically disordered world

> Whirled in a vortex that shall bring
> The world to that destructive fire
> Which burns before the ice-cap reigns
>
> ('East Coker' 2).

The meaning of its time is darkness – a darkness pointing to the one possibility of healing, the sharp compassion of the Cross – 'East Coker' 4. In a phrase of Dietrich Bonhoeffer about our own day – 'only the suffering God can help'.[23]

So Love means engagement, in some intensity. It means a compassion and a compassionate concern. In this dimension, a man's resentment at the loss of the quietness to which he had looked forward for his later years is overtaken by another and different resentment – the helpless sense of anger and revolt when men and women have been betrayed by the quiet-voiced elders as they had been ('East Coker' 2). The humiliation of that is what gives Eliot this new flash of insight into what humility means, releasing him, one may surely see him saying, from any potential arrogance of the seer, and making him take up his pen, however despairingly, to start again to convey a more considered meaning ('East Coker' 5). But that is the moment at which the whole poem comes to new life, as the poet comes to his new poetical life: the poem that began 'In my beginning is my end', ends 'In my end is my beginning' – newly purposive. And it is

> Not the intense moment
> Isolated, with no before and after,
> But a lifetime burning in every moment
> And not the lifetime of one man only

that is his concern; a dying to himself into a deeper human communion in which his vocation, his poetic apprehension of meaning, will be, in his own word for it, explored. ('East Coker' 5)

If the most moving of all the lyrics for me, as someone for whom the war of 1939–45 was a war largely at sea, must always be the sestina of 'The Dry Salvages'

> Lady, whose shrine stands on the promontory
> and her prayer for those who ended their voyage in the sea's lips
> Or wherever cannot reach them the sound of the sea bell's
> Perpetual angelus
>
> ('Dry Salvages' 4),

it may be, here again, because of personal echoes. Yet it is precisely the poet's ability to speak in a reverberating depth of *compassionate* understanding that makes the poetry: and it is surely *theologically right* – this poem which makes from out of the imagery of the endless drift of wreckage the poetry of an endless drift of human agony, endless and hopeless unless by the compassionate intervention of God (through Mary's yes at the Annunciation) time should be redeemed. Into that redeeming compassion we must let ourselves be taken, by taking seriously the agony of others which we are never to expect to get away from – unlike, perhaps, our own:

> For our own past is covered by the currents of action,
> But the torment of others remains an experience
> Unqualified, unworn by subsequent attrition
> ('Dry Salvages' 2).

That is the meaning of Incarnation. It is to that resolution of life's mystery in a radiance which has at the heart of it the darkness of a death, that the poetry moves.

In the last movement of the last of *Four Quartets* – after that first movement which is the quintessential presentation of what a 'genetic moment' can be, with its symbolism (in the sparkling hoar-frost) of the promise of renewal and new life from 'outside time's covenant'; after the reminder that the meaning, even so,

> Is only a shell, a husk of meaning,
> From which the purpose breaks only when it is fulfilled
> If at all . . .
> ('Little Gidding' 1);

after the questioning (the 'compound ghost') of whether it is indeed the case (as he had said in prose) that his own culture has proved to have nothing else to offer but disillusion and the invitation to remorse (and with what brilliant precision the symbolisms of human life from the early poems are gathered into an immediate apocalyptic dimension by the symbolism of the air raid, the dead water and dead sand and the gaping bomb craters – 'Little Gidding' 2); after the purification of the patriotic notion of victory and defeat by the acceptance that all of us together are folded into the constitution of silence in our mortality ('Little Gidding' 3); after the ultimate committal of all to the consuming fire of Love ('Little

Gidding' 4) – after these things, the space on the page around the words that set out the meaning

> With the drawing of this Love and the voice of this Calling
> ('Little Gidding' 5).

Life may go forward with a purpose: with the promise of a newness in which 'the serious question of the world' has flowered, and will flower, into the light:

> We shall not cease from exploration
> And the end of all our exploring
> Will be to arrive where we started
> And know the place for the first time.

It is, then, our own world, not any distracting foreign land, which we are to see with our own eyes, renewed in their vision by the discerning compassion of Christ for us to see the Christian meaning of all time in the Christian meaning of our times, in the present call to love. To see things so is to have received the revelation – the vision of God. Is there language that can offer it? It would be like a dance of words – of words redeemed by their purgation from all self-assertiveness: an always-to-be-remembered new start

> The complete consort dancing together . . .

And yet, says the poet, there is at each point a dying at the heart of it, for

> Every phrase and every sentence is an end and a beginning,
> Every poem an epitaph.

We have argued that a particular moment of a nation's darkness was for a particular poet the moment of transformation, a new beginning.

We spoke at the beginning of this essay of a new experience on the part of men and women of today of an emptiness of inspiration, the unavailability of speech. I am not indeed sure, on thinking about it, that a *stunned* silence is the appropriate description of this deadness of spirit which is being spoken of under the oppression of the global threat, environmental or nuclear – the one foreboding the desert, the other that nothingness which the human mind cannot quite begin to get itself round, and understandably so. But I know what I come to see as the urgent religious question which begins to emerge towards the light. In the term borrowed from our theologian, are we face-to-face here not with *a* but with *the* genetic moment for humankind?

If that is the question for religion, for poetry the question is not more or less than this: *Shall this moment of humanity have its poetry?*

We should not too quickly despair, or accept the language of the ultimate integrity of silence of which Hill was rightly so suspicious as the deceitful thing that it can be. The same Peterkiewicz whom we quoted earlier has the comment, late in his book, that the twentieth century is 'intensely dark and intensely luminous'.[24]

If that is true, it is the *both at once* of it that matters if the insight we have followed in these pages has been true: and not to have seen that (and I am not sure that Peterkiewicz does), would be to be as one who

> had the experience but missed the meaning.

I think at this point of the language of Paul Celan's later poems, affirming, in their very darkness and impenetrability, 'the enduring possibility of response'.[25] I think of the identification, compassionate yet so deliberately matter-of-fact, of the poet with the agony of others in Geoffrey Hill's poem on the holocaust, 'September Song';[26] or of his 'Two Chorale-Preludes on melodies by Paul Celan',[27] open to the desolations of space and to the poignant vulnerability of our own world in it. I see here poetry addressing, as only poetry can, human experiences of our own day that are of a new order in human history. I see the Eliot of *Four Quartets* as belonging with these writers, his poetry, surely, on the final count of things, proleptic of such poetry.

I think, too, of that 'radical' theologian whom I have mentioned only once in this paper, but deliberately at the heart of it where he belongs: the Dietrich Bonhoeffer who (eighteen years the junior of Eliot and so, like him, crossing the frontiers of two worlds) taught us to see this world of the penultimate, in his own genetic phrase, as held, in its here and now, in God's immediate compassion in Christ: held, that is to say, in its *being*, and to its *meaning*, in Christ crucified, risen, and present in his suffering world.[28] He said once that to pray is to be silent and cry out at once. At that point most clearly one sees theology and poetry meet, the one illuminating the other, nor can they finally dwell apart.

POSTSCRIPT

This essay ventures to suggest a certain congruence between the 'radical' theologian, Dietrich Bonhoeffer, and the poet, his senior by nearly twenty years, and the reader may judge this matter. What may be of interest, and to my knowledge has not been noted in Eliot scholarship, is that the two men shared the friendship of the great churchman and patron of poetry and the arts, Bishop George Bell of Chichester, the senior of Eliot by five years. It was to Bell that Bonhoeffer sent his final message when Hitler's men took him to his execution for his part in the assassination plot: 'Tell him that for me this is the end, but also the beginning'.[29]

What the official biography of Bishop Bell does not convey, but is documented in Dame Helen Gardner's *The Composition of Four Quartets*, is that Eliot was with Bell for the visit to the neutral country, Sweden, on an inter-church initiative, during which Bonhoeffer came, as it were by night, to disclose to Bell the secrets of the assassination plot.[30] I do not suppose for a moment that anything was said of that by Bell to his friend Eliot. But did he *ever* speak to him of the German pastor? Eliot and Bell had minds which thought alike (Bell was a great encourager of the poet, sponsoring 'The Rock' and 'Murder in the Cathedral'). And it was Bell's greatness to be open to the young German churchman. I write as one who himself had the great privilege of George Bell's very senior friendship.

Notes

1. David Spurr, *Conflicts in Consciousness. T. S. Eliot's Poetry and Criticism* (University of Illinois Press, 1984), p. 106.
2. David Gascoyne, 'Orpheus in the Underworld', *Collected Poems*. ed. with an Introduction by Robin Skelton (OUP, 1978), p. 37.
3. Rowan Williams, 'Poetic and Religious Imagination', *Theology*, Vol. LXXX, May 1977, No. 675, p. 180; Jerzy Peterkiewicz, *The Other Side of Silence. The Poet at the Limits of Language* (OUP, 1970).
4. Colin Macleod, *Poems* (Hillview Press, 1983), pp. 14, 17.

5. Geoffrey Hill, *Collected Poems* (André Deutsch and King Penguin Books, 1985), p. 17.
6. Geoffrey Hill, 'Poetry as Menace and Atonement,' in *The Lords of Limit. Essays on Literature and Ideas* (André Deutsche, 1984), p. 9.
7. Cornelius Ernst, OP, *Multiple Echo. Explorations in Theology*, ed. Fergus Kerr, OP and Timothy Radcliffe, OP, Foreword by Donald MacKinnon (Darton, Longman and Todd, 1979).
8. Ibid., p. 151.
9. Ibid., p. 34.
10. Ibid., p. 35.
11. Cleo McNelly Kearns, *T. S. Eliot and Indic Traditions. A Study in Poetry and Belief* (CUP, 1987).
12. Ibid., pp. 219ff.
13. Helen Gardner, *The Art of T. S. Eliot* (Cresset Press, 1949), p.54.
14. C. M. Kearns, *T. S. Eliot and Indic Traditions*, pp. 226–7.
15. Stephen Spender, *Eliot*, (Fontana Modern Masters, Fontana/Collins, 1975), pp. 158, 170, 165–6.
16. C. M. Kearns, *T. S. Eliot and Indic Traditions*, p. 232n.
17. Juliette Huxley, *Leaves of the Tulip Tree* (John Murray, 1986), p. 56.
18. C. M. Kearns, *Eliot and Indic Traditions*, op. cit., p. 119.
19. The reader of Professor Kearns' *T. S. Eliot and Indic Traditions* will find an impressive presentation (pp. 232–9) of the theme that in 'Burnt Norton' the poet is *deliberately* 'writing down' or 'writing off' (in what is *meant* to be recognised as a 'worn out poetical fashion') the 'mystical or primal vision' as the sole criterion for wisdom. Her conclusion on this, the first of *Four Quartets*, that the reader is 'returned firmly to the "here and now"' (p. 235), and that 'the reality, as opposed to the thought, of mystical liberation, comes into play only when it infuses the present and informs the ongoing sense of community and history through faith' (p. 239) is the account offered by the present paper of the movement of *Four Quartets* as a whole. It is part of Professor Kearns' deeply sympathetic perception of this writing, infused with her understanding of the Indic points of reference, that she brings out the way 'the pathos and the power of the vision of a lost immediacy' are seen by the poet as not ceasing to illumine (p. 233). The whole of the chapter 'Wisdom in "Four Quartets"' (pp. 230–66) is singularly rich reading.
20. Lyndall Gordon, *Eliot's Earlier Years* (OUP, 1977).
21. For example, A. D. Moody, *Thomas Stearns Eliot, Poet* (CUP, 1979), pp. 203ff, noted Kearns, op. cit., pp. 239ff.
22. T. S. Eliot, *The Idea of a Christian Society* (Faber and Faber, 1939), pp. 63–4.
23. Dietrich Bonhoeffer, *Letters and Papers from Prison*, enlarged edn., (SCM Press, 1971), p. 361 (letter of 16 July 1944).
24. J. Peterkiewicz, *The Other Side of Silence*, p. 106.
25. Michael Palmer on Paul Celan, *Last Poems*, English translation by Katherine Washburn and Margaret Guillemin (North Point Press, San Francisco, 1986).
26. *Collected Poems*, p. 67.

27. *Collected Poems*, p. 165.
28. Dietrich Bonhoeffer, *Ethics* ed. Eberhard Bethge (SCM Press rearranged edition, 1963, and Collins/Fontana, 1964), pp. 133–43. Compare *Letters and Papers from Prison*, of which the critical passages for comparison are the letter quoted already (see note 23) and, from the 'Outline for a Book' (p.381):
'Our relation to God is not a "religious" relationship to the highest, most powerful, and best Being imaginable – that is not authentic transcendence – but our relationship to God is a new life "in existence for others", through participation in the being of Jesus.'
29. See R. C. D. Jasper, *George Bell, Bishop of Chichester* (OUP, 1967), p. 279.
30. Helen Gardner, *The Composition of 'Four Quartets'* (Faber & Faber, 1978), p. 20.

7

The Very Dead of Winter: Notes Towards an Enquiry into English Poetry after Eliot

MICHAEL ALEXANDER

Interviewer: Have you found a professional criticism of your work illuminating or helpful? Edmund Wilson, for example?
Evelyn Waugh: Is he an American?
Interviewer: Yes.
Waugh: I don't think what they have to say is of much interest, do you?[1]

What happened to modernism in English poetry? This question used to bother me a good deal. What followed *The Waste Land* in the poetry of the thirties and later seemed, when I first began to read it thirty years ago, to have had nothing to do with *The Waste Land* – and the literary history (or polemical theory) I had learned at school had made a development onwards from modernism seem morally imperative, and its non-appearance reprehensible, a verdict upon England, a verdict confirming the tragic diagnosis of its postwar condition by D. H. Lawrence.[2] Pound wrote off England when he was thirty, or in the thirty-first year of his age, as he says in opening *Hugh Selwyn Mauberley*. Hugh Kenner seems to follow this root-and-branch historiography: apart from Basil Bunting and Evelyn Waugh, nothing: modern English writing is to be found in Paris, Ireland or America – not an uncommon American view.[3] Leavis had said it in *New Bearings in English Poetry* in 1931: Hardy, Edward Thomas, Rosenberg, all dead, and the ghost of G. M. Hopkins, long dead. In his 1950 postscript Leavis confirmed his pathologist's report: an American and an Irishman had 'gone on', but one was anti-life and the other believed in fairies. Auden, it appeared, had not (as erroneously reported in *Scrutiny*) fizzled out; rather (like Dylan Thomas) he had never started. A later bulletin from Bulstrode Gardens indicated that searchers for true poetry by an *English* writer would have to go back to Dickens.

English novelists of Waugh's generation seemed to have reacted to the apocalyptic appearance of Lawrence and Joyce somewhat in the manner of Lord Nelson to the unwanted signal, by ignoring it.[4] The case for English non-modernism is not so clear with the poets – Auden, for example, or, later, Larkin. Now that post-modernism is being touted, Auden is lost in the dead ground of the non-modernist middle ages, between the -ism and the post-. And Larkin, as a blaspheming anti-modernist, is out of the race where that mortal garland is to be run for. The canon-making, even of academic critics, often has its polemical or commercial aspect: market-making, with modernism as an academic gold standard, for modernist works require interpreters. Do common readers uncorrupted with literary prejudice believe or heed the posterior rationalising of critics? Do writers, common or uncommon?

Of course, English reactions to what we now call modernism in the 1920s were often hostile or suspicious – witness Forster or Virginia Woolf – and the reaction of, for example, Waugh, Greene and Powell to Joyce and Lawrence was perhaps reactionary – which shows again that a cartoon version of literary history in terms of quasi-political movements is not to be taken seriously. Waugh and Co. are minor novelists, but the common reader would be hard to persuade that the experimental novels of Beckett or more recent postmodernistic efforts have produced better fiction than the continuators of the conventional novel of social narrative. In poetry David Jones seems to have been the only modernist of the heroic history-of-the-world sort to persist in England; Eliot and Auden recognised his greatness.[5] But David Jones is a very special case. (More modernism, of the same sort as the first wave, was not really to have been looked for. To ask is here a sign that you have not received. A lineal notion of literary development offers too simple a norm: it leapfrogs, swings, spirals, bloweth where it listeth. For all that can be claimed for general cultural factors, writing is in any case done by persons, not by schools; and the selectivity of hindsight, when they are all folded into a single party, is your only true simplifier.)

What was it, then, that Pound and Eliot had that the poetry of the thirties lacked? A historical sense of the crisis in European culture? Or, perhaps, a discontinuous discourse, obscurity, multi-cultural allusiveness, portentousness? By these signs shall ye know modernists, say some recent anti-elitist voices. But there is enough difficulty in Auden, though his allusiveness is more discreet: 'A gentleman shows as much of his Greek as he does of his lace' (Dr Johnson). It was Auden's use of short conventional verse forms and his disbelief in the idea of a Fall from a more golden age of literature, the arts and of living, which differentiated him from Yeats, Eliot, Pound, early Joyce, and Lawrence. He seems an unnostalgic journalist in comparison with that generation: he was not disgusted specifically with modern life, nor did he in the thirties hanker for a pre-industrial culture – as the modernists, following the Romantics, had. As Edward Mendelson says in the preface to his selection of Auden's poems: 'Auden was the first poet writing in English who felt at home in the twentieth century'.[6] Later he says, 'the surest way to misunderstand Auden is to read him as the modernists' heir. Except in his very earliest and latest poems, there is virtually nothing modernist about him. Most critics of twentieth-century poetry, however, still judge poems by their conformity to modernist norms; consequently, a myth has grown up around Auden to the effect that he fell into a decline almost as soon as he began writing'. In 'A Thanksgiving' (1973), a very late poem, Auden thanks his poetic mentors: Hardy, Thomas, Frost, Yeats, Graves, Brecht, Horace, Goethe. My experience is that few poets or critics under fifty today admire Auden – Norman MacCraig, Gavin Ewart and Roy Fuller of his generation, and Peter Porter, do greatly admire him, as do John Fuller and some other playful Oxonians – which partly supports Mendelson's view. Most other English critics of Auden think, as do Larkin and Geoffrey Hill, that he went off before he left our shores. My experience of teaching Pound, Eliot and Auden is that British students tend to like Auden, and partly because he isn't trying to be great all the time. Unlike Eliot, he did not issue some of his own work as Minor Poems.

Philip Larkin is also a casualty of the critical preference for modernism, although he has become very popular indeed in England. American critics generally don't seem to be able to tune in to him. His contempt for Pound and Picasso is very close to a philistine rejection of what is still called Modern Art. Just as American critics seem to be deaf to Larkin's English tones, so students, British and American, often swallow him whole, deaf to any of his ironies. For them he succeeds all too simply in his aim of being, as he once said great poetry is, 'heart-breaking'. Stendhal's motto, *Ne pas être dupe*, not to be taken in, which might have been Larkin's, is not a bad one. Without faith, and without love, life may be authentic, but it *is* sad.

I contemplate an investigation of what followed *The Waste Land* in English poetry, particularly in Auden and Larkin, and eventually in Geoffrey Hill and Tony Harrison, but I confine myself here to a very limited look at what Pound gave Eliot. Studies of indebtedness and influence often end in emphasising the differences between authors in the ways they treat the same idea, image or formulation. Chaucer, for example, borrows from Dante many striking lines and images. But his relaxed social tone resolves the classical terseness of Dante into the homely, the humorous, the pathetic or the human: there is a loss of terror. Such a domestication has often been said to constitute the Englishness of English art, and such an assimilation seems to have happened with modernism.

To begin with Pound's relation to Eliot: Eliot has evident debts to him in many poems written between 1916 (when they met) and 1931; between Eliot's *Poems, 1920* (which Pound says they planned together) and *Coriolan*. The quatrain-poems imitating Théophile Gautier are evidently of a piece with *Hugh Selwyn Mauberley*. More interesting to investigate might be the debt of *The Waste Land* to *Cantos 1–7*, which preceded it: the cross-cutting of cultural samples left to speak for themselves is a procedure fundamental to Pound's work; the reader is to compare quiddities and draw conclusions as to the state of civilisation they imply. Modern life often emerges from such comparison and contrast as a travesty of human potentialities. There is already much of this in *Prufrock,* before Eliot met Pound; and the differences are clear, but so are some similarities and specific debts. (Eliot's view of human potentialities differs utterly from Pound's, but they share an American fascinated horror at modern Europe and at its sophistication and decay – not merely, as is sometimes said, at its wartime disintegration.)

Tiresias is perhaps borrowed by Eliot from Pound's first Canto, over which he presides, the blind seer of the 'joyless regions' of the 'sunless dead', who foresees the fate of Odysseus and his heroes not without sorrow, but not (like Eliot's Tiresias) foresuffering *all*. There are no typists on board Circe's craft. For both poets, though their purposes are so different, Tiresias is a figure of ancient authority, an oracle – and this gives rise to a general point, possibly of more substance. The figure of the ancient sage, characteristically with a cracked old voice, is to be found in Pound's very early 'twilit' poetry. A reading of Pound's *Collected Shorter Poems* shows that this sage had found a home in his orientalising poetry even before *Cathay* – in 'Ancient Wisdom, Rather Cosmic', for example – and the epitaphs on Li Po and Fu I, three little poems worked up from the literal prose versions of the Rev. James Legge's *Chinese Classics* (as were Helen Waddell's *Lyrics from the Chinese*, 1913). These poems are squibs or spoofs (like the mandarin 'Meditatio'), but in *Cathay* (1915–16) the mask of the sage fits. The longest, most personal and serious poem in this collection of translations from Tang poets (via the notes of Ernest Fenollosa) is 'Exile's Letter' by Li Po.[7] 'Exile's Letter' is addressed in its first line to an 'ancient friend' (an ancient as well as an old friend) and ends with the 'white-headed' exile calling in the boy:

> I call in the boy,
> Have him sit on his knees here
>   To seal this,
> And send it a thousand miles, thinking.

There are many similarities between 'Exile's Letter' and Eliot's 'Journey of the Magi' (1927), which begins:

> A cold coming we had of it,
> Just the worst time of year
> For a journey, and such a long journey:
> The ways deep and the weather sharp,
> The very dead of winter.

Eliot's Magus, like Yeats's, was not 'satisfied' with the uncontrollable mystery on the bestial floor, and he leads into his overwhelming final question with a direction to an amanuensis:

>   but set down
> This, set down
> This: were we led all that way for
> Birth or Death?

The Exile looks back and says: 'And all this comes to an end'; the

Magus: 'All this was a long time ago'. They are old, wise and puzzled, and, like the Sybil, have a secretary.

Back in 1920 Eliot's little old man, Gerontion, had introduced himself thus:

> Here I am, an old man in a dry month
> Being read to by a boy, waiting for rain.

Perhaps the boy had been reading him Li Po's letter; but his ancient glittering eyes are not gay.

Eliot is notorious for his valetudinarian tone: Prufrock grows old, Gerontion, Tiresias, the Magus, Simeon, 'Why should the aged eagle [at 42] stretch his wings?' – all what Larkin might have called old fools. Eliot had long anticipated 'the gifts reserved for age' before (in 1942) the familiar compound ghost disclosed them to him. But the Elder Statesman could not know that he was to marry again, and happily.

The insistence on superannuation has been found irritating. But it is not new: Tennyson's Ulysses and Tithonus had it, and Laforgue apes it. It was Ezra Pound who called Eliot 'Ol' Possum' (after the manner of Joel Chandler Harris's Brer Rabbit): a possum is an animal which feigns death when approached. But if Ol' Possum had not known Pound and never read 'Exile's Letter', he would have lost a gesture and a pose: the old man who dictates a letter. And remember who it was that the Elder Statesman married; according to Peter Ackroyd, T. S. Eliot proposed to his secretary in the office, not at teatime.[8]

To return to the reminiscences of Li Po, Rihaku or Ezra Pound and of Caspar, Melchior or Balthazar, Goodwin in his study *The Literary Influence of Ezra Pound* (1966) observed cautiously that '*Exile's Letter* and *Journey of the Magi* have a certain amount of imagery in common, the most noticeable being the valleys'. Goodwin's empirical survey is accurate (the weary physical impressions of a winter journey linked by 'And') but, while *Exile's Letter* and *Journey of the Magi* are very different kinds of poems, one could say more generally that Pound lent Eliot a wider landscape and a tone of voice. He supplemented Eliot's stock of sordid city streets, strained interiors and twisted indoor plants with a wider, more mythological, more epic use of landscape through which to travel to his dissatisfaction. Without Pound it is hard to imagine that the wise man of *Lancelot Andrewes* would have regretted 'the silken girls bringing sherbet'; the Exile's girls had got drunk about sunset and danced in transparent brocade: their green eyebrows suggest that more than sherbet might have been available. Without Pound it is hard to imagine 'You who were with me in the ships at Mylae' (*The Waste Land*) or Eliot 'knee deep in the salt marsh, heaving a cutlass' (*Gerontion*) or, from *Coriolan*:

> Meanwhile the guards shake dice on the marches
> And the frogs (O Mantuan) croak in the marshes

which is surely affected by the tone and technique of *Homage to Sextus Propertius*. But these are incidentals.

I suggest, then, that without Pound's *Cathay*, his *Cantos* 1–7, his *Propertius* (and perhaps his Dante) we would have a different Eliot. In antiquity Homer himself idealises the figure of the poet as a blind seer, honoured and humoured: 'Tiresias and Phineus, prophets old', as Milton calls them at *Paradise Lost*, III, 36. Post-Augustan English poets present themselves as despondent or mad. Tennyson and Arnold feel irrelevant to the modern industrial world, and this drift develops into the aesthetic crisis of the nineties – the subject of *Hugh Selwyn Mauberley*.[9] It is striking that Pound and Eliot both adopt the persona of the superior old man who has travelled much, seen and done everything (and read, or been read to, a great deal), survived wars and sufferings, who knows too much to be happy in the modern world or in this world – an intellectual Ulysses, a Nestor, a Tiresias who had really lived. Dante, and Dante's Ulysses, contribute much of the imagery here. (It would be interesting to find out when it was that Eliot added the epigraph to *Prufrock*.) The wise old man, the sage, has a special voice, the voice of some dead master, mantic, mandarin or magian – which one can hear in recordings of Pound and Eliot reading their work. A kind of confirmation of the centrality of this slightly histrionic or stilted figure of authority and tradition is the travesty to which Samuel Beckett subjects it. It might be said that Eliot had already pre-travestied it in hanging the Sybil of Petronius outside the entrance to his Hades.

It has been customary to look to elderly poets, even to John Betjeman, for wisdom and guidance; and the authority accorded to Wordsworth and Tennyson by the hungry sheep was eventually accorded to T. S. Eliot and sought at the Roman microphone by Ezra Pound. (In wartime England the BBC broadcast E. M. Forster and

Ezra Pound's neighbour in Rapallo, Max Beerbohm.) Auden in his debunking way also assumed this role, though he played it first as an *enfant terrible* prep-school master. In 'Church Going', Larkin fled from the pulpit, though Anglicans keep trying to put him back into it.

Auden's 'In Memory of W. B. Yeats' (d. Jan. 1939) begins with a possible echo of Eliot's 'Journey of the Magi' (1927).

> He disappeared in the dead of winter:
> The brooks were frozen, the airports almost deserted,
> And snow disfigured the public statues;
> The mercury sank in the mouth of the dying day.
> O all the instruments agree
> The day of his death was a dark cold day.

The phrase 'the dead of winter' is common enough, and presumably preceded Lancelot Andrewes, so it is a slender thread upon which to hang this essay. But Auden had known Eliot's work well from 1927 onwards and, though their remedies were initially very different, they enjoyed similarly eschatological visions of the predicament of the human as an 'etherised patient', and 'The notion of an infinitely gentle/Infinitely suffering thing'.[10]

Auden chose the phrase 'the dead of winter' for the first line of a poem in memory of the poetry of his youth as well as of W. B. Yeats, in a stanza where the dead sound beats like a drum. I distinguish three senses in 'he disappeared in the dead of winter': Yeats's death occurred in January, at the low point of winter. Then, he was lost to our sight in the darkness of winter. But also, the death of the poet was unnoticeable because he was lost in the numberless throng of those whom death sweeps away every winter. 'The dead of winter' can mean midwinter, the nadir, but 'the dead' is also a collective noun: the 'so many' that 'death has undone'. I take such polysemy to be a characteristic of modernism and in this sense Auden is a modernist, though his ambiguity is covert, much less antinomian than Eliot's. 'The mercury sank in the mouth of the dying day' is another example: the ambient temperature sinks as the daylight declines, but also the mercury sinks in the thermometer in the cooling mouth of the patient. This clinically horrible image is like the reversal of expectation which is the trademark of Eliot's opening gambit: the evening spread out like a patient, April the cruellest month. The forcible yoking of discordant elements in 'The brooks were frozen, the airports almost deserted' is pure Auden, chirpily at home in the ruins of the twentieth century, but it exemplifies another assimilation of modernism, a constant sharp alteration of tone, and is indebted to Eliot. Other unsettling brief examples from the poem in memory of Yeats are 'You were silly, like us' and 'By mourning tongues the death of the poet was kept from his poems' (as if the poems recited by Yeats's mourners were also his bereaved children who had to be protected).

The poem as a whole may have a general debt to *The Waste Land* in its central images of the prison of the self and of water in the desert. But my view is that Auden shows not a specific but a general debt to Eliot; he was not a thieving magpie but (*contra* Mendelson) an inheritor. It would not be hard to multiply possible echoes, but in Auden's intense literary self-consciousness, and his confident use of a variety of English social tones, ambiguity and bathos, he has assimilated many of the essentials of Eliot's modernism – and put them to a broader social use, somewhat as Pope domesticated the spectacular wit and metaphysical vision of the metaphysicals.

Philip Larkin's hostility to modernism admits its power for him. He attacked Pound, Picasso and Parker (three foreigners) in the way the modernists and Auden attacked Tennyson, whose work they were trying to exorcise. But unlike Auden, Larkin does see progress as a deterioration; like Eliot and Pound he is a cultural pessimist, though a conservative rather than a reactionary. He sees a terrible decline in language, and mocks its impoverishment in the way he uses it: writhing under the mundane clichés he constantly quotes and tries to escape from: 'That Whitsun I was late getting away'. A satirist, he uses allusion and bathos to achieve his effects, characteristically referring to old standards, values and communal institutions – such as seaside holidays, home, agricultural shows, weddings, churches, Armistice Day, the English countryside and England itself, together with new ones like advertisement hoardings, multiple stores, and the academic study of contemporary literature, together with some perennials, like love, marriage, death, work and British Railways. Like Thomas Hardy he is a churchy unbeliever, and like him he reacted to modernism by supposing that the English would have to go on dealing with the same old themes in the same old ways. Modernism for him is an aggravated symptom of the cultural decline which the modernists attacked; in this way he is not unlike the Australian poets A. D. Hope, James McAuley or Les A. Murray. But he agreed with the

Eliot who said that if we cannot have belief then we had better just do without it. Language is not something poets can do without, and Larkin often uses it in ways which remind us of quieter, often disappearing, English social uses: 'I searched the sand for Famous Cricketers' (cigarette cards) or 'someone running up to bowl' (cricket itself). Such understatedness is not for export and perhaps does not travel well – like Auden's 'And several thousand will think of this day/As a day when one did something slightly unusual' – like mourning, weeping, praying, changing one's mind about someone, or reciting a poem. The restoration of discursiveness, connected subordinate syntax, and conventional forms, which Larkin shares with Auden, permits a more nuanced control of tone and makes for effects less fugitive than Pound's technique permits. The technique of anticlimax is one Larkin uses habitually – in the title of 'Sad Steps', for example; or, in the tradition of Eliot's 'I have measured out my life with coffee spoons', or 'And puts a record on the gramophone':

> Until the next town, new and nondescript,
> Approached with acres of dismantled cars.

He can also rise quietly (as in the next stanza of 'The Whitsun Weddings') to a surprising small climax of hope:

> An Odeon went past, a cooling tower,
> And someone running up to bowl.

This is not, what it closely resembles, a resigned acceptance of reduced expectations. In its extremely quiet way it registers all the degradation of modern England which romantic Americans – like Shakespeare's John of Gaunt – might feel, and it registers and celebrates more, including the humanity that survives within it. It also includes an assimilated contribution of what Larkin professed to despise, much of the technique and terrified honesty of modernism, grafting it on to older uses.

A much more interesting question than the fate of modernism is whether there is any good poetry written in England. (There has been, it may be necessary to state once again, a great deal of good poetry written in this century by Americans, as by Pound, Eliot, Williams, Stevens, Moore, and Lowell.) Modernism is a national as well as an international phenomenon, and the question can be asked for England (and of course for Scotland, Wales, Ireland North and South, and perhaps Britain).

The work of Geoffrey Hill and also of Tony Harrison makes it finally evident that the apparent rejection of high modernism by English poets was an illusion. Educated provincials like Larkin, they carry the cultural freight of 'the mind of Europe' without pretending, as Larkin did, that insularity makes for a more authentic Englishness. They also confirm, by and large, that the practice of modern English verse does not require a dislocated syntax nor a rejection of formal regularity. They are both, in their contrasting ways, conscious rhetoricians who make the reader conscious of their passionate rhetoric, in marked contrast to Larkin. Ambitious, allusive, compressed, ambiguous and ironical, they are learned poets who display their learning and also their concern with the tragic materials of political history, including the history of the present. From his very earliest publications Geoffrey Hill has carried an almost Germanic weight of culture, of concern and angst, and of the entropy of the word. This perilous freight has almost overwhelmed him in his own riven ambivalence, although *Mercian Hymns* and *The Mystery of the Charity of Charles Péguy* make more definite statements. Tony Harrison's angry sense of alienation by schooling from his working-class background is his most insistent characteristic. But in the volume *Continuous* he projects and focuses the material of the moment and the future of poetry against the profound perspectives of history – another characteristic of the modernist generation.

Notes

1. Quoted by M. Bradbury in *Evelyn Waugh and his World*, ed. D. Pryce-Jones (1973).
2. 'Ours is essentially a tragic age, so we refuse to take it tragically', the opening sentence of *Lady Chatterley's Lover* (Penguin, 1961).
3. See Kenner, *The Sinking Island*, 1988, *passim*.
4. But in 1934 Waugh called his bleakest novel *A Handful of Dust* (from *The Waste Land*, line 30).
5. *In Parenthesis* was acclaimed by Eliot as 'a work of genius' in his preface to the Faber edition of 1937, in which he puts Jones on a footing with himself, Joyce and Ezra Pound as the major modernist writers of his period. *The Anathemata* (1952) was considered by W. H. Auden 'very probably the greatest long poem in English in this

century'. See Alexander, 'David Jones, An Introduction' in *Scripsi*, Vol. 2, No. 4, pp. 257–98.
6. W. H. Auden's *Selected Poems*, ed. Edward Mendelson, 1979, p. ix.
7. With the exception of Canto I, the Pound poems cited here are all to be found in the Faber *Collected Shorter Poems* (1952) or the New Directions *Personae* (1926).
8. T. S. Eliot (1984), p. 319.
9. Pound's poem deals with the material of the chapters of W. B. Yeats's *Autobiographies* (1926), entitled 'The Tragic Generation'.
10. Compare the penultimate image of Eliot's *Preludes* with Auden's 'solitary man sat weeping on a bench' in 'It was Easter as I walked in the public gardens,' Mendelson, op. cit., p. 7.

[An earlier version of this paper appeared in *Scripsi* (Melbourne).]

8
Visions of Hell: Lowry and Beckett
FRANCIS DOHERTY

Part of what has happened to literature since *The Waste Land* is bound up with concepts of tragedy, and we all know that this has become not only a problematical term but a word difficult to sustain in the post-Holocaust world.

A fragment of the general history of the concept of tragedy in our time is contained in the kinds of questions and issues which are raised when we consider the work of two writers born in the first decade of our century, Malcolm Lowry, born 1909, and Samuel Beckett, born 1906. I have space for what, quite appropriately, as Beckettians might feel, is perforce minimalist, inconclusive and private, notes you could say for an abandoned work.

Malcolm Lowry's most celebrated work, *Under the Volcano*, has its dedicated admirers, and much has been said about it. All that I wish to do is to notice one or two of its features to make the commonplace point that this work stands in a modernist, Joycean tradition (though Lowry himself distinguished his work from Joyce's), a self-consciously made work which exists by using an old system of organising meaning. This is that system of interactive symbols, complexly coded, where the reader only gradually becomes aware that apparently naturalistic details of the landscape, for instance, like volcanoes and a ravine – real enough in that pictures of them can be seen in biographies of Lowry – function as a series of poetic symbols. There is the famous letter to Jonathan Cape which takes the reader through the author's account of the structures of his book, chapter by chapter, insisting on both its symbology and its systems of thought, drawn from the Cabbala and so on, making the world of the book hermetic. Who could reasonably be expected to know about *sōd* and *Qliphoth*?

(*Note* In the Cabbala, the misuse of magical powers is compared to drunkenness or the misuse of wine, and termed, if I remember rightly, in Hebrew *sōd*, which gives us our parallel. There is a kind of attribute of the word *sōd* also which implies garden or a neglected garden, I seem to recall too, for the Cabbala is sometimes considered as a garden itself, with the Tree of Life, which is related of course to that Tree the forbidden fruit of which gave one the knowledge of good and evil, and ourselves the legend of Adam and Eve, planted within it. Be these things as they may – and they are certainly at the root of most of our knowledge, the wisdom of our religious thought, and most of our inborn superstitions as to the origin of man – William James if not Freud would certainly agree with me when I say that the agonies of the drunkard find their most accurate poetic analogue in the agonies of the mystic who has abused his powers.

The Cabbala is used for poetical purposes because it represents man's spiritual aspiration. The Tree of Life, which is its emblem, is a kind of complicated ladder with Kether, or Light, at the top and an extremely unpleasant abyss some way above the middle. The Consul's spiritual domain in this regard is probably the Qliphoth, the world of shells and demons, represented by the Tree of Life upside down – all this is not important at all to the understanding of the book; I just mention it in passing to hint that, as Henry James says, 'There are depths.'[1]

Certainly a discerning reader might be able to see that the author is somehow or other trying to make his book complex in its themes, moral, political, social, metaphysical, and the same discerning reader could have recognised that the Consul is being shown to be a tragic figure, or at least that the book is aiming at tragedy. And such a reader might well anticipate Lowry's words that the beginning and the ending of the book are poetically related.

So the main point is that, like Joyce, the author aimed for a definable and regular system of analogues, allusions, learned references, which can be plotted, strung out, noted. The author himself discusses various concepts of the tragic, quotes Aristotle, leans towards Aeschylus, and writes out of a literary and cultural deposit, but a deposit where there is no priority given to any belief-system, whether to Virgil and *'facilis decensus Avernus'*, or to Dante, or to the Fates, or to pre-Christian myth, or to Mexican dark Catholicism and the Day of the Dead. All may be said to figure equally, and all are equally important (or, as I may say mischievously, unimportant, except as aesthetic thickening).

The truth seems to be that Lowry as an individual, looking into himself, his own psychopathology, his drunkenness, and being conscious of real and deep despair, writes himself at large, reinvents himself as universal man, split into four characters: the Consul, his brother, Yvonne his wife, and her former lover, the Frenchman Laruelle, as Lowry himself wrote.[2]

The writer takes his own emotional experiences, which are profound and bleak, and uses them as the fuel for his novel; he takes his experience of desolation, for which he finds analogues in varieties of damnations, Dantean, Faustian, Cabbalistic. The emotional state of the author is primary, as can be seen reflected in letters from 1937 and 1938. Take the letter to Conrad Aiken in 1937 as an example:

Dear old bird:

Have now reached condition of amnesia, breakdown, heartbreak, consumption, cholera, alcoholic poisoning, and God will not like to know what else, if he has to, which is damned doubtful.

All change here, all change here, for Oakshot, Cockshot, Poxshot and fuck the whole bloody lot!

My only friend here is a tertiary who pins a medal of the Virgin of Guadalupe on my coat; follows me in the street (when I am not in prison, and he followed me there too several times); and who thinks I am Jesus Christ, which, as you know, I am not yet, though I may be progressing towards thinking I am myself.

I have been imprisoned as a spy in a dungeon compared with which the Chateau d'If – in the film – is a little cottage in the country overlooking the sea.

I spent Christmas – New Year's – Wedding Day there. All my mail is late. When it does arrive it is all contradiction and yours is cut into little holes.

Don't think I can go on. Where I am it is dark. Lost.
                Happy New Year,
                Malcolm[3]

This novelist's procedure was an essentially romantic one with a heavy emphasis on damnation. In spite of Lowry's declared intentions for a large-scale oeuvre which would be modelled on Dante's *Commedia* with *Lunar Caustic* as the *Purgatorio, Under the Volcano* as the *Inferno*, and the lost *In Ballast to the White Sea* as the *Paradiso*, the whole to be called *The Voyage that Never Ends*, this *Inferno* remains his most central and powerful reality. As he wrote to his publisher, 'there are a thousand writers who can draw adequate characters till all is blue for one who can tell you anything new about hell fire. And I am telling you something new about hell fire'.

He has done such a good job of mythologising his primary emotional materials and experiences (whether of mescal or Mexico or frustrated ambitions and failures) that his novel demands explication of the following kind:

> The arrows are images of martyrdom and also signs offering a choice; the paths cross in ways that suggest to Yvonne on two separate occasions a crucifixion. The choice of paths leads one either to the Falls or to the Little Lighthouse, ironic source of light where the Consul will find darkness. But it is the path to the Falls that Yvonne takes, and the choice is underlined by the fact that miniature cascades are already plunging down beside them as they walk in the direction of the final fall towards which Yvonne feels her spirit being swept away. This of course is a premonitory image of the death that awaits her, but it is also a sign that this is a novel not only about eviction from paradise, but also about the Fall, in theological terms. And, of course, if anyone in the novel is unwilling victim and needless sacrifice, it is Yvonne.[4]

But the writing which calls for this kind of explication came from a profoundly superstitious man, given to finding hidden meanings and messages in coincidences in the way the world was received by him. The failure of the S in the huge illuminated SHELL skysign in Canada which glared at him across the bay seemed a paradigm: HELL. The world for Lowry is full of significances, not emptied of it, and the more the writer or his central character concentrates on the significances, the symbols at large, the less he has time for himself, and it is more comforting to believe oneself damned already than to open oneself either to oneself or to others or to God's salvation.

Given the kind of work which Lowry wrote, poetic in the old sense, densely written, replete with symbols, his biographer is right to say, as he does of *Lunar Caustic*, that there is what we might call the aesthetic of profusion, whereby beauty is created through proliferation of symbols. In this aesthetic, Lowry is a paradigm. If one prefers, however, the aesthetics of exclusion, whereby beauty is created through spareness of effect, then Lowry is not one's man.[5]

Indeed, what Lowry's work of damnation involves aesthetically gives any critic plenty to remark on, encouraged as he is to pay attention to the undertones, to the ramifications of symbol and theme, to density. By contrast, Beckett's whole work has shown a world not of the *Inferno* kind which so engaged Lowry, but rather a rewriting of the *Purgatorio*. The Lowry hero can indeed be seen as isolated, cut off from others, *l'âme damnée*, the dead dog (god backwards) thrown after him down the ravine; Beckett's isolates are never so finally cut off, and that, we may say, is their central difficulty.

In his most famous work, *Waiting for Godot*, there is a pathos to be seen in the bonding of the pseudocouple, Vladimir and Estragon, who spend the day apart, come together in the evening, then part for the night, and actually spend very little time together. They are 'free' to come and go; they are not tied:

Estragon: We're not tied?
Vladimir: I don't hear a word you're saying.
Estragon: I'm asking you if we're tied.
Vladimir: Tied?
Estragon: Ti – ed.
Vladimir: How do you mean tied?
Estragon: Down.
Vladimir: But to whom? By whom?
Estragon: To your man.
Vladimir: To Godot? Tied to Godot? What an idea! No question of it. (*Pause*) For the moment.[6]

This pair represents one of the minimal assertions which Beckett wants to make about us, absurdly companionate, caught up in others as part of what it is to be human, and yet looking for ways of evading that total freedom which we do have, comforting ourselves by the possibility of being tied to 'your man'.

The story of the earlier Beckett fiction is in part the story of the pursuit of fellow and flight from fellow, even when the pursuit and capture may well involve appalling cruelties and suffering inflicted and received (as in *How It Is*). Even when we critics speak of the isolation of Man Alone as in *Malone Dies*, we need to remember the Beckettian joke that 'dying is such a long tiresome business I always found', where there is an impossible tense of habituation for that impossible business which, looked at in one direction, we call *living*, and yet looked at from the other he calls *dying*. We remember too that the voice which is the novel's is directly addressing another, the very act of being, say Malone, involves another for its reality, say you, the reader. Isolation is impossible, and the ideal condition of not-being where the pure silence might be reached is a constant dream, but is ever beyond us, locked as we are into life, into self. Once in existence man is, and he cannot not-be.

Several times Beckett takes the theatre into a post-death condition, into a world which seems very like a Dantesque *Purgatorio*, yet which is not. In his play, *Play*, the three participants in a bourgeois adulterous triangle are interrogated by a spotlight which moves among them stimulating the illumined into confession. The story thus elicited is elicited again, and then the cycle is about to start a third time when, mercifully, we are spared that. But the model is one of an endless, pointless interrogation which will go on *ad infinitum*, that is unendingly, unendably. Put into distortion by the dramatist is the pious prayer for the dead, '*et lux perpetua luceat eis*', and we are certainly given the lie to the '*Requiescant in pace*' which so consoles us, the living, praying for our dead. How much better, we seem to be being shown, would be the lack of '*lux perpetua*', the vainly-desiring nothing. Yet Beckett turns us towards a state of being well outside the range of naturalism and modern secular humanism.

In the twelve-minute piece for mouth, *Not I*, a babbling mouth is responded to mutely if sympathetically by an obscured djellaba-clothed figure on the side of the stage, having to listen, as often in Beckett, to a repeated babble of monologue. This babble, while encompassing sex, birth, morbid isolation, catatonia, a sudden change in condition – say death – is constantly repudiated as the lived experiences belonging to 'No. She!' The Mouth is vainly trying to become detached from all that makes a person, but this attempt is unendable, infinite, beyond the capacity of the Mouth, pathetic in its ruse. Any possible attempt at self-denial is further frustrated by the self being observed unknowingly by the other, again guaranteeing existence.

Beckett's protagonists may be in a post-life state, but there's never any possible end, even if they contrive to escape, as far as they possibly can, from any response of any others; they inevitably remain 'self-conscious', a specially loaded term for Beckett who fifty years ago said of Samuel Johnson that

> there can hardly have been many so completely at sea in their solitude as he was or so horribly aware of it. Read the Prayers and Meditations if you don't believe me . . . she [Mrs Thrale] had none of that need to suffer or necessity of suffering that he had . . . he, in a sense was spiritually self-conscious, was a tragic figure, i.e. worth putting down as part of the whole of which oneself is part.[7]

The consciousness of self and suffering, the business of living as a punishment for sin, the unforgivable sin of having been born, characterises Beckett's work, and conventional comfort in religion, in religion's often diminished and anthropomorphised deity, is continuously mocked. But, as so many have said, Beckett is a mystic, or, as I prefer more fancifully to say, Beckett is an anti-theologian.

From his early to his late work Beckett has shown a scorn for naturalism in literary procedures, has been Manichean in his attitude to the body, Swiftian in his depiction of the sexuality which our century wears as its mark of liberation, and profoundly caught up in metaphysical and theological discourse. His work has increasingly been concerned with emptiness rather than the fullness of being, with impotence rather than ability, with failure rather than success. His world is one where instead of the individual's, as in Lowry, experiencing a personal damnation, a Faustian hell of exclusion, the individual endures endlessly the pain of existence, unredeemable, anguished. Yet both writers have self-reflexive central figures who suffer. For Beckett a favourite model for this suffering of being is the crucified Christ, and in recent work on Beckett's practical theatrical directorial techniques and his preferred configurations of the stage movements in *Waiting for Godot* and its stage images, we are made more and more conscious of the power of the cruciform for Beckett.[8]

There is suffering, as Beckett writes somewhere, as an endless series of stations with no hope of crucifixion; or, more appallingly perhaps, there is Estragon's suffering which has, he says, always allowed him to compare himself to Christ, and which he produces when he proposes to walk barefoot like Christ. Vladimir says, in rebuke, 'But where he was it was warm, it was dry.' Estragon's clincher is 'Yes. And they crucified quick.'

Beckett's figures, from drama or prose fiction, retreat further and further from sources of suffering only to find more and more acutely the suffering self, helpless to escape from self, from thoughts, from memory. There's enough there to be going along with. But in the prose work, *The Lost Ones* of 1972 (originally the French *Le Dépeupleur* of 1970) Beckett gives the clearest image of what has happened to his vision of man in his state of suffering. Quite patently a parody of Dante's *Purgatorio*, there is a created world presented to us where there are rumours of ways out of the closed cylinder which doubles as the Purgatorio, but, try as they may, and at some point most try, in vain, there is no way out. There are ladders for climbing, and there might be a way out through the top of the cylinder, unreachable by ladders, so climbing and failing become ways of passing the time (I almost said living). Because this is a human fiction which Beckett has unavoidably written, it takes its place among human dreams and visions or nightmares, but being a Beckettian fiction it is only too obvious that for our sake we need to have ends to stories, a cherished belief that the roughest day will end, that the last tape can be played or the last trump sounded. Consequently the final section of this short work, its conclusion so to speak, starts:

> So on infinitely until towards the unthinkable end if this notion is maintained a last body of all by feeble fits and starts is searching still.[9]

The work can only end because, being a human work and the readers of it human, we long for ends, but there are only fictional ends, never real ones. The myth is one of searching endlessly in vain, and if in the Platonic and Shelleyan ideal the soul is searching for its lost part, *The Lost Ones* seems modelled on that myth, even if in parody.

> Abode where lost bodies roam each searching for its lost one. Vast enough for search to be in vain. Narrow enough for flight to be in vain.

But the French original is much more cruel, insisting that this is

Visions of Hell: Lowry and Beckett

Séjour où les corps vont cherchant chacun son dépeupleur.

To depopulate, to unpeople, is a powerful verb to turn to, and to search for the one who could make you not is a savage parody of any myth of completion by finding the missing part of you. Such a completion myth is summoned up by the French noun, '*son dépeupleur*', 'its unpeopler', 'its depopulator', because it must call up for a French reader the well-known lines from the first poem of Lamartine's *Méditations* of 1820, 'L'Isolement' ('Isolation' or 'Solitude'). In that ruminative poem of evening and a mountain landscape, the speaker looks round to dismiss all that might be around him because he is separated from a significant other.

> *Que me font ces vallons, ces palais, ces chaumières,*
> *Vains objets dont pour moi le charme est envolé;*
> *Fleuves, rochers, forêts, solitudes si chères,*
> *Un seul être vous manque, et tout est dépeuplé.*

And if the speaker were to get beyond the boundaries of the universe, to places where the true sun illumines other skies, and if he were able to let his 'hide' fall back to the earth, then would what he has dreamt of appear to him, that *'bien idéal que toute âme désire/Et qui n'as pas de nom au terrestre séjour'*. Such is Lamartine's romanticism, such his generic theme of the soul-mate, the *âme soeur* who inevitably inhabits a different body. In Lamartine the two may gradually grow into one, but this, as one of his critics says, may be a protracted business.[10]

Beckett takes such romantic longings, but he traps them not in a sphere ('*mais peut-être au-delà des bornes de sa sphère*'), but in a cylinder, itself a cooled-down and precisely mathematical simplification in parody of the *Purgatorio*. The cylinder which contains the Lost Ones is a precisely given figure:

> Inside a flattened cylinder fifty metres round and eighteen high for the sake of harmony.

Schoolboy mathematics shows me that the circumference of the sphere is just less than sixteen metres while the height is eighteen metres, but to get there I have as many mathematical doodles on my script as, one now knows, do Beckett's own. As a creator he likes his mathematics, but likes them most when they include irrational numbers (life being, as Murphy thought, a matrix of surds) or when nothing agrees (as Mr Knott's circular sheet receives his body as it rotates one degree a day and is changed annually on St Patrick's Day, though the 365 or so days in a year are just that bit more than the 360 degrees in a circle). In the present case the flaw is the difference between 176 and 175, where 176 is the exact divisor of 22, but not what Beckett's '50 metres round' yields when you want to calculate the radius of the sphere. Ah well! If human creations are so flawed, look at the universe, as the ancient joke of the tailor and his trousers has it in *Endgame*.

Such a location for the fiction of searching for the way out, for something to release the sufferers from suffering, is the best that Beckett can imagine, given the marvellous intricacies of Dante's imagined other worlds, and it itself suffers deliberately by invoking its ancestral creation.

But when we turn from Dante to those romantic poets who had longed for the soul's completion, as in Shelley's *Epipsychidion*, by its soul-mate, the Beckettian horror is that the soul is always bound into existence, kept there by self-awareness or other-awareness. If, almost as a joke, Beckett wrote his film-script as being based on Berkeley's *esse est percipi*, and the perceived and the perceiver turn out to be self-reflexive, it is a serious joke. The Beckett-figures are all victims, making the best vain attempts at escapes they can from a condition they would never willingly have chosen, and vainly pursuing what increasingly they recognise as 'vain wishes', or 'last gasps'. As in Dante's *Inferno* there is no escape, and souls are tormented by memories, so here torment is increased by Vladimir's invocation of *'memoria praeteritorum bonorum* – that must be unpleasant', exactly that which Dante held to be the greatest torment of the damned. Or an old man reminisces as in Beckett's *A Piece of Monologue* of 1980, where the monologuist speaks as narrator for his own story, always distanced from himself, never owning his own thoughts, or memories or life, he is far from being able to reside easily in his aloneness, as had been his precursor in Irish writing, the hero of Seán O'Faoláin's *Bird Alone* of 1936.[11] Beckett's man, with a stage echo in a standard oil-lamp with a skull-like dome, exactly his height, contemplates the blackness and waits on the 'rip word' which presumably might save him, as the 'rip cord' might save a parachutist, and passing his time computing the seconds and the days: thirty thousand nights: two and a half billion odd seconds. He was born in the room, kept the memories and pictures of his 'loved ones' and is waiting ... waiting for death, one assumes, though, as the first words say, 'Birth was the death of him.' The setting for the monologue is Edwardian, with nightshirt and standard oil-lamp, but the tone is the expected acerbic, witty, tormented and measured droplets of the isolated contemporary voice of despair – 'The globe alone. Alone gone.' This is the present condition of hell, the impossible hope of dissolution, a state where 'thoughts against thoughts in groans grind'.

Beckett is a writer who has created a set of physically impossible coordinates for the ground-of-being in Mr Knott in his novel *Watt*, written in hiding during the war in the Vaucluse, and he is not someone who is merely trifling with metaphysics or making aesthetic meals from metaphysical elements. He is someone whose fundamental sounds come from man's straining to utter or eff the unutterable or ineffable. We critics may treat him as an ironic atheist who is roused to laughter simply by the mocking of texts which are the stock-in-trade of the wayside pulpit: 'The Lord upholdeth all that fall and raiseth up all those that be bowed down', or in an opposite view as a quester in the line of all mystic questers. But what has grown throughout half a century of writing is the increased concentration on man trapped in time and its successiveness, its endless repetition, its cycles, unable to escape, unable to make sense of it, yet condemned to a mind ruined by its attempts to understand the least thing. (Beckett is said to have been overheard muttering: 'I don't know why two and two must always equal four'.) This is hell; other fanciful versions which we make up as myths are only stories told, after all.

What Lowry's great novel does is to show what has happened when tragedy no longer concerns the values of a community but rather the self-destructive urge of an individual whose damnation is chosen and actively sought. But it is written in an essentially romantic mode in a highly-developed world of correspondences. Beckett's later work shows damnation to be nothing to do with choice, but part of the way we are, and the line he belongs to goes beyond the romantics whom he loves, and it goes at least to Dr Johnson. 'They can put me wherever they want, but it's Johnson, always Johnson, who is with me. And if I follow any tradition, it is his.'[12] I suppose a resonating sympathetic echo would be struck by Beckett's vision of man's hell from the opening lines of 'On the Death of Robert Levet':

> Condemn'd to Hope's delusive mine
> As on we toil from day to day

> From sudden blasts or slow decline
> Our social comforts drop away.

We are condemned, and our sin is having been born. Neither is salvation possible nor is an end ordained.

Notes

1. Harvey Breit and Margerie Bonner Lowry (eds), *Selected Letters of Malcolm Lowry* (London: Jonathan Cape, 1967; Harmondsworth: Penguin Books, 1985), pp. 71, 65.
2. Ibid., p. 15.
3. Ibid., p. 80.
4. George Woodcock, 'The Own Place of the Mind: An Essay in Lowrian Topography', in Anne Smith (ed.), *The Art of Malcolm Lowry* (London: Vision Press, 1978), p. 122.
5. Douglas Day, *Malcolm Lowry: A Biography* (Oxford: Oxford University Press, 1984), p. 212.
6. *Waiting for Godot* (London: Faber & Faber, 1956), p. 20.
7. Letter to Thomas McGreevy, 4 August 1937. Quoted in Deirdre Bair, *Samuel Beckett: A Biography* (London: Jonathan Cape, 1978; London: Picador, 1980) pp. 220–21.
8. Dougald McMillan and Martha Fehsenfeld, *Beckett in the Theatre*, (London: John Calder, 1988).
9. *The Lost Ones* (London: Calder and Boyars, 1972), p. 60.
10. J. C. Ireson, *Lamartine: A Revaluation*, University of Hull Occasional Papers in Modern Languages No. 6, University of Hull, 1969, p. 48.
11. London: Jonathan Cape, 1936; Oxford: Oxford University Press, 1985.
12. Quoted by Deirdre Bair, *Samuel Beckett: A Biography*, p. 221. Remark made to Bair, 12 April 1972.

9

Samuel Beckett's Negative Way: Intimations of the *Via Negativa* in his Late Plays
MARIUS BUNING

For more than one reason it may seem hazardous to talk about mysticism and Samuel Beckett. For one thing, mysticism is a complex but slippery subject that easily lends itself to fashionable forms of neo-orientalism or to New Age enthusiasm. For another, to foist a mystical interpretation on his work may run the risk of what the great ironist Jonathan Swift called 'Scholiastick Midwifry', the critics having 'deliver'd them of Meanings that the Authors themselves, perhaps, never conceived'. Let me assure you that I have no such intention. Nor am I going to practise what Keir Elam has called 'the sport of hermeneutic hawking within the happy hunting ground of Beckett's drama', with the critic triumphantly producing his own critical trophy.[1] My intention is a modest one, undertaken humbly before Beckett's work that calls forth both deeply personal and intersubjective resonances.

The subject of mysticism has to face up to yet another danger: that of academic hostility, even to its slightest aura or trace. As Ihab Hassan suggests in his absorbing para-biography *Out of Egypt* (1986), mysticism is easily dismissed by dogmatists intolerant of all but their own narrow portion of reality:

> A Marxist, Zionist, or feminist may prove no more rational than some 'mystics', yet no stigma attaches itself to their commitment. Is it because men forgive attachments to factions, fractions – *my* side, *your* side – but never to the whole? The threat of mysticism: not vagueness or unreason, but a loyalty wider than most of us can bear. In short, Eros diffused, the Self dispersed, the end of paideia.[2]

With all these caveats in mind, I am nevertheless going to propose that a discrete mystical reading of Beckett's work, and in particular of his late plays, will enrich our response to them. But let me say emphatically that such an approach will claim no exclusivity. Given the allegorical, that is polysemous nature of his literary and theatrical discourse, our approach is, obviously, one along with others (literary, psychological, and philosophical).[3] Above all, it can only be undertaken in conjunction with a most scrupulous attention to technique and tone.

To consider his writings in the light of and analogous to the *via negativa* (the 'negative way') of classic mysticism is, actually, not as startling as it may sound, for it has been suggested by more than one critic, although it has equally much been disputed by others. Michael Robertson calls Beckett 'a mystic without a centre', John Pilling refers to some German mystics of the Rhineland school (Johannes Tauler, Heinrich Suso); and most recently, Martin Esslin, the Dean of Beckett studies, cast his net widely indeed, when in *Beckett at 80/Beckett in Context* (1986) he links up Beckett's search for ultimate reality with that of the mystics from ancient Indian philosophy and Buddhism to the great Christian mystics like Johannes Eckhart, San Juan de la Cruz (better known as Saint John of the Cross), and Jakob Boehme.[4]

To my knowledge, the only full-length study on the subject is Helene L. Baldwin's *Samuel Beckett's Real Silence* (1981), which claims that

> the progressive stripping down of the self which takes place in many of Beckett's works is not just a search for self, but in fact the 'negative way' of mysticism, whose object is to break through the bonds of time and place and to find what Eliot has called the still center of the turning world.[5]

Although her study contains some valuable suggestions and insights, it suffers from an over-determination to find religious and mystical parallels. What is even worse, she fails to draw the line between – to use Eliot's words – the man who suffers and the artist who creates.[6] According to information from the publisher (Blackwell, Oxford), we may soon expect an interesting study by Declan Kibert, arguing that Beckett's narratives are not formed by traditional notions of plot but on classical modes of meditation. Such works have always acknowledged their final inadequacy in the face of an eternally elusive subject and consequently they self-confessedly deconstruct themselves.[7]

It is high time to turn now to Beckett himself. So far as I know there are only two direct statements, made early in his literary career, that throw some light on his attitude to mysticism. In his *Dante . . . Bruno. Vico . . Joyce* he concludes, after having discussed Vico's philosophy of culture:

> He may still appear as a mystic to some: if so, a mystic that rejects the transcendental in every shape and form as a factor in human development, and whose Providence is not divine enough to do without the cooperation of Humanity.[8]

In his unfinished and unpublished *Dream of Fair to Middling Women* he calls himself a 'dud' mystic (a failed sage, a *'mystique manqué'*) and a 'John of the Crossroads . . . a border man' – a richly ironical reference to Saint John of the Cross, a sixteenth-century Carmelite contemplative, and author of *The Ascent of Mount Carmel* and *The Dark Night* and such great poems as 'On a Night of Darkness' and 'The Living Flame of Love'.[9]

From *The Ascent of Mount Carmel* I quote some famous lines that go to the heart of mysticism of whatever type or period:

> In order to arrive at pleasure in everything,
> you must seek pleasure in nothing.
> In order to arrive at possessing everything,
> you must seek to possess nothing.
> In order to arrive at being everything,
> you must seek to be nothing.
> In order to arrive at knowing everything,
> you must seek to know nothing.
> In order to arrive at that in which you find no pleasure,
> you must go by a way in which there is no pleasure.
> In order to arrive at that which you do not know,
> you must go by a way you do not know.
> In order to arrive at that which you do not possess,
> you must go by a way of dispossession.
> In order to arrive at that what you are not,
> you must go by a way in which you are not.

Many of us will be acquainted with these lines through T. S. Eliot's poetic paraphrase of them in *Four Quartets* ('East Coker', 3, lines 134–46):

> Shall I say it again? In order to arrive there,
> To arrive where you are, to get from where you are not,
>   You must go by a way wherein there is no ecstasy.
> In order to arrive at what you do not know
>   You must go by a way which is the way of ignorance.
> In order to possess what you do not possess
>   You must go by the way of dispossesion.
> In order to arrive at what you are not
>   You must go through the way in which you are not.
> And what you do not know is the only thing you know
> And what you own is what you do not own
> And what you are is what you are not.[10]

One notices in such mystical passages, structured on negation, the foregrounding of linguistic parallelism; the highly-patterned use of paradoxes – what Nicholas of Cusa, author of *Learned Ignorance*, called the '*coincidentia oppositorum*'; the emphasis on discipline, detachment ('dispossession'), self-annihilation and on nothingness; and the prominence of the symbolism of the journey or quest. As St John of the Cross puts it: 'Hence the soul cannot be possessed of the divine union unless it has divested itself of the love of created things.'[11] Renunciation also includes the banishment of both knowledge and memory in all its forms, if the soul is to be united with God.[12] Readers of *Malone Dies* will remember how Malone's double Macmann, finds himself in a hospital of sorts, called 'The House of St John of God' (situated on a mount that recalls the *Mons Perfectionis* or Mount Carmel), where he is stripped of his few personal belongings; they will also recall the importance of the subject of memory throughout Beckett's work.

Following on the 'Dark Night of Sense', the 'Dark Night of the Soul' is the most horrendous and terrifying part of the *via negativa*; it is concluded by the part of night 'near to the light of day', although even this final climactic step is still described in terms of near-darkness and silence – unlike in affirmative mysticism, where the more conventional images of light and music prevail. It is a 'place beyond uttermost place', a still wilderness 'where no one is at home', according to Meister Eckhart, to whom I will come back later.

In the same *Dream of Fair to Middling Women* Beckett refers explicitly to another famous fifth-century mystic, Pseudo-Dionysius or Dionysius the Areopagite (the pseudonym of St Paul's Athenian convert), who must be considered the fountainhead of negative or apophatic theology. He speaks of God as the Divine Darkness beyond Light, the super-essential Darkness. In a celebrated passage in his *Mystical Theology* he exhaustively enumerates some thirty-five negative attributes of God or Godhead, including 'not understandable', 'not knowable', 'not definable', and 'not *nameable*' (my emphasis).[13] It is a splendid example of the *via negativa*, which is the converse of the *via affirmativa*; these positive and negative approaches to knowledge and God correspond (as William James put it) to the yes-function and to the no-function in us, either viewing God as super-splendent, or asserting that the Absolute is *nothing* and (according to the Upanishads) not to be described except by 'No, No'.[14]

Such apophatic or negative formulations of God and Godhead are standard practice in negative mysticism, both Christian and Buddhist. They testify to the acutely-felt inadequacy of language to intimate ultimate reality as well as to the realisation that it is, nevertheless, through language that the mystic vision must be communicated. One is reminded of a similar paradoxical situation in Beckett's well-known statement, entirely couched in negative terms, to the effect that 'there is nothing to express, nothing with which to express, nothing from which to express, no power to express, no desire to express, together with the obligation to express.'[15]

Of course, we must exercise great care in handling these intertextual references and allusions to mysticism in Samuel Beckett's work, whose number can easily be extended to include Christian writers such as St Augustine, Dante, Descartes, Geulinx, and Pascal – each of whom had a memorable mystical experience. Obviously, we have to take fully into account the narrative context in which they occur, and the narrational tone that is employed. This means with Beckett a pervasive irony, often unsparingly mocking the uselessness of man's spiritual quest, and the 'issuelessness' of his predicament. Notably in his earlier work he sardonically exposes the quasi-certitudes of conventional, anthropomorphic Christianity; throughout his work he profoundly questions the very possibility of dealing with metaphysical and transcendental truth, given the inherent inadequacy of language to speak of such matters at all.

In two valuable articles Linda Ben-Zwi has demonstrated how Beckett's *Sprachskepsis* can be traced to a large degree to the influence of Fritz Mauthner's study of the limits of language (a three-volume work of more than 2000 pages, written in 1903), which Beckett started to read about 1930 (at the suggestion of James Joyce, and with an eye to *Finnegans Wake*), and which he is reported still to cherish.[16] From my present point of view, Mauthner's thesis that the highest forms of language are laughter and silence, the 'silent howl' over the human condition (*Molloy*), is particularly relevant, as is Mauthner's conclusion that what he is left with in the end is a 'godless mysticism' ('*gottlose Mystik*') that might transcend the limits of language.[17]

I suggest that there are several parallels to be discerned between the negativistic mystic and a writer like Beckett: both are intensely aware of the inability to express (or to 'eff') and of the breakdown of language and meaning, yet both are obsessed by the need to voice the ineffable ('I must speak of what I cannot speak') and to give their experience a local habitation and a name. Both emphasise detachment and solitude as prerequisites to concentration and contemplation:

> The only fertile research is excavatory, immersion, a contraction of the spirit, a descent. The artist is active, but negatively, shrinking from the nullity of extracircumferential phenomena, drawn in to the core of the eddy.

writes Beckett, adding that art is the 'apotheosis of solitude'.[18] Both resort to metaphoricalness when facing silence, the void, and nothingness ('than which nothing is more real'); both also employ the narrative structure of the allegorical quest, the search, the journey, physical and exterior as well as spiritual, inside the regions of the mind, 'the within, all that inner space one never sees' (*Molloy*).[19]

This quest takes place on several levels at the same time: an artistic exploration of the creative process, a psychological search for identity and self, a philosophical journey into metaphysical speculation, and a religious quest in search of the ground of man's being. More particularly, his fictions can be read as successive descents into the Dark Night of the Soul, the *via negativa* of mysticism: the ablation of all desires, the dying to the body and its functions, the annihilation of the self, and the emptying of the mind of all preconceived ideas – in short, purgation and detachment as preconditions to transcendental experience.

It may be objected, however, that in Beckett's work this quest never achieves its ultimate goal – in mystical terms the attainment of the 'beatific vision', the unification or at-one-ness of man with divine being or the sacred (God in traditional terminology). Although true, this objection does not negate the quest itself, nor does it invalidate the earnestness with which 'the beyond that is within' (*Molloy*) is presented. It remains true that ultimate meaning is forever 'deferred/differed' (in Derrida's sense) and can only be intimated by negation, that is by foregrounding the 'presence of absence' (Heidegger).[20] But this process of negation is not in itself a negative activity, and we may well feel that the exposure of the illusions of consciousness such as we find it in Beckett's work, has a strangely liberating effect upon us. I quote with much approval Paul Ricoeur's view on negation:

> To play with absence is already to dominate it and to engage in active behaviour toward the lost object as lost. Hence ... do we not discover another aspect of the death instinct, a non-pathological aspect, which would consist in one's mastery over the negative, over absence and loss? And is not this negativity implied in every appeal to symbols and to play?[21]

A closer look at the writings of Johannes Eckhart (1260–1327?), the greatest and intellectually the toughest representative of the *via negativa*, may illustrate the concept of negation further. Although his name has been loosely brought up in connection with Beckett, I am not aware of any substantial comparison between these two great writers. Yet it is with Eckhart's negative mysticism more than with that of St John of the Cross that Beckett's work, particularly his late plays and prose, invites comparison. It must be added that there is no question of any direct influence, although it is tempting to think that Beckett might have read the Dominican preacher, theologian, and outstanding stylist, since he appears to be well acquainted with negative mysticism, including the Rhineland mystics Heinrich Suso and Johannes Tauler, who are quoted in his fiction.[22]

The key concept of Meister Eckhart's bold 'theology of negation' is his sophisticated notion of 'detachment' or 'releasement' (*Gelassenheit* or *Abgeschiedenheit*), which is the driving power of the mystical union between the soul or the mind and God. Of the four stages of this process, dissimilarity, similarity, identity, and breakthrough, it is the first and the last stages that are particularly relevant, as will appear from the following string of quotations.[23]

Dissimilarity, the realisation that 'all creatures are pure nothing', involves detachment from the self, or 'self-naughting': 'to be devoid of any being of his own', 'to be dead to self', since 'only dead to self one is alive to God'; detachment from one's surroundings and from other creatures, from time and place, and from knowledge and memory – in short to be stripped of all physical and mental matters. Detachment, then, equals in this stage the lower steps of mysticism that we mentioned earlier.

Breakthrough (*'Durchbruch'*) beyond anything that has a name, comprises not only abandoning the self and all things, but also God himself: man must live 'without a why', he must seek nothing, not even God. Here Eckhart discriminates between God (*deus*) and Godhead (*deitas*), who are 'as distinct as heaven and earth'. God as a personal category is not essential, unlike Godhead, 'the origin of all things that is beyond God', who is to be loved as He is: 'not as a God, not as a Spirit, not as a Person, not as an image, but as a sheer pure One. And in this One we are to sink from nothing to nothing.'[24]

This Godhead, whose 'is-ness' (*'isticheit'*) cannot be put to words since 'to say it is already negating it', can only be experienced as 'nothing' (*'niht'*), as emptiness, as a void 'bereft of matter and form, where the soul comes to *naught*' (one of Beckett's favourite words). Unlike the 'available' God of theism, this Godhead is utterly 'unknowable' and 'unfathomable' and, thus, only to be intimated symbolically as a 'still wilderness where no one is at home', a desert 'beyond the polar circles of the mind', as the Darkness, where the soul falls into 'unknowing' and 'ignorance', and as 'The Great Silence'. The Godhead, then *is* detachment itself; He is 'being without becoming', and 'all that becomes, comes to an end there'. (Notice the almost Heideggerian, Sartrian, and Zen-Buddhist overtones.)[25]

Eckhart's apophatic, negative theology can be summed up by one of his impressive paradoxes: 'God is not seen except by blindness, nor known except by ignorance, nor understood, except by fools'.[26] How relevant are Eckhart's writings to Beckett's work, which can be legitimately called apophatic or negative, or in his own words 'literature of the unword'.[27] Although it is tempting to start with the first negative utterance in *Waiting for Godot* ('Nothing to be done') or to follow up the haunting emphasis on 'nothing' and 'notness' in *Watt* and The *Trilogy* – whose last part is, significantly enough, called *The Unnamable* – I shall have to restrict myself to his late plays, starting with *Not I* (1972) and concluding with *Nacht und Träume* (1982), one of his most recent TV monodramas.

These late plays are marked by a yet further reduction or 'lessness' on all levels of drama as text and as performance (plot, character, language and gesture). This results in maximal linguistic and theatrical economy and intensity, together with an unsurpassed emblematic and visual impact, particularly in such monodramas as *Ghost Trio*, . . . *But the Clouds* . . ., *Nacht und Träume*, *Quad I & II*, written for television, a 'peephole art' which allows us, according to Beckett, 'to see what was never meant to be seen'.[28] More than ever before they concentrate on the inner life, the essentials of consciousness and the self, the philosophers' Absolute. For Martin Esslin they are 'incarnations of some of the basic questions of our existence'; Lance Butler considers them to be 'ontological parables'.[29] In my view they can also be seen as dramatic renderings of the *via negativa*, further descents into the Dark Night of the Soul, and metaphorical explorations of detachment or releasement in the Eckhartian sense, intensely longed-for though not achieved.

Compared with the earlier plays, the tone has become less ferociously ironical about religion; it is more subdued but also more desolate: God is no longer a 'bastard' as in *Godot*; instead we find sober references to Christ's suffering ('His poor arm' in *Footfalls*) and to the Psalms (*That Time*). This does not imply that Beckett has gone soft on Christianity, of course, but it does indicate a change of direction. In the late plays his characters peer over the edge of existence; like John Donne in 'Holy Sonnet VI', they are confronted by 'life's last scene', having run the 'last mile' of their pilgrimage.[30]

What characterises the late plays, above all, is the pervasive and compulsive presence of almost total darkness, only to be mitigated by subdued portions of light. Beckett's stage directions are most explicit and meticulous on this point. To give some examples: in *Not I* the stage is in darkness but for Mouth, light only faintly from close up. House lights out; similarly in *Footfalls* the Woman's Voice is heard from dark upstage, with dim lights, less on body, least on head. Stage in darkness; in *A Piece of Monologue* there is only diffuse light, with the lamp having gone out at the end; in *Rockaby* and *Ohio Impromptu* the stage is in darkness except for a subdued spot on the face and a light on the table midstage; in *Nacht und Träume* the dreamer sits in a dark room, the 'dreamt hands' appearing from 'dark beyond'. In *Quad I & II* each figure comes out of darkness and, having completed its course, returns to same.

The overall stage or television darkness is magnified by the characters, usually old men or women, dressed in black, with long white or grey hair, which gives them a ghostly, spectral appearance (in *Ghostly Trio* even further highlighted by Beethoven's ghostly music). They are shades or masks rather than alive, agents frozen into emblems.

Visibility and its absence go hand in hand with audibility and silence. Sound is always meticulously prescribed; it may range from anguished shrieking in *Not I*, to voice modulations back and forth without any break in the general flow except when silence is indicated (*That Time*), the low and slow voices in *Footfalls*, to the subtle sound orchestration of *Rockaby*, with the voice a little softer each time, and the zero language of *Nacht und Träume*, with only a few bars of music to be softly hummed.

The mysterious interplay between darkness and half-lights brings to mind the symbolic descriptions of the mystical experience of The Dark Night of the Soul, referred to earlier. As Rudolph Otto writes in *The Idea of the Holy*:

> The darkness must be such as is enhanced and made all the more perceptible by contrast with some last vestige of brightness, which is, as it were, on the point of extinguishing; hence the 'mystical' effect begins with semidarkness.[31]

As is to be expected, negation – the painful awareness of absence – is prominent in his late plays, most strongly in *Not I*, 'an exemplary negative text', structured on the 'rhetoric of negation' on all levels, including the semantic breakdown of the text: 'words were ... what ... who ... no ...SHE'.[32] James Acheson has suggested that the play's title derives from St Paul's repeated comments in his epistles that it is 'not I' who writes, but Christ [who] liveth in me (Galatians 2:20, 1 Corinthians 7:10, 15:10).[33] If so, and also considering several other biblical and religious references (especially in the French text), *Not I* may be interpreted not only as dramatising *Mouth*'s confrontation with her own Jungian shadow (as Enoch Brater has shown), or as a flight from self-perception and self-acceptance, but also as a struggle to give up the Self in order to become aware of a wholly 'other' reality, although it cannot be put in words: 'Something she had to tell . . . something she didn't know herself . . . wouldn't know if she heard . . . then forgiven . . . God is love . . .'[34] In terms of Eckhart's distinctions, one might see the play, then, as symbolising the first mystical stage of detachment – dissimilarity – the renunciation of selfhood and the banishment of memory and desire; the mysterious Auditor can, perhaps, be seen as an icon of unfathomable, detached Godhead. Her desire to express: 'perhaps something she had to . . . had to . . . tell . . . could that be it . . .' is thwarted by her inability to express, although the voice rattles on, without yielding any decidable meaning.[35]

That Time, 'brother to *Not I*' according to Beckett himself, and thus equally concerned with the struggle to come to terms with the Self and the past, is 'just another of those old tales to keep the void from pouring in on top of you'.[36] Its protagonist, like the biblical Job split into three characters, faces 'the last things' more squarely than other Beckett characters. The play, shot through with biblical referentiality (as well as an allusion to Lao Tse), culminates in voice three, perceiving 'not a sound only the old breath and the leaves turning and then suddenly this dust whole place suddenly full of dust . . . nothing only dust and not a sound.' *That Time* perfectly illustrates Eckhart's conviction that 'Earth cannot escape sky', nor the confrontation with the void and with absence: 'not knowing where you were or when you were or what for place might have been uninhabited'.[37] Such allusions to the void might be seen in the light of Eckhart's concept of the breakthrough, the perception of 'the quiet desert of Godhead . . . neither image nor form nor condition'. The play ends ambiguously with the stage direction 'smile (toothless for preference)'; in *A Piece of Monologue* it is called 'that nevoid smile', 'signifying perhaps the smile that nullifies the void, if only temporarily'.[38]

In *Footfalls* we encounter yet another example of a tormented soul, who subsists in a nine-step stage world, trying to come to terms with her memories of 'presence' that might equally well be 'absence'. She wonders whether or not she has been present at Evensong and if she has responded to the Christian blessing at the end of the service; even if she has, May concludes that 'I saw nothing, I heard nothing . . . I was not there'. As Knowlson and Pilling write, the play 'gives a sense of inexplicable seeking' as well as of 'the distillation of absence and loss'.[39]

It is only in *Nacht und Träume*, whose televisual image is aptly described by one critic as seemingly 'created out of a kind of medieval woodcut, entitled 'a dark night of the soul', or 'the scholar dozing at his books', that some kind of equilibrium is reached between absence and presence, resistance and resignation.[40] Whether that last but one of Beckett's printed plays is to be seen as definitive, it is as yet too early to say. Hitherto it is the only play in which the 'darkness throughout Space' is positively welcomed into 'men's silent breast' (by way of an intertextual allusion to Schubert's late song). It embodies in pure abstract form an unconditional communication between the dreamer's self and 'the beyond' – symbolised by the cup of water and the cloth with which to wipe the dreamt self's brow. Beckett's *Nacht und Träume* is his furthest (allegorical) journey into nowhere and into nothing, which is at the same time everywhere and everything.

Note At the time of going to press I became acquainted with 'Comment ne pas parler. Dénégations' by Jacques Derrida in his *Psyché* (Paris, 1987), pp. 535–96. In this fundamental article (originally the opening lecture at the Jerusalem conference on 'Absence and Negativity', 1986) he clarifies his ambiguous position towards 'negative theology' with substantial quotations from both Pseudo-Dionysius and Meister Eckhart. This article, answering in part Nicolas Tredell's wish (see n. 20), deserves to be closely studied by modern theologians and critics alike.

Notes

1. Keir Elam, '*Not I*: Beckett's Mouth and the Ars(e) Rhetorica' in Enoch Brater (ed.), *Beckett at 80/Beckett in Context* (New York, 1986), p. 125.
2. Ihab Hassan, *Out of Egypt* (Illinois, 1986), p. 79.
3. For a summary of recent views on allegory, see my *T. F. Powys: a Modern Allegorist* (Amsterdam, 1986), Chapter 1, discussing Northrop Frye, Edward Honig, Rosemond Tuve, Gay Clifford, Maureen Quilligan, and in particular the seminal work by Angus Fletcher, *Allegory: the Theory of a Symbolic Mode* (Ithaca, New York, 1964; reprinted 1982).
4. Martin Esslin, 'Infinity and Eternity', in Brater, *Beckett at 80*, op. cit., p. 122.
5. H. L. Baldwin, *Samuel Beckett's Real Silence* (Pennsylvania, 1981) p. 6. See also her earlier *The Real Silence: Intimations of Mysticism in Samuel*

Beckett's Trilogy (Pennsylvania, 1973), published under the name H. L. Webner.
6. Kristin Morrison in *Journal of Beckett Studies*, IX (1984), 142–5.
7. Declan Kibert, *Samuel Beckett* (Oxford, 1988).
8. Samuel Beckett, *Disjecta: Miscellaneous Writings and a Dramatic Fragment*, ed. Ruby Cohn (New York, 1984), p. 26.
9. John Pilling, *Samuel Beckett* (London, 1976), p. 122.
10. *The Complete Works of Saint John of the Cross*, English translation F. Allison Peers (Westminster, Maryland, rev. ed. 1953). See also M. Gaudreau, *Mysticism and Image in St John of the Cross* (Frankfurt, 1976).
11. Epigraph to T. S. Eliot's *Sweeney Agonistes*.
12. Richard Woods, *Understanding Mysticism* (London, 1980), p. 245.
13. John Ferguson, *An Illustrated Encyclopaedia of Mysticism and the Mystery Religions* (London, 1976), pp. 47–8.
14. William James, *Varieties of Religious Experience* (London, 1901–2; reprinted London, 1960), pp. 366–414.
15. Samuel Beckett, *Proust* (London, 1931; reprinted New York, 1957), p. 103.
16. Linda Ben-Zwi, 'Samuel Beckett, Fritz Mauthner, and the limits of language' in *PMLA*, 95 (1980), pp. 183–90, and 'Fritz Mauthner for Company' in *Journal of Beckett Studies*, IX (1984), pp. 65–88.
17. Linda Ben-Zwi, first article, p. 197.
18. *Proust*, pp. 64–66.
19. For the constitutive features of allegory in Beckett's work, see my 'Allegory's Double Bookkeeping: Joyce and Beckett' in *Joyce/Beckett: New Essays*, eds P. H. Carey and E. Jewinsky (Milwaukee, forthcoming).
20. For a critical discussion of Derrida's notion of 'absence', as part of his 'totalizingly theological' philosophy, see Nicolas Tredell, 'Euphoria (Ltd) – The Limitations of Post-structuralism and Deconstruction' in Peter Barry, ed. *Issues in Contemporary Critical Theory* (London, 1987), pp. 91–105. Tredell's conclusion that 'the whole question of [Derrida's] relationship to religion, Western and Eastern, merits detailed examination' (p. 103) is worth following up, including its connection with negative mysticism.
21. Cited in Eloise Knapp Hay, *T. S. Eliot's Negative Way* (Harvard, Mass., 1982), p. 31 and pp. 192–3.
22. Whether or not Beckett has read Heidegger, who was much preoccupied with Eckhart, I am not in a position to say. See on this moot question, Lance St John Butler, *Samuel Beckett and the Meaning of Being* (London, 1984). On Heidegger and Eckhart, see John D. Caputo, *The Mystical Element in Heidegger's Thought* (Ohio, 1978).
23. All subsequent quotations are from Franz Pfeiffer, *The Works of Meister Eckhart* (Leipzig, 1857, London, 1924), 2 vols. On Eckhart see C. F. Kelley, *Meister Eckhart on Divine Knowledge* (New Haven, 1977).
24. *Understanding Mysticism*, p. 40.
25. For Heidegger's *Being and Time* and Sartre's *Being and Nothingness*, see Lance St John Butler, op. cit., Chapters 2–3. For the connection with Zen Buddhism, see Paul Forster, *The Beckettian Impasse: a Zen Study of Ontological Dilemmas in the Novels of Samuel Beckett* (Heidelberg,

1980). For links between Eckhart and Buddhism, see in particular D. T. Suzuki, 'The Basis of Buddhist Philosophy' in *Understanding Mysticism*, pp. 126–46.
26. Meister Eckhart, Vol. 1, p. 188.
27. German Letter of 1937, in *Disjecta*, pp. 53–54 [Translation, pp. 172–3].
28. Cited in Linda Ben-Zwi, *Samuel Beckett* (Boston, 1986), p. 208.
29. Lance St John Butler, Chapter 5. Since the voice of Molly, God, the Absolute, the author, the self, consciousness, can 'under a certain light' be considered identical, the author concludes that 'this mystical intuition is perhaps the final depth in Beckett' (p. 204).
30. John Donne, 'Holy Sonnet VI', lines 1–2.
31. Rudolph Otto, *The Idea of the Holy* (1917, London, 1923; reprinted 1959), p. 83. Darkness, silence, emptiness and empty distances are the most striking and effective indirect means of representing the 'numinous' in art, in his view. He adds that they are in a noteworthy way negative.
32. According to Keir Elam, synecdoche and litotes are Beckett's privileged figures of 'negative affirmation' (see above n. 1).
33. James Acheson, 'Madness and Mysticism in Beckett's *Not I*' in *AUMLA* (1980), pp. 91–101. For the more explicitly religious references in the French text, see ibid., p. 97. The author concludes that Mouth's dialogue is at times similar to that held between the mystics and God, but not the same (p. 97).
34. Enoch Brater, 'The "I" in Beckett's *Not I*', in *Twentieth Century Literature*, XX (1974), pp. 189–200.
35. Meister Eckhart, Vol. 1.
36. James Acheson, 'The Shape of Ideas: *That Time* and *Footfalls*' in *Beckett's Later Fiction and Drama: Texts for Company*, eds James Acheson and Katernyna Arthur (London, 1987), pp. 115–35. The author considers *That Time* to be a post-Romantic variation on Wordsworth's 'Tintern Abbey', though taking a much darker view of man's relationship to Nature (p. 120).
37. Meister Eckhart, Vol. 1.
38. Linda Ben-Zwi, *Samuel Beckett*, p. 168.
39. James Knowlson and John Pilling, *Frescoes of the Skull: the Later Plays of Samuel Beckett* (London, 1979), p. 222.
40. See n. 38, p. 205. For the text of Schubert's song, see Martin Esslin, 'Towards the Zero of Language' (p. 45, n. 36).

10
Redemption and Narrative: Refiguration of Time in Postmodern Literature
IRENA MAKARUSHKA

INTRODUCTION

In *Six Memos for the Next Millennium*,[1] Italo Calvino discusses the qualities of literature that merit becoming part of the legacy for the future. He identifies multiplicity as one of the most significant and valuable dimensions of writing. Present in 'hyper-novels' such as his own *If on a winter's night a traveler*, as well as in the works of writers such as Borges and Perec, multiplicity allows the writer 'to unite density of invention and expression with a sense of infinite possibilities'.[2] As 'a network of possibilities', multiplicity sustains the ambiguities Calvino locates at the heart of other qualities he considers praiseworthy. Though he expresses a preference for lightness, quickness, exactitude and visibility, in each case he recognises that these qualities are contingent and embedded in the thickness of human experience. The significance Calvino attributes to multiplicity is informed by his perception of the individual as complex: as both subject and object, knower and known, writer and reader. 'Who are we?' he asks:

> who is each of us, if not a combinatoria of experiences, information, books we have read, things imagined? Each life is an encylopaedia, a library, an inventory of objects, a series of styles, and everything can be constantly shuffled and reordered in every way conceivable.[3]

Attentive to the multifariousness of human experience, Calvino credits both the uniqueness of individual lives and their connectedness to history and nature.

Calvino's tribute to multiplicity is echoed by Milan Kundera in *The Art of the Novel*, where he observes that

> a novel examines not reality but existence. And existence is not what has occurred, existence is the realm of human possibilities, everything that . . . (one) can become, everything . . . (one is) capable of. Novelists draw up the map of existence by discovering this or that human possibility.[4]

Like Calvino, Kundera perceives the fictive world as mirroring difference, diversity and the free play of the imagination. The privileged position accorded to multiplicity and possibility in the thought of these two writers is instructive. In the following reflections, I propose that the qualities of multiplicity and infinite possibility cherished by Calvino and Kundera can illuminate a reconsideration of the relationship between literature and religion within a postmodern frame and consequently, a reassessment of the nature of the wasteland.

Long before T. S. Eliot described the spiritual bankruptcy of his generation as a wasteland, Hölderlin grieved that the gods had fled and Nietzsche mourned the death of God. For Hölderlin and Nietzsche, the default of the gods signalled both an end and a beginning. As Nietzsche's Zarathustra observes, 'only where there are tombs are there resurrections'.[5] Though the gods have fled, the need to create meaning out of chaos remains a compelling and immediate concern, a concern common to both literature and religion. Once the traditional metaphysical interpretations of experience lost their absolute claim, the task of naming the conditions of existence fell to the poet-philosophers. How this task is taken up by postmodern poet-philosophers such as Calvino and Kundera is the focus of this essay. Reflecting on Kundera's *The Book of Laughter and Forgetting*, a work he describes as a meditation on existence,[6] I suggest that it is paradigmatic of the fictive worlds of contemporary European literature that mirror the struggle to refigure the empty tomb. Before turning to *The Book of Laughter and Forgetting*, I propose to situate Kundera within the postmodern context in order to discuss some of the issues that have led postmodern writers to think of meaning not as an event, but as a process that is open to multiplicity and infinite possibilities.

POSTMODERN PERSPECTIVES[7]

The privileged position of multiplicity and possibility in the discourse of writers such as Calvino and Kundera as well as their rejection of the atomisation of experience reflects a postmodern world-view. Postmodernism is a cultural construct that functions as a descriptive category. It names a diversity of perspectives that by their nature resist definition. Despite the limitation of any attempt at definition, the taxonomy Ihab Hassan offers in his essay: 'Toward a Concept of Postmodernism'[8] and the categories Brian McHale suggests in *Postmodernist Fiction*[9] are particularly useful. Either implicitly or explicitly, they frame the following discussion.

To suggest that Kundera, like Nietzsche and Freud before him, reacts against the atomisation of experience is to argue that his writings illustrate the failure of modernism to come to terms with the illusion of totalising truth-claims. In *The Art of the Novel*,[10] for example, Kundera comments that humanity is at risk when it is 'caught in a veritable whirlpool of reduction' that obscures the richness of the lifeworld. The postmodern project is directed at overcoming the tendency toward reductionism and totalisation that is characteristic of modernism. The modernist substitution of the god of reason for the god of revelation promoted foundational values under the guise of secular and subjective claims that were continuous with pre-Enlightenment values. With regard to literary expression, for example, within modernism this tendency is recognisable in the effort to promote traditional claims of an absolute autonomous creator in the guise of an omniscient author. Organised around binary oppositions that assumed the possibility of alternatives such as faith or reason, good or evil, master or slave, transcendent or immanent, modernism created its own belief system that remained wedded to the priority of absolutes.

Master narratives of modernism, including the notion of the authoritative subject, political mastery and utopian progress rehearse the narratives of the pre-Enlightenment engodded universe. Modernism, after all, is heir to the world suffering what Hölderlin laments as the absence of the gods. The reaction of modernity to the flight of the gods is couched in a hierarchy of values grounded in the privileged role of reason and the purposefulness of human experience. Postmodernism, on the other hand, regards the very possibility of hierarchy and *telos* as fundamentally suspect and devoid of authoritative claims. Inasmuch as postmodernism is a reaction to modernism, it is continuous with the western tradition. It is the legitimation of dissent and difference that had always played a decisive role in the development of culture and civilisation. The postmodern poet-philosophers, like the prophets and mystics before them, herald the bankruptcy of the regnant truth-claims and prepare for the possibility of change. Recognising that creation is of necessity bound to decreation, postmodernism engages in a critical deconstruction of tradition which includes questioning its cultural codes and exploring its social and political affiliations.[11]

Modernity maintained a vigil for the absent gods by worshipping reason and authorial authority. The postmodern alternative to absolute truth-claims is indebted to Hölderlin who locates the traces of the fugitive gods in the creative activity of poets and to Nietzsche, the precursor of deconstruction, who focuses on the creative will of the poet-philosophers. Freed from the constraints of referential truth, postmodern literature privileges difference, silence and the unknown. According to McHale, the world observed in postmodern fiction differs from that circumscribed within modernist fiction owing to the difference in their interpretative strategies. In order to differentiate between the two, McHale makes use of the term 'dominant' – a term for which he is indebted to Jakobson, who in turn is indebted to Tynjanov. Dominant is defined as 'the focusing component of a work of art: it rules, determines and transforms the remaining components'.[12] Within McHale's schema, modernist literature engages in an interpretative strategy under an epistemological dominant. The questions raised concern the relationship between the knower and the known: 'How can I interpret this world of which I am a part? . . . What is there to be known? Who knows it?'[13] On the other hand, postmodern strategies, under an ontological dominant, raise questions concerning the nature of meaning, of existence and of the text.[14] Postmodern fiction does not assume that meaning is an object to be known. Rather, it reflects the creation of diverse worlds of meaning. Under an ontological dominant, postmodern literature articulates Calvino's multiplicity and Kundera's infinite possibilities.

TELLING FICTIONS

The Book of Laughter and Forgetting is a novel whose seven parts constitute variations on the theme of existence. Kundera privileges the variation form as reflecting the 'infinity of internal variety concealed in all things' (*BLF*, p. 164). Resisting the formalities of genre, Kundera creates a dense, thematically-interconnected narrative transparent to the myriad of fragments that conspire to recraft the parts into a hypothetical whole. 'This entire book', Kundera reminds the reader,

> is a novel in the form of variations. The individual parts follow each other like individual stretches of a journey leading toward a theme, a thought, a single situation, the sense of which fades in the distance (*BLF*, p. 165).

Abdicating the role of omniscient creator by refusing to provide unity prescribed by traditional novelistic forms, Kundera compels the reader to order the fragments. The reader, therefore, becomes complicit in the meaning-making process. The fictive worlds created in *The Book of Laughter and Forgetting* have the tentativeness of images in a kaleidoscope that captivate the imagination, invite participation and seduce by the promise of infinite possibilities.

The seven parts that comprise *The Book of Laughter and Forgetting* signal the array of possibilities encoded in narrative processes and reflect the reinterpretation of temporality in postmodern literature. The subversion of traditional unities in this novel mirrors the fragmentation experienced. A similar awareness of the fragmentary nature of experience, is expressed by the narrator in Calvino's *If on a winter's night a traveler*, who observes that the end of this millennium bears witness to the fact that

> the dimension of time has been shattered, we cannot love or think except in fragments of time each of which goes off along its own trajectory and immediately disappears.[15]

The shattering of time into fragments precludes not only the writing of long novels, as Calvino points out, but also novels that unfold in a linear progression.

The expectation that stories unfold linearly is met in part two, 'Mother' and, to a lesser extent, in part seven, 'The Border'. The other parts betray a postmodern frustration with linearity, with history as teleologically orientated, with the security offered by definition and closure. The remaining five parts are composed of narrative dissonances, Kundera's intrusive editorial voice and the *thematized reality? → governing terms?*

narrators' commentaries. The sequence of oneiric narratives, particularly in part six, 'The Angels', functions to disengage experience from the illusion of a solid mooring in reality. The plurality of voices and narrative strategies in these diverse fictive worlds can be read as commentaries on the creative process directed toward the recovery of memory out of the oblivion of forgetting, voice out of silence, of self out of a self-negating oppression.

'The struggle of memory against forgetting' (BLF, p. 3) is situated in a worded world. Kundera describes 'certain fundamental words',[16] among them forgetting, laughter, angels, border and *litost* – an untranslatable word that 'designates a feeling that is the synthesis of many others: grief, sympathy, remorse, and an indefinable longing' (BLF, p. 121) as the focus of his meditation on existence. The exploration of words, leads to reflection on the nature of narrative, the power of language and the experience of finitude. The tensions that animate Kundera's meditation are addressed by Foucault in 'Language to Infinity' where he writes that perhaps

> there exists in speech an essential affinity between death, endless striving, and the self-representation of language. Perhaps the figure in the mirror of infinity erected against the black wall of death is fundamental for any language from the moment it determines to leave a trace of its passage. . . . speech discovers the endless resourcefulness of its own image and where it can represent itself as already existing behind itself, already active beyond itself, to infinity.[17]

Like Foucault, Kundera sees language as the arena where battles are fought in the struggle described by Mirek, in part one, 'Lost Letters', as 'the struggle of memory against forgetting' (BLF, p. 3). Ultimately, it becomes the struggle between life and death. In part six, 'The Angels', for instance, a historian comments on the occupation of Czechoslovakia. He observes that, ' "The first step in liquidating a people . . . is to erase its memory. Destroy its books, its culture, its history" '(BLF, p. 159). Then the destruction of language is incontrovertible. The relationship between a nation and its oppressors is one of the iterations of the experience of finitude that haunts Kundera's fictive worlds.

Kundera's struggle with memory reflects his struggle with the *modernism – series of false expectations.*

Refiguration of Time in Postmodern Literature 149

capacity for texts to act as repositories of the past and with the interpretative process itself. How do individuals locate themselves in history, Kundera asks, when history itself seems to deny that possibility? What is to be done when the perfidities of history are played out by both the victim and the victimisers? In the first part, 'Lost Letters', Kundera observes that Mirek's efforts to reclaim the letters he had once written to Zdena make him

> as much of a rewriter of history as the Communist Party, all political parties all nations and all men. People are always shouting they want to create a better future. It's not true. The future is an apathetic void of no interest to anyone. The past is full of life, eager to irritate us, provoke and insult us, tempt us to destroy or repaint it. The only reason people want to be masters of the future is to change the past (BLF, p. 22).

Memory does not presence the past as though the past were an object to be reclaimed. Rather, the recovery of the past is always a recreation and reinterpretation of an experience always already interpreted. What is recovered is not the moment but the process of remembering. In 'The Border', a reverie on the erotics of experience, the narrator's observations concerning the recurrence of the border as a remembered image are illuminating. He notes that though with every repetition of a remembered image its meaning is diminished, nevertheless, the issue is not the recurring image, *per se*. Rather, he insists, 'the border is constantly with us . . .' (BLF, p. 217). What recurs, therefore, is the process of recalling it, of surfacing it, of recovering it out of our forgetfulness. *Augustine*

A similar attentiveness to the recurrence of process is evident in 'The Angels', a meditation on death described as a journey toward the forgetfulness of forgetting, toward unbearable lightness where things weigh nothing at all. In this variation on the theme of memory, the narrator describes how Tamina becomes aware of the significance of the process of interrogation which she understands as the process of being questioned about one's life. Attracted to the young man who comes to lead her on the journey toward death, she discovers that she is drawn to him not 'by what he asked, but [by] the fact that he asked anything at all' (BLF, p. 163). The process of being interrogated redeems Tamina from the loneliness of being caught within the web of her memories – both remembered and forgotten ones. Kundera, however, does not fail to point to the irony

being interrogated.*   *fact that he asked*

of logic that leads one to conclude that if, as Tamina insists, love is a constant interrogation, then 'no one loves us better than the police' (BLF, p. 163).

The lives that unfold in Kundera's fictive worlds reflect the displacement and dislocation of the narrative process itself. The telling of the story discloses the attempt to relate particular themes as they emerge out of experience, as well as the other possibilities that could have been, the lives that could have been lived. Kundera is attentive to the profound ambiguity inherent in experience that resists a reductive either/or. To choose, Kundera insists, is to choose both memory and forgetting, laughter and *litost*, lightness and weight, life and death. In each of the fictive worlds, Kundera's characters struggle to redeem the past not by recovering a fragment of a memory but by choosing to remember. In this process, memory reveals as it conceals, something is retrieved but something remains hidden. The possibilities cannot be exhausted, even in death, Kundera suggests, as evidenced by the refiguration of Tamina into a world of infinite multiplicity.

CONCLUSION

By resisting the temptation of reductive interpretative frames and traditional genre constraints, the fictive worlds of *The Book of Laughter and Forgetting* reveal the mystery of existence. Kundera's imaginative refiguration of time affirms that existence is always more than the sum of the parts and that the process of narrative unfolding reveals as much as it conceals. The autonomy of fictive worlds is subverted by the possibilities that remain eternally and infinitely possible and by the multiplicity of interpretations that attempt to make these worlds meaningful. The nature of narrative that emerges from Kundera's reflections mirrors the open-endedness of existence and experience.

Like other postmodern European writers, Kundera redirects the reader's attention from a nostalgia for the absolute[18] toward the creative process itself. As heir to poet-philosophers such as Hölderlin and Nietzsche, Kundera's task is to remind us that the primordial creative power of the gods still permeates the very fabric of human existence. Attention to process allows postmodern literature to reclaim the mystery of the text. Just as the mystery that God is, unfolds and yet remains eternally absolutely Other, so the text as created and interpreted, unfolds and yet remains eternally mystery. Fascination with the opacity of the text is also reflected in postmodern interpretative strategies that insist on a diversity of frames in order to illumine and refigure existence. The multiplicity of frames can be seen as a chorus of prophetic voices rehearsing the timeless narrative in quest of redemption.

In *The Book of Laughter and Forgetting*, Kundera considers the fate of individuals caught between laughter that offers <u>'a modest promise of salvation'</u> (*BLF*, p. 71) and the oblivion of forgetting. His narratives describe how individuals participate in making their existence meaningful and retain some degree of dignity and sanity in spite of the oppression wrought by absolute, reductive, totalising and controlling power. In effect, he raises the fundamental question of the Christian tradition, namely, 'what must I do to be saved?' For Kundera, individuals experience the need for redemption in their confrontation with the narrowness of totalising frames, with the literal-mindedness of authoritarian systems, with the betrayals of lovers, parents, friends and with their own finitude.

What Tamina discovers in death, is essential to Kundera's understanding of the relationship between creation and redemption and its analogue: the interplay of aesthetics and ethics, of religion and literature. Existence is profoundly ambiguous, both in life and in death: 'perfect buoyancy ... [becomes] a terrifying burden of buoyancy ...' (*BLF*, 188). As Tamina swims for her life, she comes to understand that salvation is not a question of choosing a specific destination toward which to escape, rather, <u>salvation is choosing to continue choosing</u>, to continue to take responsibility for creating meaning amidst the ambiguities of human experience, amidst the multiplicity of infinite possibilities. Kundera confesses an empathy with Tamina with regard to the losses that she, like everyone else, suffered in life. He notes that 'we all lose in whatever we do, because it is perfection we are after, we must go to the heart of the matter, and we can never quite reach it' (*BLF*, p. 165). Knowing that perfection is beyond our grasp, we continue to create infinite variations on the theme. The most we can hope for is that in creating variations we can overcome a degree of estrangement by arriving at a contingent unity in difference.

In *The Art of the Novel*, Kundera describes art as the echo of God's laughter in the imaginative realm where no one owns the truth.[19] He recognises that the survival of the creative imagination is contingent on its ability to remain free to dissolve, diffuse and dissipate, following Coleridge, in order to recreate, recraft and refigure. In that creative process, religious experience and artistic practice recover a common bond with the infinite realm of God's laughter. Like Nietzsche's Zarathustra, Kundera believes in a God who can laugh and dance.

Notes

1. Italo Calvino, *Six Memos for the Next Millennium*, (Cambridge: Harvard University Press, 1988), pp. 120–22.
2. Ibid., p. 120.
3. Ibid., p. 124.
4. Milan Kundera, 'Dialogue on the Art of Composition', in *The Art of the Novel*, English translation Linda Asher (New York: Grove Press, 1987), p. 42.
5. Friedrich Nietzsche, *Thus Spoke Zarathustra*, English translation Walter Kaufmann (New York: Penguin Books, 1954), p. 113.
6. Kundera, 'Dialogue . . .', p. 83.
7. This part of the present paper is a substantively rewritten version of part of 'Religious Imagination and Postmodern Narrative', a paper presented at the Arts and Religion Section of the College Theology Society in May, 1988.
8. Ihab Hassan, 'Toward a Concept of Postmodernism', in *The Postmodern Turn* (Columbus, Ohio: Ohio State University, 1987), pp. 84–98.
9. Brian McHale, *Postmodernist Fiction* (New York and London: Methuen, 1987), pp. 3–11.
10. Kundera, 'The Depreciated Legacy of Cervantes', in *The Art of the Novel*, English translation Linda Asher (New York: Grove Press, 1987), p. 17.
11. Hal Foster (ed.), 'Introduction', in *The Anti-Aesthetic: Essays on Postmodern Culture* (Port Townsend, Washington: Bay Press, 1983), p. xii.
12. McHale, *Postmodernist Fiction*, p. 6.
13. Ibid., p. 9.
14. Ibid., p. 10.
15. Italo Calvino, *If on a winter's night a traveler*, trans. William Weaver (San Diego, New York and London: A Harvest/HBJ Book, 1979), p. 8.
16. Kundera, 'Dialogue . . .', p. 84.
17. Michel Foucault, 'Language to Infinity', in *Language, Counter-Memory and Practice*, English translation Donald F. Bouchard (Ithaca, Cornell University Press, 1977), p. 55.
18. George Steiner, *Nostalgia for the Absolute* (Toronto: CBC Publications, 1974).
19. Kundera, 'The Depreciated Legacy of Cervantes', p. 8.

11
Apocalyptic Fiction and the End(s) of Realism
ROBERT DETWEILER

THE MODERN AND POSTMODERN APOCALYPSE: MAKING ENDS MEET

Apocalyptic awareness is not something rediscovered in the late twentieth century. Paul Tillich, not long after the end of the Second World War, sketched the dawning of the modern apocalyptic mentality like this:

> A new element has come into the picture, the experience of the 'end'. Something of it appeared after the first World War; but we did not feel it in its horrible depth and its incredible thoroughness. We looked at the beginning of the new more than at the end of the old. We did not realize the price that mankind has to pay for the coming of a new theonomy; we still believed in transitions without catastrophes. We did not see the possibility of final catastrophes as the true prophets, the prophets of doom, announced them.[1]

Another German, Hans Werner Richter, put it more dramatically in 1947, referring also of course to the Second World War.[2] 'The apocalypse transformed the living. What was before this time is no longer comprehensible, and appears like a fairy tale, sunken and silent. Another tone determines life, a tone born out of the world of ruins' (p. 93).

John Lukacs, writing in 1970, reviews how apocalyptic thinking has come to dominate all aspects of our lives:

> At the beginning of the century the notion that Western civilization might collapse occurred but to a handful of people . . .

By 1950 this notion had become a commonplace in the minds of many millions of Europeans and, for the first time in their history, even in the minds of some Americans. Most of us could still put this notion out of the conscious portions of our minds for long periods of time, relatively reasonably so. By the 1960's this became less and less possible. The notion that the breakdown in our civilization is actually occurring has been flooding the unconscious portions of our minds; it is now swimming up to the very surface of our consciousness. (p. 5)[3]

In his 1972 book, *Where the Wasteland Ends*, Theodore Roszak could refer bleakly to 'Environmental collapse, world poverty, technocratic elitism, psychic alienation, the death of the soul' (p. 407), but still posit with some optimism the possibility in our time of 'apocatastasis', the actualising of the Gnostic myth of the great restoration (pp. 409–27). This vision nowadays seems merely quaint.[4] With the emergence of the postmodern era (however makeshift and maligned that term may be) has come a deepening, if measured, conviction that these may indeed be the latter days. Robert Jay Lifton's *The Future of Immortality*, published in 1987, is more characteristic of the present temper.[5] Without giving in to either the religious or secular 'Armageddonists who . . . renounce responsibility for the holocaust they anticipate and, in some cases, press toward bringing about' (p. 6), Lifton tries to 'think the unthinkable' (itself a controversial concept these days) both to comprehend this intensified sense of an ending and to see if it can be mediated.

This essay will try to accommodate both senses of the term 'apocalypse' and show how contemporary apocalyptic fiction, having come into its own via the urgencies of both information/communications technology and the threat of global destruction through nuclear force or ecological contamination, plays with and plays out these two senses. *Apokalyptein* means to reveal or to disclose, and that sense is rendered in the Christian canon by the designation of John's apocalyptic vision that ends the New Testament as The Book of Revelation. But as we know from that text and others, such revelation is always of a violent eruption of natural and supernatural powers, usually involving the destruction of the world, so that apocalypse has also come to mean the event of final cataclysm. Apocalyptic fiction, then, consists of a narrative that somehow significantly 'reveals' the end of the world.

Apocalyptic Fiction and the End(s) of Realism

I will argue that the apocalyptic fiction of approximately the past two decades, in its double concern with revelation and cataclysm, persists as a uniquely transitional subgenre, oscillating between modernist and postmodernist performance. Its stress on revelation signals a strong epistemological quality that marks it as characteristically modernist; its focus on global cataclysm provides it with ontological substance and thus renders it postmodern.

My claim needs literary–historical elaboration. Critics of twentieth-century literature and its poetics such as Patricia Waugh and Brian McHale distinguish between modernist and postmodernist on the basis of epistemology and ontology. For them, to put it oversimply, the obsession of modernism was with the problems of knowing: how the mind works, how consciousness and the unconscious apprehend reality. The preoccupation of postmodernism, in contrast, is with the nature of being: what the world/self/text consist of, how they interact, whether they or anything else are real. Waugh says, 'Post-modernism clearly does not involve the modernist concern with the mind as itself the basis of an aesthetic, ordered at a profound level and revealed to consciousness at isolated "epiphanic" moments' (p. 23), and McHale uses Faulkner's *Absalom, Absalom!* to argue that it (at its conclusion a transitional text itself) 'dramatizes the shift of dominant [the controlling and organizing element of an art work] from problems of *knowing* to problems of *modes of being* – from an epistemological dominant to an *ontological one*' (p. 10).[6]

Both Waugh and McHale know, of course, that things are not this easy, and McHale in particular describes the postmodernist fascination with ontology as a matter of order and choice:

> A philosopher might object that we cannot raise epistemological questions without immediately raising ontological questions, and vice versa, and of course he or she would be right . . . Literary discourse, in effect, only specifies which set of questions ought to be asked *first* of a particular text, and delays the asking of the second set of questions, *slowing down* the process by which epistemological questions entail ontological questions and vice versa . . . In postmodernist texts, in other words, epistemology is *backgrounded* as the price for foregrounding ontology. (p. 11)

It is precisely this tension – and rhythm – that I wish to explore as they are held more provocatively in balance in contemporary apocalyptic fiction than in other current writing: epistemology and ontology, modes of knowing and being exercised in modes of revelation and destruction, both to qualify the recent literary–historical assumption that we have passed chronologically from modernism to postmodernism and to inquire into how the imagining of the end as the ultimate reality influences the nature of fictional presentation.

I did not write 'fictional *re*presentation' above for good reason. The study of contemporary apocalyptic fiction raises a complex set of questions about mimesis, literary representation, reference, definitions of realism that need to be addressed as a first step toward understanding the significance of this literature for other kinds of literary narrative, indeed for other kinds of discourse.

The epistemological challenge that arises in this connection is how the author can create – and inhabit – a consciousness that experiences what no consciousness has ever experienced: the end of the world. It is not unlike the attempts of novelists to portray, from a first-person perspective, what it is like to die – although as I shall show later, there are also telling differences. In any case, what controls or models can an author devise to make her portrayed experience of the apocalypse plausible, compelling, 'realistic'? How does her 'revelation' communicate if she cannot compare it to 'the real thing'?

The ontological problem is similar, although perhaps even more perplexing: how can existence and being in death or after death be imagined and depicted? Does not a fundamental paradox arise here? Is it possible to think, let alone think through, the process of annihilation and the mode of nothingness? One could recast both of these narratological problems in structuralist language and ask, what signifiers does an author choose to engage a signified that has no tangible reality, and that, unlike abstractions such as love, fear, and hate, cannot be experienced self-reflectively? To comment on the epistemological challenge of composing apocalyptic fiction, I will borrow Derrida's concepts of the trace and the *representamen*. To discuss the ontological dilemma I will use Baudrillard's concept of the *simulacrum*.

THE NUCLEAR END AND THE ABSOLUTE *REPRESENTAMEN*

From Derrida one learns a theory of (non)representation – better said, a theory of signification – that entertains the possibility that all writing is, in a sense, apocalyptic. His concept of the trace as a foundational absence contributes to a radically different view of referentiality that can be related to apocalyptic revelation and nihilation. The trace, the track, the clue, Derrida argues, are what we encounter, instead of whatever it is that makes these, when we search for a referent for our experience and expression. This is not just the case with philosophical or theological speculation, when we discover nothing outside language to substantiate our projections of, say, the transcendent. Rather, Derrida says, this is the way it is with all knowing: there is no 'thing itself' that corresponds to our conceptions of experience, only traces of such things, which traces are all there ever was. At the 'origin', in other words, is an imaginative memory that fashions for us clues as – we might say 'modernistically' – *existentialia* out of nothing.[7]

For the literary artist, then, who fashions a fictional world that somehow evokes the real one, the operation becomes one of exercising the language of representation in a final non-representational or ultimately self-reflexive world. Unlike Plato's poet, who creates a representation of a representation and thus is progressively further distanced from the Truth in the mind of God, the contemporary artist finds himself with nothing to represent – or with the task of representing nothing. It is this very process, this very dilemma, that the postmodern novelist incorporates into his art, making the writing of fiction, and often the difficulty of writing fiction in a self-reflexive world, the focus of his fiction and doing so in ways that neutralise the illusion that this fictional world is the real one.

One might suppose that at this point postmodern literature becomes, in a way, representational after all: it reflects a world, has as its referent a world, which knows itself via the trace of the perpetually absent subject. But Derrida argues resolutely that this is not so. Rather, he declares that the signifier, or the *representamen*, like the world it constitutes, never 'represents' 'back' but only 'ahead'. The *representamen* signifies before it 'is' (because like the trace it has no origin) and hence can only signify or present as it goes in a 'perpetual dispersal'.[8]

Such signifying out of absence, the *representamen* always ahead of 'itself' and always toward perpetual dispersal, is very much in the apocalypic mode, and Derrida himself addresses apocalyptic writing in a number of texts. Most appropriate to my study is his essay 'No Apocalypse, Not Now' in a 1984 *Diacritics* issue on 'Nuclear Criticism'.[9] I cannot summarise this profound essay here but will sketch its most salient points as they apply to my interpretation of Derrida's trace and *representamen* and what these mean for apocalyptic fiction.

In the 'fable' of the nuclear apocalypse Derrida finds the single possible, tangible, (post)historical referent that would give the trace a presence, that would, in a sense, fulfill the trace (in modernist phenomenological terms, the trace is always *'aufgehoben'* in a perpetual suspension but could be *'aufgehoben' qua* fulfilled only through confronting and disappearing into its nuclear wholeness). Or: the *representamen*, always signifying ahead of itself in normal existence, would finally know itself, complete its identity, in the cosmic cataclysm. True and full revelation, then, when representation catches up with itself, happens only and paradoxically at the moment of annihilation. Literature lives in a terrified, fascinated anticipation of that moment and generates itself in perpetual dispersal toward that moment, simultaneously hoping and not hoping that it will ever arrive.

Derrida writes, 'If we are bound and determined to speak in terms of reference, nuclear war is the only possible referent of any discourse and experience that would share their condition with that of literature' (p. 28). He goes on to argue that death for every individual can be experienced as equally catastrophic – 'there is no common measure adequate to persuade me that a personal mourning is less serious than a nuclear war' (p. 28) – and at this point his argument recapitulates that of Kermode's 'sense of an ending': our little deaths take on meaning by their assumption into apocalyptic monumentality. But then, Derrida says, eloquently and passionately:

> Culture and memory limit the 'reality' of individual death to this extent, they soften or deaden it in the realm of the 'symbolic'. The only referent that is absolutely real is thus of the scope or dimension of an absolute nuclear catastrophe that would irreversibly destroy the entire archive ['the juridico–literary ... basis of literature and criticism'] and all symbolic capacity, would destroy the 'movement of survival', what I call *'survivance'*, at the very heart of life. This absolute referent of all possible literature is on a par with the absolute effacement of any possible trace; it is thus the only ineffaceable trace, it is so as the trace of what is

entirely other, '*trace du tout autre*'. This is the only absolute trace – effaceable, ineffaceable. The only 'subject' of all possible literature, of all possible criticism, its only ultimate and a-symbolic referent, unsymbolizable, even unsignifiable; this is, if not the nuclear age, if not the nuclear catastrophe, at least that toward which nuclear discourse and the nuclear symbolic are *still beckoning* the remainderless and a-symbolic destruction of literature. Literature and literary criticism cannot speak of anything else, they can have no other ultimate referent, they can only multiply their strategic maneuvers in order to assimilate that unassimilable wholly other. They are nothing but those maneuvers and that diplomatic strategy, with the 'double talk' that can never be reduced to them. For simultaneously, that 'subject' cannot be a nameable 'subject', nor that 'referent' a nameable referent. Then the perspective of nuclear war allows us to re-elaborate the question of the referent. What is a referent? (p. 28)

It is in this sense that, as Derrida writes a bit earlier in this essay, 'The nuclear age is not an epoch, it is the absolute *épochè*, it is not absolute knowledge and the end of history, it is the *épochè* of absolute knowledge. Literature belongs to this nuclear epoch, that of the crisis and of nuclear criticism, at least if we mean by this the historical and ahistorical horizon of an absolute self-destructibility without apocalypse, without revelation of its own truth, without absolute knowledge' (p. 27).

THE TRACE AT THE END

All this is excellent preparation for my treatment of contemporary apocalyptic fiction that fluctuates between modernist and postmodernist modes, between depictions and incorporations of epistemology and ontology as provoked by visions of the end, and it is excellent preparation not least because Derrida's heavily epistemological argument – far beyond the reflexes of modernist thinking – helps to modify McHale's assertion that the postmodernist stress (which Derrida surely shares) is focused mainly on ontology. Yet in 'No Apocalypse, Not Now', Derrida also reveals a curious, and 'modernist', prejudice against contemporary apocalyptic fiction, even though such fiction might augment his own argument. He writes, 'Literature has always belonged to the nuclear epoch, even if it does not talk "seriously" about it. And in truth I believe that the nuclear epoch is dealt with more "seriously" in texts by Mallarmé, or Kafka, or Joyce, for example, than in present-day novels that would offer direct and realistic descriptions of a "real" nuclear catastrophe' (pp. 27–8). Fredric Jameson has seen more acutely what science fiction can contribute to the comprehension of a future that may instruct our sensibilities on how to approach the end when he writes that 'the apparent realism, or representationality, of science fiction has concealed another, far more complex temporal structure: not to give us "images" of the future – whatever such images might mean for a reader who will necessarily predecease their "materialization" – but rather to defamiliarize and restructure our experience of our own *present*, and to do so in specific ways distinct from all other forms of defamiliarization' (p. 244).[10] Although the contemporary apocalyptic narrative I will examine is, for the most part, science fiction merged with 'serious' fiction, much of it is far beyond traditional realistic writing. Thus the advantages of such conventional science fiction for understanding our lives in light of our future that Jameson sees are greatly enhanced through the complications of the novels I will discuss.

I will discuss six novels with apocalyptic qualities, novels which I will treat as illustrating a range of difference between realistic and non-realistic modes. I will be concerned to show how the apocalyptic element affects and is affected by the degree of realism, and how the less realistic fiction depends less, of course, on traditional literary strategies of representation and more on the fiction representing itself, which is to say displaying in various covert and overt degrees its fictionality. This fictionality, however, in the cases of those novels furthest removed from realism, attempts to replace that 'reality' that traditional realism assumes and does so by evoking the ultimate reality, *qua* Derrida, of apocalyptic revelation. These works do not constitute any sort of chronological movement from realism to anti/post/sur/realism, whereby the oldest texts would be more realistic and the newest less so. Indeed, the newest I will treat is the most realistic and the oldest is the least so.

Paul Auster's *In the Country of Last Things,* published in 1987, incorporates a skilfully wrought marriage between modernist realistic narrative and apocalyptic disclosure.[11] The short novel consists of a letter written by the narrator Anna Blume, a young woman who has left her wealthy family environment to search for her brother, who has disappeared into a devastated city. This unnamed metropolis still has a perfunctory government, but its citizens are barely functional. Resources are depleted, masses of homeless people roam the streets, and many survive by thievery, scavenging, and selling off their possessions from better days. The death toll is great and corpses litter the terrain, but people are still encouraged to commit suicide or to allow themselves to be killed in various civically sanctioned ways. Anna Blume does not find her brother during her years in this blighted place but stays alive by her own scavenging and by sharing space and meagre goods with a series of other people, most notably with the owner and tenants of Woburn House, a mansion now serving as a shelter for the homeless. She barely escapes death in a black market butcher shop that sells human flesh, endures grimly cold winters and other hardships, and at novel's end is scheming to leave the city – a difficult task, once one is in it – with a few friends, for a vaguely-conceived better life elsewhere.

Anna Blume writes this long letter, probably to a former lover, toward the end of her sojourn in this hellish city but has no confidence that it will reach its destination. Like its author, it may or may not survive.

This is realistic apocalyptic fiction in that the approaching end of a civilisation – or part of one – is described on a single narrative plane in ways that do not challenge the limits of physical possibility. Things are extreme here, but they could conceivably happen. That much is unexplained (why is this city in such bad shape when other parts of the world are not? Why does Anna Blume not attempt to return home?) does not make the text's rendition any less realistic, only less comprehensive and comprehensible. Yet the condition of no actual city or even combination of cities serves as the referent here – although one can think of cities (such as Pnom Penh during the Cambodian genocide of the 1970s) in which certain horrific parallels obtained. The realism of Auster's work depends on a combination of two things: on our imagining of a waste land stimulated by actual experiences (not necessarily first-hand) of devastation, but also on an imagined exceeding of that experience by universalising and/or intensifying it. Auster achieves his relatively unsensational evocation of apocalyse first by intense focus: he concentrates on the desperate circumstances of a single urban area. But this depiction then calls to mind the frequency and proliferation of such conditions in literary, religious, and historical narrative. We are able to 'believe' in Auster's apocalypse because – to put it oversimply – the religious tradition has already projected it, the literary imagination has elaborated it, and history has confirmed its possibility if not to say its likelihood.

That a 1987 novel could employ apocalyptic realism so powerfully does not suggest so much the durability of the realistic tradition as it does the role of the apocalypse in directing the writer's and reader's imagination toward a substantial future referent. That is to say, if realism is on the wane because the world of objective absolutes and of logocentrism, where realism found its security, has been made uncertain, one can still project the apocalypse and draw on the force of that projection, as an endpoint at which the representation and its object *will* coincide, where the trace's origin will be made manifest.

Anna Blume's letter to her past, to her former lover, is a narrative of her suffering that she hopes will in some way memorialise her. She wants it to be a trace of her; although she has an origin (unlike Derrida's trace), she expects to die, so that this trace made of inadequate words will be all that remains. It is important to her that she be remembered in this state, out of the time after she left home, so that her trace will arrive (if it arrives at all), in a sense, from the future.

Anna Blume's own perception of what is real changes as she reflects on time running out – on her own apocalypse: 'I've been trying to fit everything in, trying to get to the end before it's too late, but now I see how badly I've deceived myself. Words do not allow such things. The closer you come to the end, the more there is to say. The end is only imaginary, a destination you invent to keep yourself going, but a point comes when you realize you will never get there. You might have to stop, but that is only because you have run out of time. You stop, but that does not mean you have come to the end' (p. 183). 'The end is only imaginary' runs counter to the apocalyptic thinking that argues, the end is the only thing that is *not* imaginary, and Anna Blume herself, in her urgency to express everything before it is too late, displays the sense of fullness, of crisis, and also of frustration that marks the apocalypse. For language, always referring ahead of itself, is indeed both fulfilled and destroyed in its apocalyptic consummation.

Auster's epistolary novel imagines an urban society on the brink of the apocalypse. Muriel Spark's *The Hothouse on the East River*

(1973) imagines a group of urban dwellers *after* a cataclysm.[12] Whereas Auster depicts a devastated city in a vaguely delineated environment in more or less realistic terms, Spark portrays, in conventional realistic language, an impossible – which is to say – unrealistic situation out of what seems to be a normal environment. Her plot unfolds in a progression that divulges to the reader only near the end that he/she has been responding to an unrealistic premise. Spark's city is New York, and the main characters, Elsa and Paul, are well-to-do Manhattanites, native British, with their two children, their analysts, and various (fairly strange) acquaintances. The third-person narrative evolves from little inconsistencies at the start (for instance, Elsa's shadow falls the wrong way) to more perplexing problems (such as a central confusion involving a German POW named Kiel in England during the Second World War who was or was not the lover of Elsa or perhaps of Paul and who may or may not now be working in a Manhattan shoe store), and during the last third of the text focuses on the recognition and admission by these characters that they are dead – Elsa and Paul, in fact, killed by a German V-2 rocket in a London railway station in 1944.

Brian McHale classifies *Hothouse* as an example of 'parallel world' fiction – a classification I accept (pp. 34, 50). A trait of such writing, he says, is that it consigns the characters to a double existence, one in our normal world and one in a world elsewhere. The parallel world of *Hothouse* is an existence after death in which the characters continue to 'live' in our world largely as if they had not died. The relation between the two worlds becomes especially complicated regarding the couple's children, for, as Paul points out to his son, 'your mother and I were killed by a bomb in the spring of 1944. You were never conceived, never born' (p. 141).

Just what difference this dual existence makes to the characters is not clear, although they are certainly all neurotic and suffer from a sense (to the reader comic) of inauthenticity. But Spark seems less interested in exploring how the characters think and feel about their condition (the epistemological situation) and more in portraying their dilemma as a problem in being that involves the reader in ontological puzzles. One of these puzzles I introduced earlier as a challenge to the novelist: how to imagine nothingness, how to depict life after the apocalypse. Spark's 'resolution' (she has always been fascinated by death, as one sees from novels such as *Memento Mori*) in *Hothouse* is to describe it as both ongoing and discontinuous. One interacts with the world of the living but is separate from it. This is, obviously, not a satisfactory philosophical or theological answer (and it certainly begs the question of how one can describe a post-annihilation *world*, since only a few of the characters have been killed), but it does at least indicate the difficulty, if not the impossibility, of imagining *nothing*: as soon as one tries, *something* must take shape, and another world emerges. No doubt this is a main reason why depictions of the apocalypse seldom conclude with the cataclysm itself but follow it with portrayals of some new reality.

McHale argues provocatively that Spark's personae exist 'under erasure' (pp. 50, 99ff.). It is, first, in this sense that *Hothouse* assumes its apocalyptic tone. Not only are the couple annihilated by the rocket in what is at least an 'apocalyptoid' death; that they and other characters can be 'rubbed out' or 'wiped out' by their creator in a way that breaks the rules of realistic fiction introduces an apocalyptic attitude into the very act of imaginative writing. This destructive moment has always inhabited fiction writing, of course, but in postmodern narrative it is foregrounded and sometimes flaunted, perhaps as a way of declaring that all existence is but a trace, revokable, *sous rature*, and that fiction's referent is at last an instability that hovers between life and death. Spark's novel, which at first appears to be traditionally realistic and unconcerned with apocalypse, reveals itself as a subtly crafted fiction that undermines realism and shows apocalyptic art at work in creating an eternally suspenseful and suspendable reality.

J. G. Ballard's *The Atrocity Exhibition* (1970) makes no pretensions toward literary realism.[13] This fiction – which Jonathan Crary calls an 'exemplary psychotic text' (p. 291) – does not describe the occurrence of an actual world apocalypse, as does his 1960s science fiction trilogy (*The Drowned World*, *The Drought*, *The Crystal World*), but is a postmodern narrative that embodies the apocalyptic mode and tone more thoroughly than the earlier, more overt dramatisations. Representation in the settings of this story sequence is rendered dysfunctional because all possible referents are made uninterpretable. They are quantified, perverted into sheer spectacle, or 'mimetized' into simulacra that overpower the originals. Thus the title story which begins the sequence opens with the word 'Apocalypse' in bold print, goes on to sketch the setting as an annual exhibition of art by the patients of a mental institution which shows 'the marked preoccupation of the paintings with the theme of world cataclysm' (p. 7), and thereby sets the tone for the orchestration of motifs of destruction throughout the whole text, featuring events real (the nuclear bombing of Nagasaki, the assassination of John F. Kennedy, the fiery deaths of American astronauts), imagined (the death of Elizabeth Taylor), and typical (atrocities in Vietnam and the Congo, automobile crashes). A central consciousness who shifts identities (named, variously, Travis, Talbot, Trabert, Talbert, Travers, Traven, Tallis) experiences or projects many of these lethal events, but his involvement in them does not constitute any sort of conventional plot development. Rather, he and others are the spectators and actors in (and dreamers of) the repetitious interplay of these events, which interplay conspires to create spectacles so scandalous, gruesome, and atrocious as to elicit a visceral response that blocks analysis. What Ballard's text represents, then, is a world so inundated with sensational spectacle that its inhabitants can feel or think nothing else – and this viscerality becomes at once deathridden and prurient. Yet even this representation is offered in a manner that obliges the reader to abandon – or at least temper – conventional reading and replace/abet it with his own visceral response. It is a text of a world frighteningly out of control, that by its theme and style threatens the reader with a sense of chaos, and as such it is a more densely apocalyptic fiction than the novels by Auster and Spark.

An example of the book's impact can be derived from the eleventh sequence, entitled 'Love and Napalm: Export USA'. The story's nine paragraphs purport to examine, in the disinterested language of the social scientist, the effects of atrocity films on the sexual stimulation of Americans and conclude 'that it is only in terms of a psychosexual module such as provided by the Vietnam War that the United States can enter into a relationship with the world generally characterized by the term "love"' (p. 96). Yet each of the paragraphs is preceded by a phrase in bold print, which nine phrases arranged by themselves in verse form comprise a moving and disturbing poem:

> At night, these visions of helicopters and the DMZ
> fused in Traven's mind with the spectre
> of his daughter's body. The lantern of her face
> hung among the corridors of sleep.
> Warning him, she summoned him to her side

all the legions of the bereaved.
By day the overflights of B52s
crossed the drowned causeways of the delta,
unique ciphers of violence and desire. (pp. 93–6)

The necessarily indeterminate reading of this story sequence, extending even to absorbing the productive conflict of poetry and prose, illustrates how a postmodern text can toy with the conventions of realism to negate their representational force – by revealing the referent of such representation to be merely the spectacular. Yet the very spectacles, with their seductive surface radiance, project a desire for some 'deeper' fulfilment to which the vision of a final catastrophe responds.

Jameson writes that 'Ballard's work – so rich and corrupt – testifies powerfully to the contradictions of a properly representational attempt to grasp the future directly' (p. 245), and Crary says that 'For Ballard, the crisis of the spectacle in the 1960s follows from the disengagement of desire, its desultory floating-free from anchoring structures. His space explodes the possibility of cathecting with anything because every surface is available for investment' (p. 291). I will return later to *The Atrocity Exhibition* to show how this promiscuity of surfaces is heightened by the manufacture of simulacra and how the simulation of cataclysm produces the real thing.

Patricia Waugh refers to the novels of British author Christina Brooke-Rose as examples of 'intertextual overkill', and this designation intrigues me, for it displays a literary criticism itself inspired by a metaphor from the vocabulary of nuclear deterrence. In the language of such absurd strategising, overkill refers to a nation or nations possessing far more nuclear weapons than are needed to annihilate the enemy. 'Overkill' belongs to the language of excess that marks the mentality of those perpetrating the arms race.

Waugh employs the term 'intertextual overkill' to label a kind of postmodern writing in which the literary tradition and other discourse are plundered and reconstituted into madcap fictions. Characters challenge their authors and practise literary criticism, reviews of the novel being written appear in that text, characters from other novels show up, the conventions of espionage, detective, and horror thrillers as well as of cinema and pornography are incorporated, foreign languages are used and misused, and so on. The novelist is seemingly crazy, perverse, and out of control, the reader is overpowered, and the tradition of realistic writing appears to explode as things are made to represent only to have the referents mischievously destroyed. What this overkill kills, in other words, is any possibility of the reader exposed to it ever again taking literary realism altogether seriously.

Such writing is the stock-in-trade of Brooke-Rose, and I want to gloss three of her novels – *Out, Such,* and *Thru* – to show how her fiction both appropriates apocalyptic themes and imagery and becomes increasingly disintegrative.[14]

McHale calls *Out* an example of 'the *topos* of nuclear holocaust and its aftermath . . . in slightly displaced form' (p. 67). Although one cannot detect a traditional unified plot structure in this narrative, one can gather that in the modern world of the novel some sort of 'displacement' has occurred as a result of a 'battle for survival' that one group – possibly American and European Caucasians – lost. 'Resettlement' has been undertaken that places some of the characters in shantytowns and heavily restricted zones. Africans and Asians seem to be in power; the setting resembles in part the territories of South Africa, except that here the blacks rule, and the whites work for them. Some people are dying of a leukemia-like illness that could be caused by radiation or toxins, unemployment is rampant, and the government's condition is precarious.

But all of these 'facts' can only be inferred, since they are presented in the midst of surreal and absurd dialogue and along with key images that are repeated, *nouveau roman* style, but do not unite into any coherent structure (for instance, two flies mate on the knee of a woman who is a patient in some sort of institution). This fragmenting narrative, then, is fed into a final scene that begins as a description of a burning house and ends as a paroxysm of simultaneous birth and death:

> It is not possible to witness the beginning, the first ticking of the metronome, because all you are entitled to assume is that it would have been as now described if it had been seen by minds with the kind of perception man has evolved only quite recently. Those that cannot grow with it must die.
>
>   The fire leaps up bright orange, with a yellow shower, circles of red, oh, close your eyes, relax but grip the instrument and hold it up, well up, let it gush forth from the deep sphere of our being

and reach up for the sky before it turns to spray its dust over the fire that crackles . . . the dust fills up the head, bombarding the cells that run amok, emitting helium particles until the human element disintegrates and radiates into the huge consciousness of light. . . . We are merely marking time and time is nothing, nothing. A moment of agony, of burning flesh, an aspect of the human element disintegrating to ash, and you are dead. (p. 198).

One sees here, in most vivid form, an apotheosising of the trace: referentiality, whatever else it is in between, begins and ends in the imagination.

Such, published two years later, frustrates conventional summarising even more. It is a Beckettesque piece featuring a scientist, perhaps an astrophysicist, in a coffin. This 'Lazarus' has died, perhaps on an operating table, returned to life, and is absorbed in tracking his wife's suspected infidelity with his doctor. The apocalyptic moments of *Such* mainly inhabit passages that employ imagery of nuclear- and astrophysics. For example, referring to the dead/alive scientist's wife: 'she still bombards our conversation with those particles of anxiety that spiral at high velocity around the lightning zig-zag of her magnetic field' (p. 355). The novel concludes with a passage that, like *The Atrocity Exhibition* and like *Out*, but in a more extravagant and even frenzied way, combines sexual desire with cosmic violence:

Come, let me rouse your base instincts, ha! Hands grab at hands and wrists to pin them down in an angular attitude with parabolic gestures that create situations, contortions in the innumerable particles of her desire bombarded with astonishment, repulsion, fear that spiral at high velocity around the lightning zig-zags of her magnetic field . . . you give rebirth which hurts to some lost slice of you, a forgotten area of particles that come whirling back to form filaments of gas in violent motion or extragalactic nebulae colliding perhaps on the outer rim . . . Some argue nevertheless that parts of a divided nucleus recede from one another at great speed, the shock processes involving ejection of high energy particles that must ultimately form a human element, a star where the taste of love will increase its luminosity until it cools in quiet rage at all that tenderness that went to waste, accumulating only the degenerate matter of decay. (p. 390)

In *Thru*, finally, published nearly a decade later, the most radical disintegration of realism, readability, and writing itself occurs. Here is indeed intertextual overkill. *Thru* engages, among other things, structural linguistics and psychoanalysis in a number of languages and employs graphs, charts, handwritten notes and various kinds of 'concrete writing' (where the forms on the page efface the content) to overwhelm whatever plot and characterisation survive. Waugh calls this novel 'thoroughly self-referential' (p. 147), and McHale thinks that it is haunted by 'the specter of infinite regress' (p. 121). In *Thru* there is no apocalyptic theme or plot and very little apocalyptic imagery. There does not need to be: total revelation here appears as an explosion of information so intense and multifarious that it cannot be absorbed. The apocalypse here has assumed and destroyed fictive form. What is represented is the death of representation.

SIMULATING THE END

McHale's 'specter of infinite regress' suggests another shape that the end of representation can take. This is the apocalypse of implosion envisioned by Jean Baudrillard. Baudrillard's notion of the simulacrum expands its own idiosyncratic version of the apocalypse. It is one that does not consist of nuclear destruction, although it can be employed to interpret fictions of such devastation. He describes our world – meaning the mainly late-capitalist, First World society – as already out of touch with the 'real' and instead permeated by the 'hyperreal', whose signifying components are the simulacrum and simulation. In the 1983 text I am analysing here, Baudrillard is not primarily interested in the history of representation and its waning; he does not inquire intently whether there ever was a 'real' that could be represented but is concerned with contemporary, totally-simulated existence, and in that sense his regard is ontological and postmodern according to the interrelation of these *à la* McHale.[15]

According to Baudrillard, representation has been absorbed into a capitalist, consumerist, technological system that substitutes, for referents which have substance and stability, merely the interacting signs of an information and communications culture. Whereas Derrida argues that all we can discover and interpret from is the trace which precedes its own elusive identity and renders absolute referents (as the origins of the traces) nonexistent, Baudrillard says that we are left with a network of images that skate on the surface and disguise the fact that the surface is all there is. Because these images reflect only each other and themselves, they are simulacra that simulate the real.' Moreover, not unlike the movement of Derrida's trace, for Baudrillard 'Simulation is characterized by a *precession of the model'* (p. 264), so that the simulacra have no 'real' base. The representation process goes on, in other words, according to Baudrillard, but it does so in a single dimension, for the simulation unit is itself a machine whose purpose it is to reproduce, infinitely, imitations of its circuitry, which itself is an imitation of a mathematical abstraction. At fault here (and Baudrillard views simulation in intensely negative terms) is, apparently, capitalist-controlled electronic technology: 'This representational imagining ... disappears with simulation – whose operation is nuclear and genetic ... The real is produced from miniaturized units, from matrices, memory banks, and command models – and with these it can be reproduced an infinite number of times ... In fact, since it is no longer enveloped by an imaginary, it is no longer real at all. It is a hyperreal, the product of an irradiating synthesis of combinatory models in a hyperspace without atmosphere' (p. 254).

Baudrillard continues his argument via a strategy that, in effect, gets rid of the problem of representation by dismissing the possibility of our culture ever again generating the real – whatever this real may have been:

> [T]he age of simulation thus begins with a liquidation of all referentials – worse: by their artificial resurrection in systems of signs ... It is no longer a question of imitation, nor of reduplication, nor even of parody. It is rather a question of substituting signs of the real for the real itself, that is, an operation to deter every real process by its operational double, a metastable, programmatic, perfect descriptive machine which provides all the signs of the real and short-circuits all its vicissitudes. Never again will the real have to be produced – this is the vital function of the model in a system of death, or rather of anticipated resurrection which no longer leaves any chance even in the event of death. A hyperreal henceforth sheltered from the imaginary, and from any distinction between the real and the imaginary, leaving room only for the orbital recurrence of models and the simulated generation of difference. (p. 254)

One gets some sense of what the real might have been further on in the essay, when Baudrillard discusses the process by which God has been simulated. He concentrates on the iconoclasts in religious history who wished to destroy images of divinity out of fear, ultimately, not that the images desecrated God but that they would cause worshippers to sense the 'omnipotence of simulacra, this facility they have of effacing God from the consciousness of men, and the overwhelming truth which they suggest: that ultimately there has never been any God, that only the simulacrum exists, indeed that God himself has only ever been his own simulacrum' (p. 255). Baudrillard connects this anxiety (which seems based on a recognition that the simalacrum occupies an 'originary' position very much like Derrida's trace) to the dissolution of representation itself:

> All of Western faith and good faith was engaged in this wager on representation: that a sign could refer to a depth of meaning, that a sign could *exchange* for meaning, and that something could guarantee this exchange – God, of course. But what if God himself can be simulated, that is to say, reduced to the signs which attest his existence? Then the whole system becomes weightless, it is no longer anything but a gigantic simulacrum – not unreal, but a simulacrum, never again exchanging for what is real, but exchanging in itself, in an uninterrupted circuit without reference or circumference. (p. 256)

Baudrillard sees no help for our world dominated by simulation, short of urging it to its end by accelerating the dynamics of the hyperreal into a state of total excess, a hyperentropy, that becomes paralysis. Harland in *Superstructuralism*, in fact, insists that 'His thinking is essentially nihilistic; he seems to welcome the prospect of a final apocalypse, and his main concern is to have it arrive as soon as possible' (p. 182). It is the semiotic version of capitalist expansion to the point where further development is impossible, or where consumerism reaches an absolute glut and a sated catatonia results. But this universe of simulation this endpoint will be experienced, Baudrillard says, as an implosion, a complete collapse of all artificial (the only kind) images into themselves. It is a process that socialist countries will not escape, for they are also complicit with the spread of simulation technology, and Baudrillard sees the event in apocalyptic terms. 'The nuclear is the apotheosis of simulation' (p. 275), he writes, and in the ensuing discussion of nuclear deterrence he declares that the fearful scenario of global destruction by atomic weapons is itself part of the staged hyperreality of the simulation environment that controls us and that depends on the model of electronic information/communications technology. Mutual assured destruction will remain a fiction (a component of a postmodern myth?) – and as such it is the perfect sign for societies dominated by simulacra: no one believes that this fiction represents a reality that will come to pass. Rather, deterrence is a 'pretext' for a 'universal system of security, linkup, and control' (p. 276) whose task it is to prevent any sort of disturbance, nuclear or otherwise, of our (d)evolution toward stasis. 'It isn't that the direct menace of atomic destruction paralyzes our lives. It is rather that deterrence leukemizes us' (p. 276). And: 'The balance of terror is the terror of balance' (p. 276).

Even nuclear accidents are not capable of shaking us (back) toward a grasp of a non-simulated reality: 'these events no longer make any sense; they are nothing more than a duplex effect of simulation at the summit' (p. 278). Thus the nuclear system, operating under the sign of deterrence, 'institutes a universally accelerated process of *implosion*; it conceals everything around it, absorbs all living energy', and Baudrillard sees this process as one 'where all these energies are abolished in a catastrophic process' (p. 281). What shape this inverted apocalypse will take he does not say, but he clearly conceives of it as a world ending.

This vision of a horribly perfected world of simulacra behind which there is no other reality is, of course, itself excessive. As Jonathan Crary points out, Baudrillard's 'virtuoso delineation of the utterly monolithic surfaces of contemporaneity becomes complicit, at a certain point, in the maintenance of the myths of the same cybernetic omnipotence he intends to deplore. What his texts exclude is any sense of breakdown, of faulty circuits, of systematic malfunction: or of a body that cannot be fully colonized or pacified, of disease, and of the colossal delapidation of everything that claims infallibility or sleekness' (pp. 290–91).[16] But beyond this, Baudrillard's failure to consider the insistent reality of waste in his world of the hyperreal renders his version of apocalypse curiously benign. As our awareness of the immense problem of waste grows (I could meditate on the fact that the computer screen I watch as I type these pages has an icon labelled 'trash'), and with that proliferating waste an accelerating pollution, apocalyptic (and other) fiction worries more and more about the possibility of a world obliterating itself through garbage and toxins.

Baudrillard's vision of a cataclysmic implosion has an aesthetic neatness about it that is perversely appealing – not unlike the psychology of Kermode's 'sense of an ending'. The prospect of the world suffocating in its own detritus is decidedly less attractive but much more likely. It is a major irony of our era that the universe of simulation produces real garbage, and that this trash may be the palpable, unavoidable, ultimate real beneath the trace and the simulacra. One unhappy way of responding to the theme of this conference is to remark that beyond the waste land is the waste land: beyond the metaphoric aridity exploited by the artists and scholars of modernism is the literal junk of the postmodern age. Since trash is worthless (except that which can be recycled, at which point it is no longer trash), it is, of course, an apt kind of simulacrum itself, a stand-in for the final meaninglessness of a world *based* on simulation. But more than this, the imagining of a world smothered in its own waste offers a more compelling version of Baudrillard's apocalypse by implosion.

THANATOXIC ENDS

With Baudrillard's concept of the simulacrum as my point of departure, I will show how five apocalyptic novels, all of them set in degenerate information-technological societies, significantly use simulation in various ways as a replacement for traditional representation, and how these simulated worlds, even when they turn hyperreal, do not generate the kind of implosion that Baudrillard predicts but rather break down under the weight of the waste – literal and psychological – that they produce.

Even the most realistic of these narratives, an 'airport trade' novel by Whitley Streiber and James Kunetka called *Nature's End* (1986), depends in good part on simulation technology and its interaction with a world dying in ecological disaster.[17] It is the year 2025, and overpopulation, pollution, and depletion of natural resources threaten to make humankind extinct in two decades. Yet at the same time the First World at least is a wonderland of electronic high-tech, and a wealthy upper class enjoys great advantages, such as treatments to stop the ageing process, while the masses suffer. In these circumstances a charismatic leader, Gupta Singh of Calcutta, emerges as the champion of the depopulationist movement, which advocates global participation in voluntary genocide that would kill off one-third of the world's population (three billion people) so that the rest could survive. It becomes the perilous task of John Sinclair, a professional convictor (a combination of super-prosecutor and computer expert) to expose Singh as a fraud: rather than an Indian mystic, he is a mad American genetics researcher who wishes to control the future by manipulating the 'voluntary' deaths of the three billion.

We need not linger over the plot of *Nature's End*. More to my purposes is to describe the treatment of simulation in the narrative. Singh, a genius at media manipulation, has been able to project himself worldwide as something other than he is. His public, political persona as the wise old figure who will save two-thirds of humankind by inspiring the deaths of the others, is a computer and television creation and projection, and he has even undergone cosmetic surgery to make his physical appearance resemble the electronic one. Sinclair, in turn, has access to computers that can break through this simulacrum and compose another one out of myriad information bits (bytes?), gradually piecing together a relentlessly honest, sociopsychological profile of the man. Once launched, this process moves inexorably toward exposure and conviction, and after many cliffhanging moments, Sinclair triumphs. *Nature's End*, an entertainment fiction, offers as its action a war of simulacra against a backdrop of environmental doom.

Ballard's *The Atrocity Exhibition* provides a more complicated and less realistic version of the contest of simulacra in a waste land. This is a world of battlefields, car crashes, vaporised cities, broken and diseased bodies – all 'apocalyptic landscapes' (p. 45), as the narrator calls them. Yet many of these are projected at a remove: they are 'mimetized' and simulated electronically, and through 'modula', mimicry, replicas, mannequins. This mania for the replication of reality that accelerates into hyperreality is caught neatly in the concept of the 'modulus', which seems to be, variously, a mental image, something like a hologram, and an animated model. Whatever it is, the modulus is not real, yet stands in so effectively for it that the real becomes unnecessary – indeed, even an irritating obstacle to experience. Yet all such simulation functions degenerately, often as voyeuristic metaexperiencing in which the observer/participant is aroused by watching violence on the television and film screen. In Freudian/feminist terms, the spectacular and specular converge on images of vulnerable, violated otherness to satisfy the libido.

McHale marks a more formal narratological role for the modulus in *The Atrocity Exhibition*. 'This theme of the "modulus" at the level of story-content . . . exactly duplicates the formal organization of the stories, in which a fixed repertoire of modules, many of them repeated from the earlier apocalyptic novels, are differently recombined and manipulated from story to story' (p. 70). According to McHale, this is a strategy that puts science fiction in the service of the postmodern ontological challenge, which is to say, requesting that we rethink the nature of the real or (in Derrida's terms) the question of the referent in the light of our technologically enhanced ability to alter our perception of reality and even, alas, to end reality.

'I have the uncanny feeling of being in someone else's old film set' (p. 128), one of the voices remarks in William Burroughs' *The Wild Boys* (1969),[18] and this novel indeed, as much of Burroughs' work, uses the cinema tradition and cinematography to create a simulated reality that confuses our experience of ordinary existence. It is impossible to distill a single storyline from the chaos of settings, characters, imagery, and voices of *The Wild Boys*, and most readers coming unprepared to Burroughs' perverse sexual fiction would probably be too shocked to try. But one does gradually absorb the impression of a corrupt and wasted world (some of it set, from the time of Burroughs' composition, in futuristic 1988) in which resources are running out and packs of wild boys – vicious, lust-crazed, and devilishly armed – battle 'suppressive police states . . . set up throughout the Western world . . . under the pretext of drug control' (p. 138). Most of the depiction is, like *The Atrocity Exhibition*, acutely voyeuristic in theme (repeated scenes of homosexual intercourse) and execution: five of the chapters are labelled 'The Penny Arcade Peep Show' and trade on the old cliché of surreptitious, titillating watching.

Because the referent of *The Wild Boys* is moviemaking, the reader does not need to decide between what is represented as 'real' or as already cinematically represented. McHale thinks that Burroughs 'represents characters as stepping out of the ontological level of the movies . . . to some higher (or lower) level' (p. 130), but I do not think it is clear (little is clear in Burroughs' fiction) that they ever leave the ontological level of film.

What does happen is that at various points in the narration the reader is drawn into both the film-making process (shot directions are given; a camera shooting a scene being described is destroyed, and the cameraman shouts for another one) and the film-watching, and thus becomes involved in a second-level simulation. Fiction here, however sketchily, simulates cinematography, and the novel becomes a simulacrum of the film, which is itself already a technological model of some reality – but a model, as Burroughs deploys it, so compelling that it effaces the 'original'. The apocalypse itself occurs as just one of many cinematic clichés: 'Armored cars, sirens screaming, converge on a rocket installation. / Too late. The rocket blasts off a mad tycoon at the controls. The earth blows up behind him. As his ship rides the blast he screams: "HI HO SILVER YIPPEEE". He is riding ahead of the posse tossing sticks of dynamite over his shoulder. Sharp smell of weeds from old Westerns' (p. 169).

Burroughs' world is overcome by the junk of Hollywood, the waste of the illusion industry. His novels come closer than most to confirming Baudrillard's vision of a simulation society, except that they do not project an implosion via technological hegemony but rather the modulation of that technology into sadomasochistic reflex.

If it were possible for apocalyptic fiction to be charming, Russell Hoban's *Riddley Walker* (1980) would be a candidate for that designation.[19] Its setting is anything but delightful, though, consisting of the ravaged countryside of Kent many millennia and generations after ours and long after the nuclear devastation of the Third World War. Riddley is a twelve-year-old boy who belongs to one of the small groups of descendants of the survivors, a band of primitive scavengers who salvage the wreckage of the high-tech age buried underground and sell it as scrap metal. Drawing on a lifetime of writing children's fiction, Hoban manages to portray Riddley in the first person as an enterprising and reflective boy able to intuit the great loss that his post-holocaust diaspora suffers and to try, however pitifully, to mitigate it.

Riddley participates in both of the simulation activities that determine this fine novel. One of them is the poignant and doomed effort of this remnant to recapture what is to them the magnificence of the era of technology – our own – via religious ritual, magic, and crude science. In both comic and moving ways that I can only hint at here, they evoke the grandeur and complexity of nuclear physics, information technology, and space travel by apotheosising theorums and formulae from our culture – these already distorted almost beyond recognition – but actually comprehending nothing of them. Their worship of the age of technology intensifies their already pathetically wrongheaded attempts to simulate it; gunpowder, for example, becomes the false simulacrum for nuclear fission, and when they manage at last to combine potassium nitrate, charcoal, and sulphur to set off the first postwar explosions, the results are both ghastly and funny: ghastly in that a number of the mutants kept on hand as high priests of the science cult (they are the descendants of the computer and political 'elite') are blown to bits; and funny through Riddley's (second-hand) laconic recounting of it in the butchered English that these people speak: 'they lit the fews . . . thats when it gone bang and peaces of iron pot and Eusa folk [the mutants] wizzing all roun' (p. 200).

The concept of a false simulacrum is perhaps an oxymoron, for one could argue that a model which does not adequately represent its original is, in fact, not a simulacrum; it is simply a bad model. Nevertheless, Hoban's depiction of what is intended by these heirs of the apocalypse as a simulacrum contributes valuably to the epistemology and ontology of representation. It suggests what might happen to a society *after* representation, after the world of familiar referents is so totally abolished that one needs to start over. Even then, it seems, the nostalgia for the absolute is so compelling that one deifies the annihilating past that somehow incarnated the absolute. The trace is glorified, mythologised into a narrative of the lost absolute, and representation is thereby reinvented.

Mythologising takes place in Hoban's novel in another way in which Riddley and the reader participate and that shows still another role of the simulacrum. Hoban, namely – and this is one of the admirable achievements of *Riddley Walker* – creates a religion with both story and ritual for this degenerate remnant that is unlike any extant or dead one. It is a simulated myth, in other words, but it is developed so thoroughly and multidimensionally as to provide material for one to sense how a group of survivors who live in the harshest of circumstances might still shape a faith out of the very catastrophe that made them what they are. Robert Jay Lifton discusses some of this in *The Future of Immortality* in his analysis of the Hiroshima A-bomb survivors, but it is still a relatively unexplored subject. Hoban's fiction embodies a simulation of religious faith born out of crisis that, however grotesque to our minds, nonetheless projects a mode of being based on hope. When Riddley Walker at the end of the novel heads out on the road like a post-holocaust Huck Finn to perform his Punch and Judy show, relying on his wit and the ravaged communities' goodwill to inspire the proper interpretations, he is simultaneously risking the end of representation and recuperating it. It is a foolhardy act of dissemination but one that, unlike Baudrillard's vision, simulates hope.

Finally, I will treat Margaret Atwood's 1986 dystopian novel *The Handmaid's Tale* in terms of simulacra and waste.[20] One could call this text, indulging a minor pun, a thanatoxic fiction, for it deals with a society in our near future in which the severely poisoned environment has badly damaged human reproductive capacities – brought on large-scale infertility, miscarriages, and mutation. Atwood has been taken to task for offering such an unremittingly bleak vision, yet a recent issue of *Time*, which contains one article on garbage disposal 'approaching the crisis stage throughout the U.S.' and another on the growing fear of pesticides contaminating our food, makes her appear prophetic rather than excessive.[21] To meet this realised catastrophe in *The Handmaid's Tale* a fascist military group has taken over the United States, now the Republic of Gilead, in a bloody coup and runs the country as a police state in which women above all suffer the loss of their rights and live in total subservience to men. The narrator is a woman in her thirties renamed Offred (Of Fred = belonging to Fred), taken from her family and placed, like many others of childbearing age, into concubinage with an elderly high-ranking military figure – the Commander – as a surrogate for his barren wife. Because procreation is difficult, it has become the privilege of the elite, but because so many upper-class women cannot bear children, this fundamentalist militaristic culture has adopted a biblical 'precedent' that endorses surrogate motherhood. It is found in Genesis 30, where Rachel, who is infertile, proposes to her husband Jacob: 'Behold my maid Bilhah, go in unto her, and she shall bear upon my knees, that I may also have children by her'.

The Republic of Gilead has formalised this vignette into a central sacred ceremony. The handmaid reclines literally between the thighs of her mistress while, in the company of the household, their master copulates with her. It is not an erotic situation. As Offred reflects on it (with Augustinian overtones), 'It has nothing to do with sexual desire . . . arousal and orgasm are no longer thought necessary; they would be a symptom of frivolity . . . / . . . This is serious business' (pp. 94–5). It is surely serious business for the handmaids, for if they do not conceive after a few such attempts they will be replaced and sent away to die in the highly toxic atmosphere of outlying work camps.

This ceremony can be viewed as a simulacrum in various ways. For one, of course, it simultaneously substitutes for and imitates conjugal intercourse, and it is not as naive a representation as it seems at first if one considers that in slave-holding societies a person-as-possession can be used easily in such a symbolic/material fashion. For another, the ritual literalises the described action of a sacred text and thus becomes not only a simulacrum but a sacrament. Here another dimension of representation emerges for consideration: in what ways does reflection on the enacted repetition of a sacred event in a believers' culture contribute to the definition of representation?

What is evoked in the ceremony of intercourse with the handmaid is the power of absolute authority. The old military leaders of this fundamentalist theocracy purport to emulate a Hebrew patriarch in order to save the human species (at least in Gilead). The procreative ritual finally simulates the creative potency of the Judeo-Christian God. It is a representation that works, of course, only because those who perpetrate it are powerful enough to enforce it. Actually, it is as arbitrary a signification process as any other and an absurdly flawed simulation; if the main concern of the Gilead government were truly the survival of its populace, it would make far more sense to mate the handmaids with healthy young men – but that strategy would clearly not reinforce the theocratic power structure, with its attendant privileges.

Offred indeed discovers that her Commander, like many other senior leaders, is not really a believer in the state religion of Gilead, and that the sacramental simulation is a sham – a representational act that destroys its own meaning. Although its ostensible referents (and hence its validation) are God, family, and community, none of these is foundational but only a disguise for the real referent, which is totalitarian power.

Language itself is involved in the interplay of simulation and waste in a crucial way. Books have been destroyed in Gilead, and reading and writing are forbidden except among the leaders. The society is controlled by television, mass meetings, and, of course, surveillance technology. Yet although writing has been wasted in this sense, it is employed 'religiously' in grotesquely profligate ways such as by the Soul Scrolls franchises. These are empty shops in which unattended computers print out rolls of prayers ordered by 'Compuphone' by the pious. 'There are five different prayers: for health, wealth, a death, a birth, a sin. You pick the one you want, punch in the number, then punch in your own number so your account will be debited, and punch in the number of times you want the prayer repeated./The machines talk as they print out the prayers: if you like, you can go inside and listen to them, the toneless metallic voices repeating the same thing over and over ... There are no people inside the building: the machines run by themselves' (p. 167). Here is an excellent example of Baudrillard's simulacrum accelerated to the hyperreal. What was once a human act of devotion and commitment has been automated, quantified, rendered excessive and, in its utter tastelessness, obscene.

But this humiliation of religious utterance via its reduction to computerised chatter is just one instance of the effacement of language in a culture dying of waste. More significant is what happens to Offred in this regard and how her narrator's situation influences the narration of *The Handmaid's Tale*. Offred is not allowed to write, yet needs desperately to relate her story, above all in the hope of having it somehow reach her husband and daughter, who may still be alive somewhere. She attempts to tell it as if it were a written narrative, hoping somehow, sometime, to get it down. Thus the story is a simulacrum of a written tale. Yet the nature of this telling is still more complicated than that. The final section of the novel is called *'Historical Notes'* and is offered as *'a partial transcript of the proceedings of the Twelfth Symposium on Gileadian Studies'* (p. 299), held in 2195, some two centuries after the era that Offred describes. Gilead no longer exists, and the scholars at this international conference look back on it merely as the object of disinterested research. No explanation is given as to how this new world has overcome the ecological catastrophes that Gilead had suffered. From a Cambridge scholar's conjectures at this meeting we learn that Offred escaped the Commander's household, went underground, and probably spent sufficient time at a safe house in Bangor, Maine to record her story on tape. The transcription of these recordings constitutes the novel, and as the scholar points out, Offred (assuming the tapes are not a forgery) relates her story on tape as if she were still a captive handmaid. Thus her recorded story is a simulation of a simulation: she acts as if she were telling in the present the story she had projected, during the time of her enslavement, as a substitute for a written tale. Even during her imprisonment Offred herself realises the complicated nature of her narration. At one point she says, 'When I get out of here, if I'm ever able to set this down, in any form, even in the form of one voice to another, it will be a reconstruction then too, at yet another remove' (p. 134).

We thus conclude these pages on fictions of apocalypse by waste with an instance of how narrative complexity produces simulacra that, in turn, generate a hyperreality. At the end of Offred's telling – in fact, two hundred years after the end – nothing remains but a possibly faked, technologically preserved narration of a society thoroughly corrupted by its own poisons. As far as we know (as readers buying into this fiction), Offred may never have existed; all we have is a trace of a (literally) fugitive trace. Yet as this narrator's voice insists, out of such telltale clues we must construct our reality and that of others. Addressing her lost family, Offred says, 'By telling you anything at all I am at least believing in you, I believe you're there, I believe you into being. Because I'm telling you this story I will your existence. I tell, therefore you are' (p. 268).

Although these fictions of cataclysmic waste are, in part, less postmodernistically experimental and thus, superficially, more realistic, they turn out to be as elusive as those employing intertextual overkill. These too, by demonstrating how simulation finally only simulates itself, leave us endlessly reflected and reflective. But whereas according to Baudrillard such hyperreality should implode into a dense nothing, these narratives show instead a vast messiness. Nothingness is revealed, but not as a tidy abstraction. It translates into chaos, which translates into waste.

Yet waste by its very materiality can create, if not hope, at least awareness. Frances Ferguson in an essay called 'The Nuclear Sublime' argues that our efforts to think the unthinkable, meaning here to imagine the nuclear apocalypse, generally not only turn into 'something very much like calculations of exactly how horrible life would be after a significant nuclear explosion' (p. 7); they also allow us to evade our acute contemporary problems of 'the pressures of intersubjectivity' (p. 9) – a fairly tame term for the vast difficulty we humans have in coexisting in a rapidly shrinking, increasingly overcrowded and contaminated world.[22]

I believe that over much of the globe we are already *living* the unthinkable, to the extent that my freedom to think the unthinkable at a literature and religion conference is a First-World luxury.

Jameson argues in 'Progress Versus Utopia' that the deepest lesson we can learn from science fiction is defamiliarisation – to recover from its futurist fantasies an awareness of the impoverished relationship we have to our present world – and I have been trying to interpret apocalyptic writing according to that strategy. But I think that the revelation embedded in the apocalyptic mode is now rebuking our forgetfulness with a vengeance. Apocalyptic narrative marks at least the beginning of the end of realism because, perhaps paradoxically, that realism no longer represents much of the world as it is. And how 'is' the world? If it is true, as Ronald Aronson writes, that 'For 100 million people, perhaps one out of every hundred people who have lived in this century, Doomsday has happened', we are already living in the apocalyptic mode and have just not figured it out.[23] And if this is so, then apocalyptic fiction may be our special genre of revelation, a trace rapidly taking shape, gaining definition from the future: warning us against its fulfilment, inviting us to work toward the end of this new kind of realism.

Notes

1. Paul Tillich, 'Religion and Secular Culture', in *The Protestant Era*, English translation James Luther Smith (Chicago: University of Chicago Press, 1948), pp. 59–60.
2. Quoted in Ralf Schnell, *Die Literatur der Bundesrepublik: Literatur in der Entscheidung – zur Konstitution der westdeutschen Nachkriegsliteratur (1945–1949)* (Stuttgart: J. B. Metzlersche Verlagsbuchhandlung, 1986). My translation.
3. John Lukacs, *The Passing of the Modern Age* (New York: Harper & Row, 1970).
4. Theodore Roszak, *Where the Wasteland Ends: Politics and Transcendence in Postindustrial Society* (Garden City, New York: Doubleday, 1972).
5. Robert Jay Lifton, *The Future of Immortality and Other Essays for a Nuclear Age* (New York: Basic Books, 1987).
6. Patricia Waugh, *Metafiction: The Theory and Practice of Self-Conscious Fiction* (London and New York: Methuen, 1984). Brian McHale, *Postmodernist Fiction* (London and New York: Methuen, 1987).
7. Richard Harland, *Superstructuralism: The Philosophy of Structuralism and Post-Structuralism* (London and New York: Methuen, 1987), has an excellent discussion of the trace and the *representamen* in relation to Freud's Magic Writing Pad, pp. 142 ff.

8. "Perpetual dispersal" is Harland's term, p. 148.
9. Jacques Derrida, 'No Apocalypse, Not Now (full speed ahead, seven missiles, seven missives)', *Diacritics* 14/2 (Summer 1984), pp. 20–31.
10. Fredric Jameson, "Progress Versus Utopia: or, Can We Imagine the Future?" in Brian Wallis (ed.), *Art After Modernism: Rethinking Representation* (Boston: David R. Godine, 1984), pp. 239–52.
11. Paul Auster, *In the Country of Last Things* (New York: Viking Penguin, 1987).
12. Muriel Spark, *The Hothouse on the East River* (New York: The Viking Press, 1973).
13. J. G. Ballard, *The Atrocity Exhibition* (London: Triad/Panther Books, 1979). First published by Jonathan Cape in 1970.
14. Christina Brooke-Rose, *Out* (London: Michael Joseph, 1964); *Such* (Michael Joseph, 1966); *Thru* (London: Hamish Hamilton, 1975). I have used these texts collected in *The Christina Brooke-Rose Omnibus* (Manchester: Carcanet Press, 1986).
15. Jean Baudrillard, 'The Precession of Simulacra', *Art After Modernism* pp. 253–81.
16. Jonathan Crary, 'Eclipse of the Spectacle', Wallis (ed.), *Art After Modernism*, pp. 283–94.
17. Whitley Strieber and James Kunetka, *Nature's End: The Consequences of the Twentieth Century* (New York: Warner Books, 1986). Strieber and Kunetka have also written an earlier novel, *Warday*, describing the effects of nuclear war.
18. William Burroughs, *The Wild Boys: A Book of the Dead* (New York: Grove Press, 1969).
19. Russell Hoban, *Riddley Walker* (New York: Washington Square Press, 1980).
20. Margaret Atwood, *The Handmaid's Tale* (Boston: Houghton Mifflin, 1986). For more detailed interpretations of both *Riddley Walker* and *The Handmaid's Tale* see my *Breaking the Fall: Religious Readings of Contemporary Fiction* (London: Macmillan, 1989).
21. *Time*, 132/10 (5 September, 1988), pp. 51, 81.
22. Frances Ferguson, 'The Nuclear Sublime', *Diacritics* 14/2 (Summer, 1984), pp. 4–10.
23. Ronald Aronson, *The Dialectics of Disaster: A Preface to Hope* (Thetford: The Thetford Press, 1983), pp. 7–8.

Index

Absalom, Absalom! (William Faulkner) 155
Acheson, James 138
Ackroyd, Peter 110
Acts of the Apostles 78
Adler, Alfred 22
Aeneid (Virgil) 71
Aeschylus 118
Aiken, Conrad 119
Alexander, Samuel 59, 63
America and Cosmic Man (Wyndham Lewis) 65
Anathemata, The (David Jones) 115
Andrewes, Lancelot 110, 112
Apocalypse (D. H. Lawrence) 34, 38, 39, 44, 49, 50
Apocalyptic 153–83
Apollo in Picardy (Walter Pater) 38
Appearance and Reality (F. H. Bradley) 64–5
Aristotle 118
Arnold, Matthew 82
Aronson, Ronald 182
Art of the Novel, The (Milan Kundera) 144, 145, 151
Ascent of Mount Carmel, The (St John of the Cross) 75, 131–2
Ash-Wednesday (T. S. Eliot) 72, 80
Aspects of the Novel (E. M. Forster) 23–4
Atrocity Exhibition, The (J. G. Ballard) 164–6, 168, 174–5
Atwood, Margaret 178–81
Auden, W. H. 106, 107, 108, 112–13, 114
Augustine of Hippo, St 133
Auster, Paul 160–62

Bakhtin, Mikhail 28
Baldwin, Helene L. 130
Ballard, J. G. 164–6, 169–73
Baring, Maurice 18, 19, 20, 27

Barth, Karl 18, 30, 34, 52
Baudelaire, Charles 4, 82
Baudrillard, Jean 156, 169–73, 178, 181
Beckett, Samuel 79, 80, 106, 117, 121–8, 129–40, 168
Beckett at 80/Beckett in Context (Martin Esslin) 130
Beerbohm, Max 112
Beethoven, Ludwig van 11, 138
Bell, George 102
Ben-Zwi, Linda 133–4
Berdyaev, Nickolai 25, 27, 29
Bergson, Henri 57–8, 59, 62, 63
Berkeley, George 59
Betjeman, John 111
Bird Alone (Sean O'Faolain) 126
Birth of Tragedy and the Genealogy of Morals, The (Friedrich Nietzsche) 10
Boehme, Jakob 130
Bonhoeffer, Dietrich 50, 98, 101, 102
Book of Laughter and Forgetting, The (Milan Kundera) 144, 145–52
Borges, Jorge Luis 143
Bosanquet, Bernard 60
Bradley, F. H. 58, 63–5
Brater, Enoch 138
Brecht, Bertold 107
Brémond, Henri 59
Brer Rabbit (Joel Chandler Harris) 110
British Writers of the Thirties (Valentine Cunningham) 65
Brooke, Rupert 75
Brooke-Rose, Christina 166–9
Brothers Karamazov, The (F. Dostoyevsky) 21, 23–4
Browne, Sir Thomas 82
Buchan, John 38
Buddhism 130, 133, 136
Bultmann, Rudolf 35, 53

Index

Bunting, Basil 105
Burroughs, William 175–6
...But the Clouds... (Samuel Beckett) 137
Butler, Lance St John 137
Byron, George Gordon 4

Cabbala 117–18, 119
Calvino, Italo 143–4, 145, 146, 147
Cambodia 161
Campbell, Roy 65
Canterbury Tales, The (Geoffrey Chaucer) 75, 76
Cantos, The (Ezra Pound) 39, 108, 111
Cape, Jonathan 117
Carr, E. H. 25
Cathay (Ezra Pound) 109, 111
Celan, Paul 101
Chamberlain, Neville 96
Chaucer, Geoffrey 75, 76, 81
Chinese Classics (Rev. James Legge) 109
Christ 27, 50, 100, 101, 119, 123–4, 137
Christianity 8–10, 13, 19, 50, 57
Church Dogmatics (Karl Barth) 52–3
Classical Temper, The (S. L. Goldberg) 63
Coleridge, Samuel Taylor 152
Collected Poems (T. S. Eliot) 74, 76, 79
Collected Shorter Poems (Ezra Pound) 109
Colossians, Epistle to the 50
Composition of Four Quartets, The (Helen Gardner) 102
Concept of Dread, The (Søren Kierkegaard) 6–7
Conrad, Joseph 16, 21, 75
Continuous (Tony Harrison) 115
Corinthians, First Epistle to the 44, 138
Corinthians, Second Epistle to the 45
Crary, Jonathan 162, 162, 172
Crime and Punishment (F. Dostoyevsky) 17, 21

Crystal World, The (J. G. Ballard) 164
Cunningham, Valentine 65
Czechoslovakia 96, 148

Dangerous Corner (J. B. Priestley) 56
Dante, Alighieri 75, 77, 79, 82, 111, 118, 119, 122, 124, 126, 133
Dante... Bruno. Vico... Joyce (Samuel Beckett) 131
D'Arcy, Martin 60–61, 63
Dark Forest, The (Hugh Walpole) 16
Dark Night of the Soul, The (St John of the Cross) 131
Daughters of the Vicar (D. H. Lawrence) 37, 40
Debussy, Claude Achille 5
Democracy (D. H. Lawrence) 39
Denys l'Auxerrois (Walter Pater) 38
Derrida, Jacques 135, 140, 156–60, 169, 170, 171, 175
Descartes, René 133
Diacritics 158
Dickens, Charles 17, 106
Dionysius the Areopagite 133, 140
Divine Comedy, The (Alighieri Dante) 75, 82, 119–20, 122, 124, 125, 126
Doctor Faustus (Thomas Mann) 1–14
Dr Zhivago (Boris Pasternak) 51, 55
Don Giovanni (W. A. Mozart) 4
Donne, John 82, 137
Donoghue, Denis 80
Dostoyevsky, Fyodor 15–33, 49
Dream of Fair to Middling Women (Samuel Beckett) 131, 133
Drought, The (J. G. Ballard) 164
Drowned World, The (J. G. Ballard) 164
Dunciad, The (Alexander Pope) 76
Dunne, J. W. 56, 58, 65, 67

Ecclesiastes 79–81, 83
Eckhart, Johannes 130, 132, 135–6, 137, 139, 141
Education of the People (D. H. Lawrence) 39
Edwards, Michael viii, 54
Einstein, Albert. 59, 62
Either/or (Søren Kierkegaard) 3
Eliot, T. S. viii, 36, 56, 57–8, 60, 63, 70–85, 86–104, 106, 107, 108–14, 130, 132, 144
Eliot's Early Years (Lyndall Gordon) 96
Empson, William 39
Endgame (Samuel Beckett) 126
Epipsychidion (P. B. Shelley) 126
Epstein, Sir Jacob 59
Ernst, Cornelius 46–7, 89–90, 93, 95
Escaped Cock, The (D. H. Lawrence) 40, 43–4, 47–8, 49, 50
Essays on Truth and Reality (F. H. Bradley) 64
Esslin, Martin 130, 137
Ewart, Gavin 107
Exodus 45
Experiment with Time, An (J. W. Dunne) 56
Ezechiel 75

Faerie Queene, The (Edmund Spenser) 71
Family Reunion, The (T. S. Eliot) 80
Faulkner, William 155
Feminism 174
Fenollosa, Ernest 109
Ferguson, Frances 181
Finnegans Wake (James Joyce) 63, 134
Fleurs du Mal, Les (Charles Baudelaire) 75
Flying Fish, The (D. H. Lawrence) 40, 42–3
Footfalls (Samuel Beckett) 137, 138, 139
Ford, John 82
Forster, E. M. 23–4, 28, 38, 106, 111
Foucault, Michel 148

Four Quartets, The (T. S. Eliot) viii, 36, 70–85, 88, 90, 91–102, 132
Fragment of Stained Glass, A (D. H. Lawrence) 37
Freud, Sigmund 22, 145, 174
Frost, Robert 107
Fuller, John 107
Fuller, Roy 107
Future of Immorality, The (Robert Jay Lifton) 154, 177

Gaboriau, Emile 17
Galatians, Epistle to the 138
Galsworthy, John 21
Gardner, Helen 90, 102
Garnett, Constance 18
Gascoyne, David 86, 93
Gauguin, Paul 60
Gautier, Théophile 108
Genesis 77, 78, 176
Germany 11–12
'Gerontion' (T. S. Eliot) 74
Geulinx, Arnold 133
Ghost Trio (Samuel Beckett) 137, 138
Gide, André 21, 25, 28
Gissing, George Robert 17
Gnosticism 154
Goethe, Johann Wolfgang von 107
Goldberg, S. L. 63
Golden Bowl, The (Henry James) 79
Gordon, Lyndall 96
Gosse, Edmund 21
Grand Inquisitor, The (F. Dostoyevsky) 22, 49
Graves, Robert 107
Great Russian Realist, A (Lloyd) 19
Greene, Graham 106

Handful of Dust, A (Evelyn Waugh) 115
Handmaid's Tale, The (Margaret Atwood) 178–81
Hardy, Thomas 48, 105, 107, 113
Harland, Richard 171
Harris, Joel Chandler 110
Harrison, Tony 108, 115

Index

Hassan, Ihab 129, 145
Heart of Darkness, The (Joseph Conrad) 75
Heidegger, Martin 51–2, 135, 136
Hesse, Hermann 25
Hill, Geoffrey 87–8, 101, 107, 108, 115
Hiroshima 177
History and Eschatology (Rudolf Bultmann) 35
Hoban, Russell 176–8
Hölderlin, Friedrich 38, 39, 144, 145, 146, 150
Hollis, Christopher 66
Holy Sinner, The (Thomas Mann) 14
Homer 111
Hope, A. D. 113
Hopkins, Gerard Manley 105
Horace 107
Hothouse on the East River, The (Muriel Spark) 162–4
How It Is (Samuel Beckett) 122
Hugh Selwyn Mauberley (Ezra Pound) 105, 108, 111
Hulme, T. E. 58
Human Age, The (Wyndham Lewis) 65, 66
Hume, David 59
Huxley, Juliette 92

Idea of a Christian Society, The (T. S. Eliot) 96
Idea of the Holy, The (Rudolf Otto) 138
If on a winter's night a traveller (Halo Calvino) 147
In Ballast to the White Sea (Malcolm Lowry) 120
Incarnate Lord, The (Lionel Thornton) 61
In Parenthesis (David Jones) 115
In the Country of Last Things (Paul Auster) 160–2
Introduction to Metaphysics (Henri Bergson) 58
Ivanov, Vyacheslav 28

Jakobson, Roman 144

James, Henry 17, 21, 82
James, William 60, 63, 133
Jameson, Frederic 160, 166
John, Gospel according to 44, 50
John of the Cross, St 73, 75, 130, 131, 132, 135
Johnson, Samuel 79, 82, 107, 123, 127
Jones, David 106, 115
Journals and Papers (Søren Kierkegaard) 4
'Journey of the Magi' (T. S. Eliot) 109, 110, 112
Joyce, James 59, 60, 61–2, 65, 68, 106, 107, 117, 118, 134, 160
Jung, Carl Gustav 138

Kafka, Franz 160
Kangaroo (D. H. Lawrence) 44
Kearns, Cleo McNelly 89, 90–1, 92, 93, 103
Keats, John 38, 39, 77
Kennedy, John F. 163
Kenner, Hugh 66, 105
Kermode, Frank 158, 173
Kibert, Declan 130
Kierkegaard, Søren 3–9, 12
Kings, First Book of 53
Kipling, Rudyard 82
Kropotkin, Peter 17–18, 27
Kundera, Milan 144, 145–52
Kunetka, James 173

Lady Chatterley's Lover (D. H. Lawrence) 40, 115
Laforgue, Jules 82
Lamartine, Alphonse 125
Larkin, Philip 106, 107–8, 110, 112, 114, 115
Lavrin, Janko 22
Lawrence, D. H. viii, 21–2, 27, 29, 34–55, 105, 106, 107
Learned Ignorance (Nicholas of Cusa) 132
Leaves of the Tulip Tree (Juliette Huxley) 92
Leavis, F. R. 23, 105–6
Legge, Rev. James 109
Leibniz, Gottfried Wilhelm 59

Index

Lewis, Wyndham 56–69
Lifton, Robert Jay 154, 177
Literary Essays (Ezra Pound) 68
Literary Influence of Ezra Pound, The (Goodwin) 110
Little Gidding (T. S. Eliot) 36
Locke, John 59
Lost Ones, The (Samuel Beckett) 124–5
'Love Song of J. Alfred Prufrock, The' (T. S. Eliot) 74, 79, 80, 108, 111
Lowell, Robert 114
Lowry, Malcolm 117–21, 123, 127
Lukacs, John 153
Luke, Gospel according to 50, 78
Lunar Caustic (Malcolm Lowry) 119, 120–21
Luther, Martin 10
Lyrics from the Chinese (Helen Waddell) 109

McAuley, James 113
MacCraig, Norman 107
McHale, Brian 145, 146, 155, 159, 163, 164, 167, 168, 175
Mackinnon, D. M. 46
Macleod, Colin 87
Maestro – Don Gesualdo (Giovanni Verga) 51
Malign Fiesta (Wyndham Lewis) 65
Mallarmé, Stephane 82, 86, 160
Malone Dies (Samuel Beckett) 122, 132
Man who Loved Islands, The (D. H. Lawrence) 40
Mann, Thomas 1–14
Many Inventions 79
Marcel, Gabriel 57
Maritain, Jacques 57
Matthew, Gospel according to 44, 45
Mauthner, Fritz 134
Meditations (Alphonse Lamartine) 125
Meier-Graefe, Julius 25
Memento Mori (Muriel Spark) 163
Mendelson, Edward 107, 113

Mercian Hymns (Geoffrey Hill) 115
Merezhkovsky, Dmitri 18, 19, 25
Merton, Thomas 91
Michaelangelo, Buonarroti 59
Milton, John 75, 82, 83, 84, 111
Mirsky, D. S. 24
Modern Fiction (Virginia Woolf) 23
Molière 4
Møller, Poul Martin 6
Molloy (Samuel Beckett) 134–5, 137
Monstre Gai (Wyndham Lewis) 65
Month, The 60
Moore, George 17
Moore, Marianne 114
Mouth (Samuel Beckett) 137, 138
Mozart, Wolfgang Amadeus 4, 52
Mr. Noon (D. H. Lawrence) 40
Muchnic, Helen 15–16
Murder in the Cathedral (T. S. Eliot) 80, 102
Murphy (Samuel Beckett) 79
Murry, John Middleton 19–21, 22, 23, 24, 27, 29
Murray, Les A. 113
Mystery of the Charity of Charles Péguy, The (Geoffrey Hill) 115
Mystical Theology (Dionysius the Areopagite) 133

Nacht und Träume (Samuel Beckett) 137–8, 139–40
Nagasaki 165
Nature's End (Whitley Streiber and James Kunetka) 173–4
Nero 7
New Bearings in English Poetry (F. R. Leavis) 105
New English Weekly 65
New Immorality, The (J. W. Dunne) 56
Nicholas of Cusa 132
Nietzsche, Friedrich Wilhelm 10, 19, 24, 27, 59, 60, 144, 145, 146, 150
Nihilism 2
Ninth Symphony (Beethoven) 11

Index

'No Apocalypse, Not Now' (Jacques Derrida) 158–60
Not I (Samuel Beckett) 122, 137, 138, 139
Notes From Underground (F. Dostoyevsky) 24

'Ode to a Nightingale' (John Keats) 77
'Ode to the West Wind' (P. B. Shelley) 75
Odour of Chrysanthemums (D. H. Lawrence) 37
Odyssey (Homer) 71
O'Faolain, Sean 126
Ohio Impromptu (Samuel Beckett) 137
'On the Morning of Christ's Nativity' (John Milton) 75
Orpheus (David Gascoigne) 86
Other Side of Silence, The (Jerzy Peterkiewicz) 86
Otto, Rudolf 50, 138
Out (Christina Brooke-Rose) 167–8
Out of Egypt (Ihab Hassan) 129

Pannenberg, Wolfhart 34, 53
Paradise Lost (John Milton) 71, 75, 76, 111
Parker, Dorothy 113
Pascal, Blaise 133
Pasternak, Boris 51
Pater, Walter 38
Paul, St 13–14, 45, 70, 79, 138
Peterkiewicz, Jerzy 86, 91, 101
Petronius Arbiter 111
Phelps, Gilbert 19, 21
Phnom Penh 161
Picasso, Pablo 59, 107, 113
Piece of Monologue, A (Samuel Beckett) 126, 137, 139
Pilling, John 130, 139
Plato 59, 157
Play (Samuel Beckett) 122
Plotinus 59
Plumed Serpent, The (D. H. Lawrence) 38–9, 40–41, 44–6
Poe, Edgar Allan 82

Poor Folk (F. Dostoyevsky) 17
Pope, Alexander 76, 113
Porter, Peter 107
Postmodernism 145–52, 155–6, 164
Postmodernist Fiction (Brian McHale) 145
Pound, Ezra 38, 39, 58, 59, 60, 68, 82, 105, 107, 108–12, 113, 114
Powell, Anthony 106
Powys, John Cowper 10, 20, 23, 27
Prelude, The (William Wordsworth) 76
Preston, Raymond 80
Priestley, J. B. 56–7, 67
Princess, The (D. H. Lawrence) 40
Proust, Marcel 59, 61–2
Prussian Officer, The (D. H. Lawrence) 37
Psalms, The 137
Psyché (Jacques Derrida) 140

Quad I & II (Samuel Beckett) 137, 138

Rainbow, The (D. H. Lawrence) 37, 43, 48
Ravel, Maurice Joseph 5
Reflections on the Death of a Porcupine (D. H. Lawrence) 42, 43
Reformation 13
Renga 82
Resurrection of the Dead, The (Karl Barth) 34
Revelation, Book of 35, 38, 44, 154
Revenge for Love, The (Wyndham Lewis) 65
Richter, Hans Werner 153
Ricoeur, Paul 135
Riddley Walker (Russell Hoban) 176–8
Rivière, Jacques 25
Robertson, Michael 130
Rock, The (T. S. Eliot) 56, 102
Rockaby (Samuel Beckett) 137, 138
Rodin, François-Auguste-René 59
Roman Russe, Le (Vicomte de Vogue) 28

Romans, Epistle to the   13–14, 50, 79
Romanticism   5
Romaunt of the Rose, The (Geoffrey Chaucer)   76
Rosenberg, Isaac   105
Roszak, Theodore   154
Rousseau, Jean-Jacques   60
Rousselot, Père   60
Rowland, Christopher   53
Rozanov, Vasily   18
Russell, Bertrand   59

St. Mawr (D. H. Lawrence)   37, 44, 49, 50
Saintsbury, George   18, 27
Samson Agonistes (John Milton)   75
Samuel Beckett's Real Silence (Helene L. Baldwin)   130
Sartre, Jean-Paul   136
Schopenhauer, Arthur   10, 59, 63
Science and the Modern World (A. N. Whitehead)   63
Scrutiny   106
Self-Condemned (Wyndham Lewis)   65
Shakespeare, William   82, 114
Sheldrake, Rupert   65
Shelley, Percy Bysshe   75, 82, 124, 126
Six Mementos for the Next Millennium (Italo Calvino)   143
Solovyov, Vladimir   18, 25
Spanish Tragedy, The (Thomas Kyd)   75
Spark, Muriel   162–4
Speculations (T. E. Hulme)   58
Spender, Stephen   91–2, 93
Spengler, Oswald   25, 59
Spurr, David   86, 93
Stein, Gertrude   59, 60, 62
Stendhal   108
Stevens, Wallace   114
Stevenson, Robert Louis   17, 18
Streiber, Whitley   173
Studies in Classic American Literature (D. H. Lawrence)   39
Study of Thomas Hardy (D. H. Lawrence)   48

Such (Christina Brooke-Rose)   167, 168
Sun Also Rises, The (Ernest Hemingway)   79
Superstructuralism (Richard Harland)   171
Suso, Heinrich   130, 135
Swift, Jonathan   82, 83, 123, 129

Tang poets   109
Tauler, Johannes   130, 135
Taylor, Elizabeth   165
Tennyson, Alfred Lord   82, 110, 111, 113
That Time (Samuel Beckett)   137, 138, 139
Thomas Aquinas, St   89
Thomas, Dylan   106
Thomas, Edward   105, 107
Thorn in the Flesh, The (D. H. Lawrence)   37
Thornton, Lionel   61, 63
Thru (Christina Brooke-Rose)   167, 168–9
Thurneysen, Eduard   29, 30
Thus Spoke Zarathustra (F. Nietzsche)   144
Tillich, Paul   13, 153
Time and the Conways (J. B. Priestley)   56
Time and Western Man (Wyndham Lewis)   58–62, 63–4
Times Literary Supplement, The   25–6, 28
Tolstoy, Count Lev Nikolaevich   17, 18, 21, 65
Tomasevskij, Boris   31
Tomlin, Frederick   65–6
Tourneur, Cyril   82
Towards a Christian Poetics (Michael Edwards)   54, 82
'Tradition and the Individual Talent' (T. S. Eliot)   57–8, 83
Traherne, Thomas   92
Traversi, Derek   29, 30
Tredell, Nicholas   141
Tristan and Isolde (Richard Wagner)   75

T. S. Eliot and Indic Traditions (Cleo Kearns) 90–91, 103
Turgenev, Ivan Sergeevich 17, 21, 26
Tynjanov, Jurij 146

Ulysses (James Joyce) 63
Under the Volcano (Malcolm Lowry) 117–20, 127
Under Western Eyes (Joseph Conrad) 16
Unnamable, The (Samuel Beckett) 137
Upanishads 133

'Vanity of Human Wishes, The' (Samuel Johnson) 79, 82
Vedas 75
Verga, Giovanni 51
Via negativa 132–3, 134, 135, 137
Vietnam 165
Virgil 82, 118
Virgin and the Gipsy, The (D. H. Lawrence) 40
Visions and Revisions (John Cowper Powys) 19
Vogue, Vicomte de (Eugene Melchior) 28
von Hartmann, Edouard 63
von Hügel, Baron Friedrich 57
Vulgar Streak, The (Wyndham Lewis) 61

Waddell, Helen 109
Waiting for Godot (Samuel Beckett) 121, 123, 136, 137
Waliszewski, Kazimierz 17, 27
Walpole, Sir Hugh Seymour 16
Waste Land, The (T. S. Eliot) viii, 36, 70–85, 90–91, 94, 105, 108, 111, 117
Watson, J. B. 60, 63
Watt (Samuel Beckett) 127, 137
Waugh, Evelyn 105, 106, 115
Waugh, Patricia 155, 166
Weimar 12
White Peacock, The (D. H. Lawrence) 40
Whitehead, Alfred North 59, 63
Where the Wasteland Ends (Theodore Roszak) 154
Wild Boys, The (William Burroughs) 175–6
Williams, Rowan 86
Williams, William Carlos 114
Wilson, Edmund 105
Women in Love (D. H. Lawrence) 37, 39, 40, 41–2, 49
Woolf, Virginia 23, 28, 106
Wordsworth, William 76, 111

Yarmolinsky, Avraham 25
Yeats, William Butler 60, 70, 82, 83, 84, 107, 109, 112, 113

Zweig, Stefan 25, 27

Irena Makaruska: "Redemption and Narrative: Refiguration of Time in Postmodern Literature."

- ✓ Multiplicity and possibility → "god of revelation"
- ✗ Omniscient author → "god of reason"
    ↓
    differing questions inherent in reading

→ "postmodern frustration with linearity"
    ↓
    reductive framework
    authorial control
    epistemological dominant.

"modest promise of salvation" (Kundera)
- choice — choosing to choose   • asking
- Memory — creative
    in imaginative realm of possibility
    — redemption (fragmented; interrogative; refigurative)
        "Common bond with the infinite realm of God's laughter."

※

→ ontology

→ epistemology

How to interpret in which?
What is there to be known?
Who know it?

that he was asked
interruption
↓
fragments
↓
order
and reshuffle

nature of meaning
existence
and text

Crowder.

Incarnation & resurrection cannot be read in Dostoyevsky apart from the problematic, equivocal contexts (29)